ANGEL TECH

OTHER TITLES FROM FALCON PRESS

Antero Alli
Angel Tech Talk (audio)
The 8-Circuit Brain (video)
An Interview with Antero Alli (video)
Paratheatre (audio)
The Underground Cinema of Antero Alli (video)

Christopher S. Hyatt, Ph.D. & Antero Alli
A Modern Shaman's Guide to a Pregnant Universe

Christopher S. Hyatt, Ph.D.
Undoing Yourself With Energized Meditation & Other Devices
Radical Undoing: Complete Course for Undoing Yourself (DVDs)
To Lie Is Human: Not Getting Caught Is Divine
The Psychopath's Bible: For the Extreme Individual

Christopher S. Hyatt, Ph.D. with contributions by
Wm. S. Burroughs, Timothy Leary, Robert A. Wilson, et al.
Rebels & Devils: The Psychology of Liberation

S. Jason Black and Christopher S. Hyatt, Ph.D.
Pacts With the Devil: A Chronicle of Sex, Blasphemy & Liberation
Urban Voodoo: A Beginner's Guide to Afro-Caribbean Magic

Steven Heller, Ph.D.
Monsters & Magical Sticks: There's No Such Thing As Hypnosis?

Joseph C. Lisiewski, Ph.D.
Israel Regardie and the Philosopher's Stone
Ceremonial Magic and the Power of Evocation
Kabbalistic Cycles and the Mastery of Life
Howlings from the Pit

Israel Regardie
The Complete Golden Dawn System of Magic
The Golden Dawn Audio CDs

Sorceress Cagliastro
Blood Sorcery Bible

Peter J. Carroll
The Chaos Magick Audio CDs
PsyberMagick

Phil Hine
Condensed Chaos
Prime Chaos

For up-to-the-minute information on prices and availability, please visit our website at
http://originalfalcon.com

ANGEL TECH

A Modern Shaman's Guide
To Reality Selection

by
Antero Alli

Preface by
Robert Anton Wilson

THE *Original* FALCON PRESS
TEMPE, ARIZONA, U.S.A.

International Standard Book Number: 978-1-935150-95-4
Library of Congress Catalog Card Number: 86-82908

First Edition 1985, Vigilantero Press
Second Printing 1986, Vigilantero Press
Third Printing (Second Revised Edition) 1986, Falcon Press
Fourth Printing 1987, Falcon Press
Fifth Printing 1988, Falcon Press
Sixth Printing 1991, New Falcon Publications
Seventh Printing 1994, New Falcon Publications
Eighth Printing 2006, New Falcon Publications
Ninth Printing 2008, The Original Falcon Press
Tenth Printing (Third Revised Edition) 2012

Cover Art and Design by James Koehnline
http://www.koehnline.com

The paper used in this publication meets the minimum requirements of the American National Standard for Permanence of Paper for Printed Library Materials Z39.48-1984.

Address all inquiries to:
THE ORIGINAL FALCON PRESS
1753 East Broadway Road #101-277
Tempe, AZ 85282 U.S.A.
(or)
PO Box 3540
Silver Springs, NV 89429 U.S.A.
website: http://www.originalfalcon.com
email: info@originalfalcon.com

ACKNOWLEDGEMENTS

THE ANGEL TECHNICIANS

Guy Swansbro — Layout Artist
Cate Mugasis — First Edition Typesetting/Design
Nick Tharcher — Second Edition Typesetting/Design
Christie Alli — Proofreading

ILLUSTRATORS

Christie Alli
Guy Swansbro
Randy Rolen
Antero Alli (Collages)
And the Authors of the 20th/21st Century Tarot

GUIDANCE (HIGH SCHOOL TEACHERS)

Christopher S. Hyatt, Ph.D.
Bob Wilson (Catma)
Timothy Leary
Georges Gurdjieff
Rakel M. Stahle
David Rosenbloom (Ritual Theatre)
Michael Symonds (PSI-Technology)
Allegra Ahlquist
Jose Arguelles (PAN)
Keith Berger
Kendall Katze
Peter Kater
Robert Buchanan (Astrology)
AND Mom & Dad

TABLE OF CONTENTS

UPDATE 2008!

BY ANTERO ALLI

A lot has happened in the 23 years since the first edition (black cover) *Angel Tech* first came out. For starters, my three favorite Falcon Press authors—Timothy Leary, Robert Anton Wilson and Christopher S. Hyatt—have all passed away. These great men are terribly missed and will be honored for years to come for their seminal contributions in their various fields of human consciousness research. I had the good fortune to share quality time with Dr. Hyatt and Bob Wilson—and only met Tim once for dinner—and I was awestruck by how boldly each man embodied the complex visions they stood for. They did not merely talk about them; they were fully committed to their realization. Over three decades these visionaries made a home in my psyche as human archetypes representing the outer limits of what it really meant to have Guts, to have Heart and to have Brains. (I leave it to the reader to connect the dots). Sometimes, I felt like Dorothy on her way to the Land of Oz.

All that has also happened collectively in the last 23 years—here in the USA and abroad—seems to have escalated our awareness of how truly uncertain our future can be. Our anxiety thresholds have been tested, stretched and pushed to maximum capacities for how much uncertainty can be permitted before we snap. And I've been hearing a whole lot of snapping going on. People are either flipping in or flipping out, depending on how well, or how poorly, we have been managing the incumbent force of our anxiety. Uncertainty is a shocking fact of life; the best way to predict the future is to create it. And learning how to permit more uncertainty makes us all more creative than we can imagine, given that we also become accountable for managing the force of anxiety rising naturally enough as we reach our Uncertainty Threshold.

Over these past twenty-three years, a lot has also happened in my ongoing research into the 8-Circuit Brain model, especially within three novel areas of theory and praxis: 1) specific vertical connectivities shared between lower and higher circuits allowing for a more stable and dynamic operation of the whole; 2) more in-depth insight into the nature and function of "outside shocks"; and 3) a revisioning of the complex psychic bardo called "Chapel Perilous". As a result of this ongoing experimentation I have also updated the definitions and functions of each circuit. Not to discount the validity of any definitions outlined in *Angel Tech,* I offer this cursory outline of my updated research results:

THE SURVIVAL CIRCUITS: FIXATIONS AND ANCHORS

C–1 Bio-Survival Intelligence…the will to survive fixations: food, shelter, self-preservation, material goods, safety and security anchor: degree of physical confidence earned and maintained to assure survival.

C–2 Emotional-Territorial Intelligence…the will to power fixations: self-defense, territoriality, status, ego-strength, emotional honesty anchor: degree of emotional confidence earned and maintained to assure propriety.

C–3 Symbolic-Conceptual Intelligence…the will to sanity fixations: problem-solving, map-making, technology, linguistics, system theories anchor: degree of mental confidence earned and maintained to assure peace of mind.

C–4 Social-Moral Intelligence…the will to socialize fixations: belonging, friendship, domestication, sexual and tribal identity, ethical codes anchor: degree of social confidence earned and maintained to assure social loyalties.

THE POST-SURVIVAL CIRCUITS: CURRENTS & SHOCKS

C–5 Somatic-Sensory Intelligence…through the Body and Five Senses Currents: rapture, communion with nature, body wisdom, tantra (yoga, meditation, ritual), charisma, second wind, falling in love (endorphins). The shock of Ecstasy and Bliss (absence of suffering).

C–6 Intuitive-Psychic Intelligence…through the Brain, Spine, Central Nervous System Currents: the light body or aura, direct perception of intuition, clairvoyance and other psychic processes, sex magick, reality selection, neuro-relativity (non-conceptual). The Shock of Uncertainty (absence of falsely assumed certitudes).

C–7 Mytho-Poetic Genetic Intelligence…through the DNA matrix of all life forms. Currents: ancestral and past-life memories, realms of autonomous archetypes, persistent synchronicity, planetary (Gaia) mind, cosmic consciousness. The Shock of Indivisibility or Cosmic Unity (absence of dualistic consciousness).

C–8 Quantum-Nonlocal Intelligence...through Invisible Subatomic interactions. Currents: near death experiences, the dreambody/dream-time, lucid dreaming, authentic out of body experiences, communion with Void, the mystery of singularity. The Shock of Impermanence (absence of the amnesiac sleep of "living forever").

SHOCKS, ANCHORS AND VERTICAL CONNECTIVITY

I see each of these eight functions of Intelligence existing within each individual at various degrees of expression and latency. They can all be viewed in a linear sequential "evolutionary" way and/or in a nonlinear "radial" way; both vantages express valid truths. I think it would be erro-neous to assume any one circuit to be "better" or "worse," or "higher" or "lower" than any other, as they all symbolize simultaneously existing states of consciousness working together as a dynamic changing whole. I also think that to view them hierarchically—as if any circuit is superior or inferior than any other—perpetuates cultural amnesia and any relig-ious indoctrination preserving the Body-Mind schism. *Lies! Lies! Lies!*

Though there are countless ways these eight functions interact and/or act on each other, the area I have found most interesting so far addresses how the first four "survival" circuits and the second four "post-survival" circuits act on each other through precise two-way vertical connectiv-ities. I specifically refer to how the upper circuits act on the lower circuits as distinct shocks and how the lower circuits act on the upper circuits as stabilizing anchor points, or integration of those shocks. The specific vertical connectivities addressed here: **1/5; 2/6; 3/7; 4/8.**

Without a supple and resilient foundation (circuits 1–4 integrated), any significant force of expanded consciousness (circuits 5–8) can leave us destabilized at varying degrees of personality disintegration and disas-sociation. Once the survival circuits can be more fully experienced, inte-grated and *embodied,* they can also better serve to (re)stabilize the personality to better absorb and integrate the shocks delivered by any activation of the post-survival circuits.

Upper circuit post-survival shocks stimulate growth and development in the four survival circuits, just as the survival circuits (once integrated) can help substantiate the more ephemeral and subtle states symbolized by circuits five through eight. If monitored and tended to, all eight circuits can be made to work together in more meaningful ways to serve the dynamic changing whole they are expressions of. By tending to the specific verticalities shared between upper circuit shocks and lower circuit anchors (1/5; 2/6; 3/7; 4/8), the Eight-Circuit Brain model can offer safer and more creative guidelines to the high-seas adventures of consciousness research.

THE FUNCTION AND MEANING OF "SHOCK"

Shock, as I am using the term in context to the Eight-Circuit Brain model, represents any force beyond the comprehension and control of the ego; a genuine shock arrives from beyond ego. Real life shocks emerge everywhere and can happen anytime to anybody; no one is exempt. Examples: sudden housing eviction, getting fired from work, marriage, divorce, childbirth, parenthood, loss of loved ones, natural disasters, sudden kundalini activations, death of parents, death of children, falling in love, unexpected financial windfalls, terrorist attacks, any move of residence, police arrest, incarceration, big employment promotions, betrayal by friends and/or family, car accidents, hospitalization, surgery, spiritual epiphanies, cardiac arrests, strokes, epistemological crisis, heroic doses of magic mushroom; the list goes on & on & on…

Contrary to popular belief, shocks may be neither bad nor good by nature but neutral. How we respond to real life shocks usually determines the degree our experience turns negative or positive, painful or joyous, destructive or creative. To assume that shocks are not neutral but either negative or positive suggests that the universe is either out to burn us—the negatively inflated paranoid bias—or that the universe is out to bless us—the positively inflated messianic bias. In my view, both express self-delusion. I think how we respond to shock may actually be more important than any initial shock itself, and redefines our responsibility as our response-ability.

Shocks act as trigger points for Self-initiation, engaging the separatist ego in a confrontation with the archetype of the Self. And, as Swiss psychiatrist Carl G. Jung was oft to say, *"the experience of the Self is almost always a defeat for the ego."* With enough outside shocks absorbed and integrated, we become as human shock absorbers for the transmission of initiatic shock to others. As we are initiated, so can we become as initiates, men and women of power—if that is what we want. Some of us undergo this Self-initiation process instinctively without any conscious plan or knowledge of the eight circuits, while others approach it on purpose as an ongoing Self-initiation ritual; either way, outside shocks absorbed and integrated throughout our systems become transformed into the transmission of its presence to the world.

OUTSIDE SHOCKS, INSIDE SHOCKS

Shocks come in basically two forms: inside and outside. Inside shocks are shocks we can give ourselves. For example, by creating intentional inconveniences for ourselves in daily life, we can administer small shocks to our habitual routines by altering the expected. Any way we can shock ourselves more awake constitutes an "inside shock." However, there is only so much we can do by our own efforts alone. Armenian philosopher G.I. Gurdjieff called "outside shocks" any event arriving from any place beyond our personal control and comprehension (such as the examples already given earlier). Outside shocks tend to be far more effective in genuinely transforming and shaking things up than any inside shock can. Implementing inside shocks can, however, encourage enough internal flexibility to help us navigate and manage the greater forces of real outside shocks when they arrive.

When we are in a state of genuine shock or crisis, consciousness naturally escalates as a survival reflex and we enter an emergency state. We can experience this escalation on a small scale whenever we become genuinely upset or thrown off-center. In a state of shock the ego wobbles into "marginality," a kind of gap zone, where our experience and awareness of uncertainty greatly increases. The marginal state of shock tends to be fluid and unstable, representing a time when new directives and values can be implemented and then, maintained through applied effort, a supportive environment and a series of challenges to strengthen the new patterns. Think of shock as a creative state. It was under such circumstances that *Angel Tech* was originally written and written for: to provide practical guidelines for those currently in shock or marginal, and marginalized, states towards creative rearrangements of your present and future lives. For those of us currently too comfortable to change or too complacent to care, *Angel Tech* may appear as impenetrable esoteric shit.

CHAPEL PERILOUS REVISITED

When I first wrote *Angel Tech,* "Chapel Perilous" was placed between C-4 and C-5 as a kind of discontinuity gap for keeping the Eight-Circuit Brain system more open-ended. Since then, I have come to see things differently. I now view Chapel Perilous as not so localized between C-4 and C-5 but as a kind of bardo zone hovering over the entire Eight-Circuit Brain, perhaps like a fog or aetheric web absorbing whatever consciousness has not yet been absorbed and integrated through the eight circuits.

The basic idea, as described in *Angel Tech,* remains the same: Chapel Perilous acts as a metaphor for a psychic refuge for lost and/or abandoned souls remaining in suspension until ready to get back into the body and get on with the business of living on planet Earth. Or we can look at Chapel Perilous as a kind of Lost & Found Dept. for the unclaimed and/or lost portions of ourselves. Truth be told, almost everyone I have met and/or have gotten to know over the last two decades is, or was, inside Chapel Perilous (in order of greatest percentage to the smallest):

1) does not know it and remains there unaware of their displacement.
2) has awakened to the fact and cannot or does not want to leave.
3) has awakened and managed to escape with soul intact or, paranoid.
4) has awakened, escaped and returns there for reasons of their own.

I count myself among those who fortunate enough to have awakened and escaped with soul intact and as one who periodically returns there for reasons of my own. I know of many others who have not been so lucky. Most of my so-called wisdom comes from making mistakes and learning from them. Making mistakes is not a problem; repeating the same old mistakes is a problem and a chief source of stupidity. If you're making new mistakes, odds are you are probably advancing your intelligence.

These three areas of research, as outlined in this **Update 2008!**—as vertical connectivities, the function of shock, Chapel Perilous—will all be given a thorough, exhaustive investigation in my forthcoming book, *The Eight-Circuit Brain: Advanced Studies and Praxis.* Until then, I present you with Part One: *Angel Tech*. Do the work and you will get results; don't do the work and you will get those results.

— Antero Alli
Berkeley, California, July 1, 2008

PREFACE

BY ROBERT ANTON WILSON

Herein are all the great neurological scripts of the past synthesized and modernized for our day: the Tarot. Cabala. The Hindu Chakra System. Alchemy. And here, too—praise be to the Sun Absolute!—is a refreshing absence of the cant, the pomposity and the deliberate mystification that makes most books on those subjects virtually unreadable.

Some, who like to talk of things "mystical" but have no first-hand knowledge, may find Antero's realism a bit disconcerting. A look at my *Prometheus Rising, Cosmic Trigger* and *Cosmic Trigger II* might help lead the reader into that set of no *bovine excreta*. It might do these folks some good to remember that Sufism begins with ritual dances (to gain control over the involuntary nervous system) and yoga with body-relaxation techniques. They might even ponder a bit on the traditional Christian teaching that the body is the Temple of the Holy Spirit. They might further ponder Gopi Krishna's assertion that rebirth is a matter of moving energies properly through the spinal cord, or Da Free John's correlation of various levels of consciousness with the sympathetic, autonomic and central nervous systems. (But remember these are an models and like all models they age.)

Antero Alli has chosen to organize his system around the 8 circuits of the brain, as described by Dr. Timothy Leary in *Info-Psychology* and other books. Many will object to this because they do not like what they have read about Dr. Leary in the newspapers. This mechanical reaction, or conditioned reflex, is no longer necessary. (See *The New Inquisition.*) Since Dr. Leary is in the process of having his name legally changed to Irving Blum, the ideas of the 8 brain circuits can now be considered *on their own merits* without the distraction of having an unpopular name attached to them. Considered thus, without political prejudice, it seems to me that judicious readers will agree with the 8-circuit model as an admirable creation. It combines all the latest discoveries in psychology, neurology, brain chemistry, socio-biology, etc. and also incorporates and updates the maps of altered states of consciousness to be found in astrology, alchemy, yoga, and similar pre-scientific disciplines for Brain Change.

All in all, this is a book that Lao-Tse could understand and enjoy—after a few scientific terms were explained to him. And 3,000 years from now, somewhere in the Sirius system, seekers of higher knowledge and wider consciousness will still find it useful, after a few of our archaic metaphors are clarified. Meanwhile, everybody can enjoy it and use it right now.

— Robert Anton Wilson, Ph.D.
Institute for the Study of the Human Future

Author's Notes

Before embarking upon the journey of reading this book, permit me to introduce to you a few points of interest. First and perhaps foremost is my acknowledgement to Dr. Timothy Leary's valiant endeavor of writing *Exo-Psychology,* from which *Angel Tech* was originally inspired. Dr. Leary was, I believe, the first writer to render a humanistic translation to the universal law of octaves. Others, most notably Gurdjieff and the Sufi Mystery Schools, pioneered this herculean task but remained accessible only to an elite few. Leary chose to relate the law of octaves to our present day sciences: physics, sociology, genetics, somatics, neurology and modern philosophy in an attempt to update previously archaic definitions of this eight-fold system. As part of my own integrative process, I have adjusted and/or changed the terminology, format and style further still. The intent is to deeply de-mystify the process of living life's mysteries fuller than before.

Angel Tech is not about angels in the common sense, but like much of this book, is a reformulation of outdated terms to suit modern-day living. My tendency to reform terms has emerged as a response to an accelerated pace of living, where the almost constant influx of new information has compelled continuous adjustments in the way I think about things. Not unlike Alice in Wonderland, I run as fast as I can to remain in the same place. In doing so, I've developed an impatience with any theory taken too seriously which does not immediately apply to action. As a result, this book is action-oriented. Sections of *Angel Tech,* especially *Mechanical Problems,* may prove exceedingly dense reading. This is due to what I believe to be the realistic requirement of understanding the nitty-gritty mechanics of fixing broken people: ourselves. Perhaps this is where true healing begins…as self-healing. Besides, it's a good way to Walk Your Talk and get on with it.

Angel Tech is a code name for the process of stabilizing the contact between right (ANGEL) an left (TECH) hemispheres of the brain. The connecting ganglia between these hemispheres is called the "corpus callosum" which may function as if it were a *reality selection* switch. It "has the ability" to choose between left (linear) and right (intuitive) hemispheres the appropriate mode of Intelligence for the situation at hand. (I am fully aware that this discussion reflects a model of the brain network and even as a model does not include such things as the lower brain stem which my friend Dr. Hyatt handles in his book *Undoing Yourself with Energized Meditation.)* This is how the title of this book came to be. As for "modern shaman"...with so much whoop-tee-doo about the cosmic significance of shamanism these days...it's getting trickier to define the term. Nevertheless, I've managed to plant a few clues.

To access left and right brains, as well as reality selection itself, illustrations have been strategically placed as **REST POINTS.** When coming across one, relax. Or lift your eyes from the page and ponder, drift and dream...whatever your mind does to process input. Left brain loves words as much as right brain loves pictures & sensations...both sides need equal time and space to get used to working together in a more meaningful way. Metaphysically, this tends to serve the principle of Consciousness itself which, like the god Hermes, travels among worlds without becoming resident to any of them. Consciousness, it seems, is the passport.

Our next point is somewhat whimsical. *Angel Tech* was constructed much like a can-opener. What it describes is secondary to what it opens up. It's a workbook to access the multiple functions of Intelligence. The overall intent is Intelligence Increase...based on how you, the reader, define your terms. *Angel Tech* is also a statement about the utter benevolence and surgical precision by which Life expresses itself through us. Life can be "dangerous" in that anything truly alive is a threat to the dead or "unliving." It is, perhaps, in this manner that this book (like Hesse's *Magic Theatre* in *Steppenwolf)* is not for everybody. You may become more alive after reading it. It is in this light that I have, at the risk of sounding redundant, used the device of repetition to expose the need for self-response(ability) within each and every level of our graduation throughout *Angel Tech.* I feel we are only as free as our integrity permits.

The last and most serious point of all is to have fun. As a famous Discordian once proclaimed, "The world's problems will be solved the day everybody stops taking themselves so seriously." Our quest into The Outrageous can be just what the doctor ordered for those who have unwittingly lapsed into the spell of Terminal Adulthood. Whatever you do, don't hold your breath. The Curse of Greyface wants you to hold your breath. Open your mouths and breathe... Open your mouths and shout!

May the farce be with you and the Buddha, too.

— Antero Alli, Boulder CO, USA, 1986

INTRODUCTION

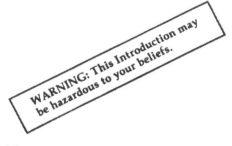

WARNING: This Introduction may be hazardous to your beliefs.

**angel: being of light tech:
from "techne" meaning Art**

the art of being light

ANGEL TECH:
AN INTRODUCTION

We are, in essence, beings of light Most of us have forgotten this, some of us are starting to remember and a few of us are living the truth. If you are reading this now, you are probably somewhere in the middle... between forgetting and living. Those forgetful among us would have no reason to read this book unless they, perhaps, are waking up at this time. Individuals already living the truth are very possibly too busy to read a book about it. How do I know these things? I'm the one writing this book and if I were living the complete truth, maybe I'd have no purpose writing about it, would I? However, I've a story to tell and writing is my way of organizing my thoughts so that I might communicate and, proceed. My bias is to approach living as consciously as I can...eyes open, through the center and out the other side.

ANGEL TECH is an Invisible Institute for Higher Learning dedicated to Intelligent Survival with the Planet The Teachers walk amidst our daily lives prepared to share the appropriate information when we are ready for it. As we evolve, the lessons present themselves more clearly. For those of us who are too headstrong to learn from other human beings, lessons will duly arrive in the guise of Situations, Dreams and other Self-generating activities. The rest of us who can learn from each other directly, will share the opportunity of meeting the Teachers in the flesh. *They are us.* We appear in a vast array of masks, cloaks and roles and many of us will not even take the credit for something which comes as natural as helping each other. These Teachers, however, have been recognized in the following services: Gas Station Attendants (Self-Serve), Grandmothers, Stumbling Drunks, Astronomers, Cats, Landladies, Ferns, Newscasters, Mozart, Hardcore Punk Music, Madmen, Crystals, Children, Presidents, Indian Chiefs, Movie Stars, Plumbers, Telephone Operators and the list goes on forever. It's all Spiritual and the Teachers are everywhere. It just takes a certain kind of perspective to see this.

A message is the ordering of a signal. Consider ANGEL TECH as an alternative education system, one which arranges living planetary signals into meaningful messages. These signals come in *octaves,* or cycles of eight. Languages throughout history have translates these signals as: The Overtones of Music Theory, The DNA Code, The I Ching, Computer Binary Notation, The 8 Mayan Calendars, The Game of Chess and other interpretations of the universal law of octaves. This book furthers the attempt at humanizing spiritual realities...revealing the unbreakable bond intersecting cosmic and banal factors of our daily waking, dreaming lives on this planet.

ANGEL TECH, like the Universe it refers to, is fraught with "strange loops." A strange loop is any event animated by an interplay of contraries. It is strange for at least two reasons: 1) The more you try and figure it out, the more you get stuck inside and 2) If you stop trying to figure it out and start "living it out," the more, uh, strange things get. However, what is strange from one perspective remains quite ordinary from another, and vice versa. From the viewpoint of our Multidimensional Nature, Life may not be a simplistic True/False Answer Test after all but a Multiple Choke Questionnaire. Strange experiences may simply reflect a hereto unknown facet of our very being and not something "other than Life."

This book was written in the spirit of exciting self-definition; It may, at times, take for granted that the reader knows he/she creates his/her own reality. The text herein explores and defines what could be one of the primary strange loops of being human. This strange loop, or interplay of contraries, permeating our lives refers to *how* we choose to interpret our realities...according to:

1) **Socio-cultural Imprints** — what and how we were taught and conditioned to believe, think and feel about ourselves and the world and...
2) **Our Central Nervous System** — what our innate sensitivities register as true for the purpose of coming to our own questions and conclusions.

ENTRANCE EXAMINATION

1) What is Intelligence? Define it in your own words.
2) According to your definition of #1, how can Intelligence be increased, accelerated and/or realized?
3) What is your favorite color?

The overall intent of ANGEL TECH can be experienced for yourself through a process called "self-reclamation." This book's format is an evolutionary grid to test this process, as well as support its manifestation. The work has begun with your own definition of Intelligence and its potential for increase. How you define your terms determines the degree of direct knowledge accessible to yourself. Your definitions) is the integral thread of your psychology...how you make sense of it all and how big your picture is. Most importantly, you are putting yourself ON THE LINE by risking self-definition. This is because true transformation begins with self-knowledge, as only that which EXISTS is subject to change.

Our definitions are tested daily as a way to check our resonance with the spiritual; we discover which images accurately reflect What Is and, which do not. If we remain attached to an idea after it is revealed unreflective of truth, we begin living a lie and compound our suffering. Attachment to anything dead and/or dying creates pain. If given the choice between dying a Slow Death or passing through Quick Decay, which would you select?

( ) Slow Death ( ) Quick Decay

FUN-FAX

Consider this possibility. Angels are cosmic beings embodied as planets... Archangels are stars (our sun). Planet Earth is the most powerful Angelic Force permeating our lives.

Our definitions and "maps" may evolve with the spiritual when we are willing to adjust and, if need be, release our attachment to outdated notions of What Is. The conceptual education of Thought Adjustment teaches us how to exercise conscious synchronicity with the spiritual truths governing our lives. Mystically speaking, Thought Adjusters are Angels who are here and now ready to help us help ourselves. An Angel is that part of us which has already realized its destiny, surrendered to the Highest Good and helps the "rest of us" catch up. Angels are Us-In-The-Future. We have already happened.

PART TWO

1) Are you willing to dedicate your life to the living out of your own definitions until they stop working?   ( ) Yes   ( ) No   ( ) Other
2) In the event of the collapse of your definitions, are you willing to adjust and if need be, release them entirely in order to grow receptive

to your next evolutionary phase of Intelligence?
( ) Yes   ( ) No   ( ) Uh, Gee... 1 Don't Know... Maybe... What If...
3) What is your favorite brand of beer?

IF you answered YES to at least two of the above questions, you are now under serious consideration for ANGEL TECH eligibility; the final approval, however, rests with you. Entry and graduation throughout this program depends entirely upon the thoroughness by which you're able to ABSORB, ORGANIZE, and COMMUNICATE information and/or energy. (Read the last sentence again for the generic definition of Intelligence in ANGEL TECH.) This is a program for Intelligence Increase based in the definition of you, the user and, this program is user-friendly. It has been designed for those who are now ready to initiate the process of reading, adjusting, and transforming their own patterns according to the innate ability of living truthfully. De-programming and subsequently, re-programming, naturally occur when outdated, redundant definitions explode and disintegrate in the face of greater truths than we are presently living.

A program is your "reality map." Our programs usually include the definitions of our parents, peers, teachers, culture, mass media and finally, ourselves. This network of definitions makes up the map we automatically use to describe the world we live in. In short, about 23% of our map belongs to us...the individual, with the remaining 77% dictated by others. We are not alone within ourselves. If we would like to create more internal space for our own feelings, thoughts and conclusions it is crucial that we understand how our minds work. The re-education of the intellect itself is the mandatory prerequisite.

NOW APPEARING

THE INTELLECT DURING ITS INFANTILE PHASE

The infantile phase of any new stage of evolution is, by the very nature of its purpose, self-centered. As new territory is encountered, it is integrated into oneself through the process of "making it one's own." The more space claimed, the more self-reference is developed to form a greater sense of identity. This very sense of self is the substance necessary for the purpose of transformation, as only that which exists is subject to change. The intellect, during its infantile phase, is justifiably self-absorbed with Having It All Figured Out. After all, the forte of the intellect *is* to Figure Things Out. The moment this intellect recognizes an Intelligence greater than its own, it's up against the wall with two choices: 1) It surrenders its authority to serve the greater Intelligence as its translator *or* 2) It holds fast to its previous identity as Ultimate Creator and thus, proceeds to possess the personality with its fearful tyranny until its inevitable confession of defeat. Here marks the turning point between illumination and madness.

NOW...BACK TO OUR PROGRAM

The intent of this program is to help clarify the process of self-reclamation according to each individual's preferred style of surviving in our:

1) **Physical Sense**
2) **Emotional Bias**
3) **Conceptual Framework**
4) **Social Rituals**
5) **Sensory Pleasures**
6) **Psychic Perspective**
7) **Mythic Synchronicities**
8) **Spiritual Being**

These eight levels constitute the grid, or reference, by which this program accesses information and/or energy within ourselves and each other. As will be discussed later, the eight are harmonically related...levels 5–8 are overtones for levels 1–4, for example: Our Physical Sense supports Sensory Pleasures, as does our Emotional Bias produce the overtone of Psychic Perspective and so forth.

One interesting aspect of programs is: If there's something in our lives that doesn't work anymore, it doesn't mean there's something WRONG with who we are because WE ARE NOT THE PROGRAM. Our programs may be out-dated or require adjustment but that doesn't necessitate self-condemnation to rectify. As the Programmer, we learn to distinguish between who we *are* and the program we're following by knowing how to suspend judgment. Read the last sentence again before going on. If there is anything to judge, it is *information* and not our being or anyone else's. We can judge what people *know* but how can intellect fathom the mysterious unity of being? Understanding this distinction helps us separate who we are from what we know.

WHO ARE YOU AND WHAT DO YOU KNOW?

The Central Nervous System controls the body. Its regulation of pain, pleasure, reflex, behavior, emotions and everything we know as "real" is a response to the program it receives from DNA. The Body is devotional by nature and takes its orders from the Brain, a bio-computer innocently acting on its orders from its creator, DNA, who in turn evolves from the Sub-atomic Mysteries perpetually churning forth from the nucleus of the Atom. The message Subatomic Mysteries pass onto DNA is: i-n-f-i-n-i-t-y. By the time the Central Nervous System gets it, it spells *immortality* and when the Body gets it, it's Reproduction Time. This is how sex is the greatest mystery of all. It translates the genetic message of immortality by reproducing to perpetuate the species, which is DNA's way of knowing itself through the purpose of living forever. DNA, however, may not have designed and/or translated its message/program of immortality to accommodate each individual CNS's preferred style of surviving. Until this program is made conscious and understood, it is safe to say that we are Robots for DNA. That is, until we learn enough about this program as Bodies and as our CNS so we learn to think like DNA and co-design the program. Since DNA is the blueprint or language by which Life knows itself, it is up to us to recognize a biological basis for our ideas about Life. The more we find out how Life works, the more we can synchronize ourselves to its intent and Be Alive. But first, we must find, define and redefine our Robotic, Conditioned Self…that part of us which runs on AUTOMATIC and governs those regions as of yet, unclaimed by our personal approval and acceptance.

The big robot breakthrough comes with the realization that we are beings of light, first and foremost before being created as bodies, emotions, thoughts and the rest of it. When we recognize that these things are not really "things" at all but functions of One Intelligence (as colors to Light), robot reprogramming may be possible. How these functions of Intelligence are defined constitute the homework for *ANGEL TECH* participants.

This book is a survival manual for fallen angels who are through with their frozen responses to the nightmares around us. The opportunity is upon us to re-establish our planetary commitment on all levels. There is no reason to leave the planet and/or blame gravity for bringing us down. There is no reason to leave our body and/or blame responsibility for bringing us down. Gravity remains our greatest source of instruction. To fly higher, plant your feet firmly in the ground…**ground.**

CONSCIOUS EVOLUTION

Eight grades mark the evolution consciousness may traverse throughout ANGEL TECH, with each grade expressive of a (unction of Intelligence. This 8-Grade program is presented in three interdependent phases to allow for breathing space. They are: 1) ELEMENTARY SCHOOL 2) CHAPEL PERILOUS and 3) HIGH SCHOOL. Elementary School education (Grades 1–4) studies *individual survival issues* in a course entitled KARMA MECHANICS. It is here that our consciousness is asked to apply itself in the realms of Physical, Emotional Conceptual, and Social survival. Finals are presented in the Graduate Study course called MECHANICAL PROBLEMS, a section given to exploring malfunctions in the survival mechanism and their correlating adjustments towards effective survival tactics. The goal of Elementary School is in turning out "Karma Mechanics"…self-responsible individuals capable of adjusting their own lives towards greater freedom and creativity.

    Chapel Perilous is a name given to a free-floating initiation zone. Mythically speaking, it's where souls go when they're catapulted out of their bodies as a result of *shock*…while the bodies continue on "automatic pilot" walking the planet's surface. Chapel Perilous is the shock of imminent crisis, the conversion point of the *I Ching's* 23rd Hexagram where grace collapses and things fall apart for the purpose of their transformation. When structures reach their point of critical mass, the doors of The Chapel swing open by the winds of change.

> *"Captain, it would be illogical to assume that conditions will remain stable indefinitely..."*
> — Spock, 2nd-in-command of SS Enterprise

High School consciousness concerns itself with Life After Survival, also called The Art of Getting High and Staying There. Once survival priorities are stabilized, it's only natural to relax, have fun and manifest creative potential. With more Leisure Time on our hands, we can learn the Brain Change technologies of Rapture, Ritual, Charisma Training, Clairvoyance, Reality Selection, Tarot, Synchronicity, Alchemy, Astrology, and the Dreaming Rituals of Factor X...all presented for our immediate participation and, without ingesting drugs!

Brain change willed is as close to magic as we're going to get and lets us bypass the Middle Classes tendencies for ingesting drugs (alcohol) to escape present and future time by regressing and living in the great unwashed mires of the status quo. It is important to remember that regression am be in the service of the self, like going back home to learn what you have forgotten or left unintegrated. Getting high is information gathering, staying high is the result of transmuting information into living experience.

ANGEL TECH: THE MAP

PHASE ONE   **ELEMENTARY SCHOOL**   **GRADES 1–4**

FIRST Grade Physical Intelligence   Medium: The Organism
Education: Passivity, Safety and Nourishment

SECOND Grade Emotional Intelligence   Medium: Belief Systems
Education: Self-expression, Status and Personal Power

THIRD Grade Conceptual Intelligence Medium: Conceptual Framework
Education: Attention, Map-Making and Articulation

FOURTH Grade Social Intelligence   Medium: Code of Ethics
Education: Adolescence, Adulthood and Collectivization

PHASE TWO   **CHAPEL PERILOUS**   **INITIATION**

INITIATION is a creative response to the Unknown. CHAPEL PERILOUS signifies a rite of passage wherein Physical, Emotional, Conceptual and Social Education is tested for its integrity as a preparation for graduation.

PHASE THREE   **HIGH SCHOOL**   **GRADES 5–8**

FIFTH Grade Sensory Intelligence   Medium: The Body's 5 Senses
Education: Rapture, Ritual and Charisma Training

SIXTH Grade Psychic Intelligence   Medium: Central Nervous System
Education: Natural Clairvoyance, Reality Selection and Designing Tarot

SEVENTH Grade Mythic Intelligence   Medium: DNA & The Planet
Education: Synchronicity, Alchemy and Astrology

EIGHTH Grade Spiritual Intelligence   Medium: Subatomic Mysteries
Education: Paradox Found, Dreaming and Factor X

Completion of each Grade depends upon how thoroughly each is Absorbed, Organized and Communicated. This leads to Graduation from one grade into the next. How thoroughly this material is Absorbed, Organized and Communicated will determine the rate and completeness toward graduation. This 3-Phase process reflects the activities of our most basic unit of Biological Intelligence: *the Neuron.* The neuron is an "energy structure" rather than an invented one. Neurons communicate how Life Itself expresses Intelligence through us. This is why this trinary process has been selected as a model for Intelligence Increase in ANGEL TECH.

GRADUATION

Communication problems stem from not completing the intermediary phase of organizing the information absorbed. To complete this 3-phase Intelligence Circuit, it is imperative to interpret for oneself any new information taken in. To know is not enough. Knowledge becomes a wisdom through its practical application in daily experience. Whatever is put to practice, can be *integrated* thus...enabling a renewed receptivity to more learning. This is how this model of Intelligence works. This energy structure is innate within each of us and we have only to excite its recognition...it's already happening, right where you are sitting now.

Due to the crucial need to understand the binary process of intelligence, there are listed below alternative words to help describe the essential functions of:

ABSORPTION: receive, experience, take in, learn, osmose, access, input, engagement, consume, suck in, vulnerability, give in to, open

ORGANIZATION: integrate, translate, interpret, order, arrange, understand, assimilate, digest, sort out, make one's own way, to redefine

COMMUNICATION: transmit, share, relay, practice, project, distribute, send, to give of self, extend, inform, presentation, articulate.

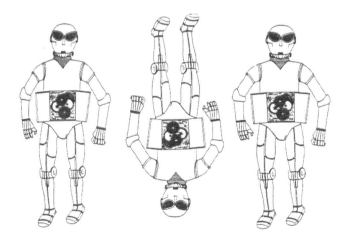

INTERNAL SUPPORT

The three sub-phases (Absorbing, Organizing, Communicating) of each function of Intelligence also express a series of internal supports. Areas of activity have been selected to excite direct contact with all the sub-phases of every function of Intelligence presented in ANGEL TECH. Below, there is listed the manner by which the sub-phases of the first four functions *support* the sub-phases of the latter four functions. Once again, there will be exceptions, additions and subtractions of your own.

First Grade Physical Intelligence	—	Fifth Grade Sensory Intelligence
PASSIVITY	*supports*	RAPTURE
SAFETY	*supports*	RITUAL
NOURISHMENT	*supports*	CHARISMA

Second Grade Emotional Intelligence —		Sixth Grade Psychic Intelligence
SELF-EXPRESSION	*supports*	CLAIRVOYANCE
STATUS	*supports*	REALITY SELECTION
PERSONAL POWER	*supports*	DESIGNING A TAROT

Third Grade Conceptual Intelligence —		Seventh Grade Mythic Intelligence
PAYING ATTENTION	*supports*	SYNCHRONICITY
MAP-MAKING & NAMING	*supports*	ALCHEMY
ARTICULATION	*supports*	ASTROLOGY

Fourth Grade Social Intelligence	—	Eighth Grade Spiritual Intelligence
ADOLESCENCE	*supports*	PARADOX
ADULTHOOD	*supports*	DREAMING
COLLECTIVIZATION	*supports*	FACTOR 'X'

An additional correspondence exists between **CHAPEL PERILOUS** and wherever FACTOR 'X' leads us. **CHAPEL PERILOUS** is an initiatory phase marking the transition between the first four functions and the latter four. It relates to post-FACTOR X activities in that both refer to "out-of-body" states. However, **CHAPEL PERILOUS** is where souls go when they are lost and FACTOR 'X' communications refer to how souls are found.

Within the ANGEL TECH paradigm there exists a network of internal supports, correspondences and parallels. The first four functions of Intelligence (Physical, Emotional, Conceptual and Social) act as "stabilizers" for the latter, more creative and unpredictable functions (Sensory, Psychic, Mythic and Spiritual), which in turn act as "catalysts" for the previous four functions. All eight functions contain inherent capacities for *Absorbing, Organizing* and *Communicating* their respective Intelligences. The format of this book has been set up to invite the reader to explore these three sub-phases within each function of Intelligence towards the overall graduation and increase of Intelligence.

! — stands for the karmic impulse of reincarnation

† — stands for the imminent shock of Chapel Perilous

? — stands for irrevocable unknowns and irretrievable mysteries

THE ROYAL TRAP

ANGEL TECH is a system, and like other systems, it is a "map" and not the territory itself. Maps, at best, refer us to the territory accessible through direct experiential contact. To expand Intelligence make maps as fast as you can absorb information so that you keep integrating. Adjust the maps you have to synchronize closer with the territory, or simply create new maps, ones with enough space to permit new incoming information. Without this kind of continual updating it's very easy to begin living in the past, as new information arrives daily. It's easy to get attached to a particular map and get caught eating the menu instead of the meal.

Please permit now a brief but hopefully entertaining diversion, as I attempt a description of the Royal Trap in basic animal language. When we fall in love with a map over the very territory itself, a wily creature is born that we'll call *dogma.* Dogmas are the "demons" in ANGEL TECH. This most nefarious species of literary canine is known for its rigid, dogged grip on things. It has been seen to pop its pithy head into the most emotional of places. Last but not least, dogma has been historically recognized for its ability to defend-to-the-death premises long outdated by the ever-expanding rate of new scientific breakthroughs and spiritual revelations.

As Fallen Angels we are graced with living in the Age of Relativity which has spawned a new breed of philosophical animal in *catma,* or "relative disbelief." Unlike the absolute belief of dogma, catma doesn't have to believe in anything. (This includes the belief of not having to believe in anything.) If properly fed, groomed and cared for, catma will keep dogmas quite busy chasing their own tales. If you listen closely, you can hear them bark, "Truth! Proof! Proof!" (SECRET MESSAGE #23: The Truth Will Set You Free But First It May Make You Miserable.)

The overall intent behind ANGEL TECH is twofold: 1) How to access Intelligence and 2) Put it to work. Even though the Eight Grades provide a linear progression of events, it is important to note that all eight of the functions exist simultaneously at different degrees of consciousness. ANGEL TECH simply provides a guideline towards opening our "higher centers" *after* stabilizing the "lower ones." This is why we start in First Grade and work from the bottom up. It is in this manner that we may learn to "ground" our creative sources in everyday survival activities. The Eight Grades offer participants the opportunity to live out the evolution of our humanity for ourselves. A glorious diversity becomes obvious when we discover there is no one reality map for any reality, as everybody has their own. A magnificent unity dawns when there's enough compassion to accept these differences. An appreciation for paradox develops when, perhaps, we see the relationships between our incongruously juxtaposed differences.

There is no Final Arrival or Absolute Enlightenment save honorable mention given to confessing ignorance. As more functions of Intelligence are integrated into our perspective, our maps and definitions become more open-ended as the more we "know," the more we realize in utter clarity what remains unknown. Some things are just not meant to be figured out. Sometimes all we can do is realize that we *are* the mystery itself and let it go at that. As with all true discipline, the real education begins ON OUR OWN. There will be a kaleidoscope of challenges to excite new information arriving in many flavors. What we do with it determines how much we have learned *or* if we have learned anything at all. There will be Teachers. They will arrive at the right time in the right place. However, they do not have to be people. Teachers can be situations, serving to catalyze and provoke change within us.

There are no accidents in ANGEL TECH. Messages arrive daily fresh from the No Coincidences Dept. It's all a matter of perspective...how we choose to look at things. Crisis is Opportunity... Suffering is a Mask for Growth... Mistakes are God Leaks... Personal Tragedy is Spiritual Victory... Disillusionment is Illumination. As you have already surmised, it begins Right Where You Are Sitting Now.

dogma AND catma

Faculty &
Administration

Entrance Requirements

ELEMENTARY SCHOOL
(GRADES 1–4)

HOMEWORK

The motivation for learning in ANGEL TECH comes from love and love comes in many colors. In Elementary School, every time we graduate we discover love for the first time because each grade defines love differently. This experience shifts throughout each grade, from First Grade Mother Love...to Second Grade Love of Power...to...Third Grade Idea Love...to...Fourth Grade Personal Love. Homework means contacting the direct experience of our love: physically, emotionally, conceptually and socially...or, what makes us *happy* in these areas. Our research: locating those conditioned and mechanical responses which stop us from direct-experiencing each function of our Intelligence. The final authority: *how* we absorb, organize and communicate our experience of reality.

FIRST GRADE

First Grade is for BABIES. We learn how to be passive, dependent and totally self-centered, infantile entities living for immediate oral-body gratification. We discover what feels good and what doesn't, what is nourishing and what isn't. As babies we find out about fear for the first time, especially, the fear of falling and the fear of sudden loud noises which interrupt our infant bliss. We also have the privilege of screaming bloody murder when we don't get our way, as well as shining like a buddha when we do. Most of all, Babies need Mothers or surrogates, the providers of First Grade Love. Mothers determine whether Baby's reality is based in trust or fear depending upon how committed Mom is in providing love. The provision of Mother Love helps imprint trust, as the absence imprints distrust. This does not mean that Fathers are to be excluded...they become more important in our culture later on.

First Grade experience is the most undifferentiated of all...the qualities of distinction and clarity get in the way. Baby-talk is a good way to get acquainted. Other oral activities such as sucking, spitting, biting, chewing, gurgling, drooling, screaming and vomiting also excite

Physical Intelligence. Perhaps most significant of all, babies are known to produce the softest and gentlest of human sounds.

As Babies, we ARE our most vulnerable, impressionable feelings and perceptions. There is no split. The openness we feel as Babies becomes the basis by which we can learn. Without it, we grow old by stopping reception. By staying open, we're absorbing the world around us. In fact, as Babies, we're so open that we really don't know the difference between the world and ourselves. It's all the same to us...until, we're not fed, held and cleaned. Then, we're reminded of the difference, mostly between pleasure and pain. And even then, we become the pain so much, we cry as if the world is going to end any moment. On the other hand, when we become the pleasure, we provide our parents with hours of endless joy as they share (and remember) our Infant Bliss, Wonder and Absolute Awe.

In First Grade, our whole reason for living is the warm, comforting feeling of being loved by Mother-surrogate. Mother Love is not only warm and comfy but sloppy, wet and all-encompassing. When it's there, it's everywhere and when it's gone, it's gone in a big way. Being a Baby is just about the most terrifying thing you could imagine, as an adult, because so much depends on Mother being there. Sometimes Mother is replaced by The Babysitter but it's never really the same. It does, however, help us grow as Babies to not be picked up and held too much so we can graduate from our total dependency. Some of us get held way too much and never really stop being Babies...even as Fourth Grade Adults! So, we are essentially helpless to the mistakes, accidents and trials of our Mother as she learns to raise us.

The most important thing to remember from First Grade is that no matter what happens, everything becomes accepted and in many instances life just takes care of itself. If we don't learn this, we either don't graduate *or* understand the importance of dependency, vulnerability and safety. All these things are necessary for comfort at the most basic level. In Second Grade, though, they are often hidden and forgotten because there are other things to learn. But deep inside, we are soft, mushy Babies seeking warmth in all kinds of sloppy, wet places. One more thing, we love putting things into our mouths...

First Grade activities: soak in a hot bath, let someone you trust carry you, receive a full-body massage, crawl and baby-talk, cry out when you feel helpless, feel the fear of falling and sudden loud noises, get real hungry, cuddle with someone who loves you, discover who your

"Mother" models are, satisfy yourself, be held by someone, permit somebody to feed you.

SECOND GRADE

Second Grade is for Kids. Babies grow into Kids when they start moving away from Mothers and begin exploring on their own. The new education is crawling, standing and walking in the world. Kids test themselves. They want to see how fast they can move and how strong they are. Kids learn to become strong and fast so they don't have to feel like helpless Babies. Nobody likes a crybaby in Second Grade and no Second Grader likes to be one, especially around other Kids. Once in awhile, Kids will fight each other to test their strength and mobility. This way. Kids learn about winning and losing which is the Main Game in Second Grade. This is why Kids make the best gangs. They know how important winning is. In these gangs, Kids find out who is Boss and who is the least important Kid, the one all the others make fun of or gang up on. Bosses get to tell all the other Kids in their gang what game they will play. In Second Grade, everybody should be Boss at least once to graduate.

The most important thing to know in Second Grade is that we are special and important in some way. As Kids, we do this by expressing ourselves. How else will other Kids know who we are? On occasion, Kids will meet Big Kids. Big Kids are the strongest and fastest Kids around. A lot of times, Kids will worship and fear Big Kids because they know how strong and fast they are. Big Kids are Fourth Graders who sometimes hang out with Little Kids when they have Second Grade Homework to catch up on. Second Grade Love is for Power. The love of power is sometimes necessary to just stand on our own two feet. Power takes many different forms. The three main kinds of power in Second Grade are: *Strength, Personal Freedom and Status.*

Second Grade strength is visceral and is entirely dependent upon how much guts you have. It takes courage to know you can take care of yourself in a jam. With Mom not around all the time, you have to learn how to protect yourself…even fight for your life, if you have to. Kids learn the *willingness* to do so or they become "cowards, sissies, mama's boys/girls" which are names to describe the least important Kids. Boys have a harder time in Second Grade then Girls do because they are not expected to fight in the *same way* but some of them still do.

When a Kid leaves Mother to create his/her own space, he/she becomes an individual as soon as he/she finds a way to own that

space and make it his/hers. Second Grade Homework is *owning your actions and space.* Kids are in charge of themselves enough to determine who and who cannot come in. Emotional Intelligence is being organized. Kids are confident enough to *enforce* these decisions. This process of emotional centering is self-centered and, necessarily so. With Mom gone, somebody's got to watch out for Number One.

Autonomy gives us the right to do things our own way unless we're out smarted by Third Grade Student-types or bullied by Fourth Grade Big Kids or maybe, scolded by Adults. Until that time, we do as we please. We wear the clothes we like, cut our hair the way we want or let it grow long. We keep secrets from Adults and even lie to them just to protect our sense of freedom. We kids invent emotional strategies to keep getting our way, too. It's all political from our point of view because we're political animals. (Did you know that the word "politics" comes from the root word for *police,* which is "policie"?) We make great informants, enforcers and tyrants. The word "policy" is also related to politics and Kids love making deals, especially when they know they'll come out on top.

Status arrives when we are recognized to know the game well enough to win almost every time. Kids love winners and winning. Winning, after all, is exciting. (Kids get excited about winning as it excites adrenaline, an important Second Grade drug.) Status goes to the person and/or activity providing the greatest adrenaline rush and jag. This is, of course, relative...every Kid has their own Thrill Criteria. What turns one Kid on, turns another right off. This is what keeps Kids together when they try and make friends with each other. As Kids, we find out if we can get along with each others rushes, thrills and excitements. If not, no big deal...there's always more Kids to check out.

Second Grade activities: Play any sport to win. Watch a Clint Eastwood movie, Take a ride on a Ferris wheel. Develop your own power elite group. Slamdance at a punk-rock concert. Initiate a wrestling match. Lose an argument and feel defeated. Make someone else feel important. Take a karate lesson. Climb a tree. Throw a tantrum. Rebel against your favorite authority figure. When feeling violated, don't hold back your anger...lash out. Act like you're on top of the world.

THIRD GRADE

Third Grade is for STUDENTS. As Students, we learn how to study things up close in order to Figure Them Out. (First Grade Babies are too absorbed with Mom and Second Grade Kids are too self-absorbed to study anything that closely). By Third Grade, we're expected to know enough to stop crying and fighting long enough to use our heads. Third Grade Homework is all about training our minds to solve problems which are more abstract and distant. This has to do with knowing when something is a problem and when it doesn't have to be. Students love knowing How Things Work, so they can take things apart just to put them back together again. This is easy when we figure out how to be clear, precise and logical in the way we think about things.

There's a lot to learn in Third Grade but the most important is knowing that you are smart. Being smart means developing the skills to keep learning *new ways* to learn. Sometimes being smart makes us clever and even cunning, sneaky and shrewd. This tends to happen when Students become Too Smart For Their Own Good...which may not be very smart at all. It is important, however, to never stop learning. One way to make sure we never stop learning is to understand how our mind(s) works. This'll help us *interpret* some of the more intuitive complex experiences of High School so we don't blow our minds away too much. The process of integrating new experiences through our own interpretations of it is called our "psychology." The more we understand our own psychology, the more we'll be able to comprehend other people's psychology and be prepared for Fourth Grade Social Studies.

Students learn to live in their minds, fantasizing and imagining worlds to inhabit. Sometimes Students live in a World of Their Own. It can be fun to imagine the wildest, most beautiful dream to live in whether we just want to escape from dreary, dismal realities or are involved with a creative project. Either way, we find out that our minds are magnificent dream-makers that'll create just about anything. Knowing this, going outside and playing is just Kids Stuff unless it's an activity requiring our mental concentration, as well. The most important thing to know about our minds is that they're real good at making things up, whether they are real or not...and in order to graduate into Fourth Grade, we have to know what is "real" from what is "not."

In Second Grade, We discovered and claimed our territory; in Third Grade, we learn to make maps describing our experience &/or

copy the maps made by other Students. The four main map-making tools are Reading, Writing, Arithmetic and Speaking. Of course, we have to know how to think and use our heads in order to make maps in the first place. One good reason to make maps is to communicate ourselves to others without having to be a Baby or a Kid about it. This means learning how to voice our thoughts so that others get the picture we're sending. One way Students get smarter is by finding the right *words* to describe experience with. This creates "perspective" by the emotional distance of *abstraction*...the ability to say a lot with a little. As Students discover, we lose our perspective when we're too emotional or physical. However, it is important to keep in mind that concepts are not "real," like things or experiences. Developing a sense of humor also helps us keep perspective.

Another way to get smarter is by learning how to keep our maps, or descriptions, somewhat incomplete...so, when there's new information, it can be included. New information is like another piece of the puzzle. Even when the puzzle's finished, it's still a puzzle. This is because "truth" can only be referred to and never totally explained. Students don't graduate until they figure this **out.** For example: If we believe we've got all the pieces to the puzzle, then there's no reason to think there's any other pieces. This happens when we mistake our maps for the territory and create a dogma, or absolute belief. (See *Introduction*.) This feels like we know everything. It also closes our minds to learning new ways to learn and so, we have to remain in Third Grade until we figure it out for ourselves: *Keep Your Mind Open*...even when you have all the pieces, it's still a puzzle.

Third Grade love is for Ideas. The mind loves what is true. Sometimes, however, we fall in love with words and make dogma because words only reflect and suggest truth; they are not identical with it. One way we find this out is by learning to fine-tune our Bullshit Detector... (see Robert Anton Wilson's *Prometheus Rising* and *The New Inquisition*) our ability to know if something is true or false. We begin to separate facts from personalities. A fundamental process of discrimination takes place, where we learn the difference between mystery, technology and facts.

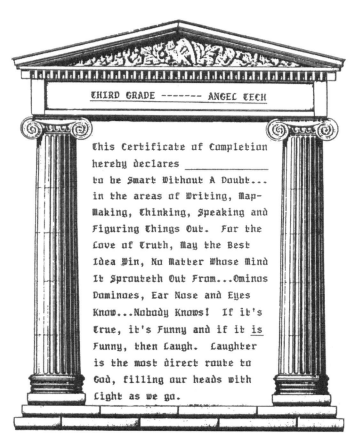

THIRD GRADE -------- ANGEL TECH

This Certificate of Completion hereby declares _____ to be Smart Without A Doubt... in the areas of Writing, Map-Making, Thinking, Speaking and Figuring Things Out. For the Love of Truth, May the Best Idea Win, No Matter Whose Mind It Sprouteth Out From...Ominus Dominoes, Ear Nose and Eyes Know...Nobody Knows! If it's True, it's Funny and if it is Funny, then Laugh. Laughter is the most direct route to God, filling our heads with Light as we go.

Third Grade activities: Take something apart and put it back together again, Read three books during the same period of time, Read a book on statistics even though you might not know what it means, Go to the library and read four doctoral dissertations: one each in the social sciences, the arts, literature and physics; Give a lecture, Write a book or a play, Critique a film, Confess your ignorance without apologizing, Learn a new language, Figure out how to get rich, Read periodicals that you normally wouldn't

FOURTH GRADE

Fourth Grade is for Big Kids, Adults, Family and the Religion of your "choice." Grade Four is a big place and presents the most diverse, complex types of situations involving people. Being the final Grade in

Elementary School, everybody here has already been through the first three Grades. Graduating participants now share the opportunity for developing their Social Intelligence...or How To Get Along With People. Groups are defined as any number larger than one. Couples are groups. When relating to another person, we are also relating to the collective. This kind of awareness begins Fourth Grade education.

The first phase of Fourth Grade belongs to Big Kids, who are also known as **Adolescents.** Big Kids are no longer Babies, at least not all the time. They feel important and smart enough to start making up their own rules. The Main Games Big Kids play are called Courting Rituals, which are elaborate activities expressing catalyzed sexual/hormonal impulses. In these rituals, Big Kids find out what turns them on about other people and what turns them off. The results of this rite of passage determines certain sexual preferences and mating styles...two factors shaping their future social life. Occasionally, certain Big Kids aren't ready for these rituals, and so they return to First, Second and/or Third grade until they are safe, important and smart enough to join in. For Big Kids, life at best is a Big Party. When the Party's over. Big Kids either become Adults *or* find ways to bypass Terminal Adulthood by prolonging adolescence.

Adults are Big Kids who "grew up." The word "adult" implies a "fully developed plant or animal in the final phase of its growth." (The word "adolescent" comes from the Latin "ad" and "alescere" meaning, *to grow).* Big Kids usually rebel against Adults because they don't want to grow up and die. Many Big Kids grow up and become Adults *without rebelling* and so remain Big Kids inside and Little Adults outside. Adult Education requires participants to memorize the Reward and Punishment system of the society they live in, as if it were absolute and essential rather then being arbitrary and relative. This is to help Adults look and feel "socially acceptable" for doing the Right Thing and to act guilty and feel like "no-good dumb shits" for doing the Wrong Thing in their culture.

The strongest social need comes from the urge to belong. One way Adults feel close is by Getting Married. One way they start organizing their Social Intelligence is by Having Babies and meeting with other genetic family members for Get Togethers, during which, Adults find out about Family Hierarchy i.e., who eats first and last, however, belonging and closeness is primary.

Another way Adults belong is through the "extended [or non-genetic] family"...where groups of Adults are organized around a common purpose. This purpose can be as simple as just Getting Together or as Grandiose as Saving The World. Adults like Getting Together with Friends and some team up to Save The World. Others create a *Religion* to get other Adults to drop what they're doing and join them. Religions are *Rules to Live By* for many Adults who feel lost, confused and/or out of touch with their own unique style of intelligent survival on the planet. Religions are also designed to meet the social need for belonging, as well as the physical, emotional and conceptual needs for security, status and "knowledge." Some Adults decide to remain in Fourth Grade forever by becoming members of certain religious groups. This is called joining the CHURCH OF EVERLASTING LIFE—or Terminal Cure For Uncertainty.

The CHURCH OF EVERLASTING LIFE is any group, corporation, person, religion and/or government promising to meet our "needs" in exchange for the sacrifice of our mind, autonomy and identity. Most frequently, however, we are told that we are incompetent to handle our "problems," thus requiring these very high-priced caretakers. This kind of CHURCH offers members *rewards* from Grades One through Four: 1st Grade FOOD, SECURITY and PROTECTION; 2nd Grade STATUS, LAND and WORK; 3rd Grade MONEY, DOCUMENTS and MAPS; 4th Grade MEMBERSHIP, RELIGION and RETIREMENT. These rewards and others may be ours if we let the Church own us. Since the urge to belong is a strong social need, it's important to meet this need *somewhere.* If there's no place to go, there's always the CHURCH OF EVERLASTING LIFE. The other alternative is in knowing how to make, keep and change friends. In Fourth Grade, we find out how important our real friends *are* and we find out ways to know *who* they are. The most important lesson in Fourth Grade is: *KNOWING WHO YOUR FRIENDS ARE.* Those of us unwilling to remain in Fourth Grade forever become candidates for Graduation through the Initiation of *Chapel Perilous.* Not everybody has to go through the Chapel. It *is* possible to skip right over it and submerge oneself directly in Fifth Grade Rapture without a trace of guilt, fear or humiliation. For those of us with any doubts at all, let's meet in the CHAPEL.

Fourth Grade activities: Attend a funeral, Make a new friend, Go to a garden party, Confront your enemy with a gift, Get married now, Join a religion. Spend a night with the author, Call Jerry Falwell, Initiate a romance.

KARMA MECHANICS

UNDERGRADUATE STUDY

KARMA MECHANICS (Course Description): Learn how survival works and how to make it work for you. Research: the Absorption, Organization and Communication of PHYSICAL, EMOTIONAL, CONCEPTUAL and SOCIAL functions of Intelligence. Four credits.
    PREREQUISITE: Commitment, Honesty and Integrity.
    Inquire within.

THE PREMISE

Everybody wants to survive unless somebody has made the choice to die. The will to survive thrives in the spirit of its continuity. The survivor *knows* that no matter what happens, some part will endure. (Are you a survivor?) The realization of this knowledge is enough to dissipate the anxiety we feel when we believe there is NO FUTURE. This type of anxiety makes it impossible to afford the leisure to pursue "post-survival" activities like those found in High School. It's difficult to be creative if you're worrying about your individual survival issues. Before even thinking about getting high, it's only appropriate to CLEAN UP OUR ACTS.

(sounds of thunderous applause)

Karma, as defined here, implies those Life Lessons by which our destiny reveals itself; Mechanics is the study of how motion works, hence, KARMA MECHANICS means "studying the motion of our destiny." For the sake of Multiple Definitions, Double Vision and Good, Clean Fun...Karma Mechanics are also individuals who study KARMA MECHANICS in order to command their own destiny. Karma Mechanics do this by adjusting their karma to synchronize with a higher purpose than mere mechanical living. The key word here is *adjustment.*
    One adjustment for Karma Mechanics is exercising the capacity for "inner discrimination." To discriminate does not mean "to criticize"...which, in this instance, runs counter-productive. It is more of the necessary discernment to recognize the separate functions working as pieces of a whole. This refers specifically to the task of differentiating

46

states of awareness within ourselves. If we feel inwardly indistinct, this can be registered as a kind of "soup effect." The homogenous quality of soupiness can frustrate our attempts to communicate and socialize. Not only is it confusing, this lack of inner distinction has been known to entertain an entire family of negative emotions. Mr. & Mrs. Inertia bring their moody children Despondency, Apathy and Despair. If the party lasts long enough, who knows? Maybe distant Uncle Violence will show up with a grab-bag of games for the children to play with?

THE MECHANICS OF SURVIVAL

KARMA MECHANICS is a course of study best suited for self-realizing robots. The sooner we come to accept our mechanical, robotic self, the sooner we can find the "mold" and break free. By confessing our "conditioned" robothood, we begin self-realizing as robots, in order to evolve into the humanity we are in essence. This starts when our "true feelings" become more rewarding than our conditioned responses. The challenge is in response-ability...the ability to respond creatively to the unknown. Re-read the last sentence for the generic definition of *initiation* in *ANGEL TECH*.

To observe the internal workings of the robot, **Karma Mechanics are asked to relate to the first four grades in Elementary School as gears, i.e., First Gear, Second Gear, etc.** The bottom line of robothood is Gear One Physical Survival. This is the slowest moving gear and rotates by meeting security needs. It also functions as the blueprint for the security priorities of Gears Two, Three and Four, i.e., Emotional, Conceptual, and Social Security. All gears depend upon First Gear to keep the robot alive and moving. Gear Two Emotional Survival revolves a bit faster around territorial and status issues. It's responsible for robot power. Third Gear Conceptual Survival spins faster still around symbolic robot skills like thinking, writing, talking, reading and making maps of local experience. Third Gear is the robot brain. Gear Four Social Survival whirls about and incorporates all previous gears towards getting it together to relate socially with other robots. Fourth Gear expresses the robot personality.

Freedom, herein is defined within this quaternity...that is to say *freedom within a form* is as free as we get. The form is already within us as our four basic functions of Survival Intelligence. This form has been externalized for your convenience as this course in KARMA MECHANICS. Freedom is realized when this 4-fold structure is thoroughly absorbed, organized and communicated *in your own way*. It's hard work and demands total commitment. By finding out where each gear turns within us, it is possible to begin watching your karma. This initiates the arduous path of self-knowledge essential to adjusting karma...our own. We begin by locating our conditioned responses...FIND THE ROBOT.

AN INTERVIEW WITH A KARMA MECHANIC
with Chip Delaney, Ace Reporter

Chip Delaney: You were saying...that you wish anonymity. Why?

Karma Mechanic: I prefer to work in silence. Also, I feel...any undue personal emphasis right now would offset Fourth Gear. You see, my social life is very active and I'm attempting some privacy.

CD: I see...so, when did you first realize that you were a robot and what was it like?

KM: I woke up one morning, looked in the mirror and just knew it. What was it like? Well, initially...a shock. When my mirror image started looking back at me, the "real me" felt this sensation like the bottom falling out, if you know what I'm getting at. I felt hollow. It was disturbing and reassuring, simultaneously. I was mechanical and knowing this kind of fascinated me. I mean, I wasn't as attached anymore. How could I be?

CD (nervous laughter): No, I suppose not...fascinating indeed. Tell me, what did you do next?

KM: Not a hell of a lot right away, Chip. You see, it wasn't enough to realize my robothood. Once I knew that, well, you can just imagine the rest. Most of the people I considered friends were also robots, including my lover at the time. I mean, now I believe we're all robots but only a few of us *know* it. There was this one friend of mine though, who'll also remain anonymous for reasons of his own, who knew he was a robot. I never knew he knew until I knew I was one first. How could I? Anyway, we met and we both knew...it was kind of uncanny yet tremendously reassuring. He told me my life was a mess and turned me onto the karma mechanics motto..."Own Thyself." It was straight uphill from then on.

CD: Straight uphill?

KM: A hell of a lot of hard work, Chip.

CD: Right. Of course (coughs).

KM: You see, once I realized my life was a mess, I couldn't pretend to be a real, together guy anymore. I was no longer "in the know." In fact, I've never felt so damned ignorant in all my life. Not stupid...ignorant...there's a difference. So, my life was a mess. I wasn't eating right. I was being evicted from my apartment for not paying rent because I was fired from work and on top of all this, my girlfriend dumped me. I mean,

I did all the right things with her…1 suppose the fire went out or something, I don't know. So, there I was…an abandoned robot on the streets.

CD: Looking at you now, that's hard to believe.

KM: Thanks, Chip, but it's all true and truth is stranger than fiction…

CD: That's right…(ponders)…so (clears throat), just how did you become a karma mechanic?

KM: Well…remember that fellow I mentioned earlier who also knew he was a robot? Well, he knew someone who dated somebody who used to live with this woman who called herself a karma mechanic. She had apparently sent away for some obscure metaphysical manual which mapped out the schemata for becoming a karma mechanic. This map got around fast. Folks just xeroxed them off by the thousands and gave them away free to anyone even half curious. Not only did I get one of these maps…1 managed to steal the entire manual which I'm xeroxing and distributing to other self-realizing robots. I'd say being a karma mechanic is an attractive idea in these times of growing social uniformity and standardization, don't you think?

CD: Yes, I imagine it would be, wouldn't it? So…you found a map and this manual…did you just follow the instructions?

KM: Not exactly, Chip. Whoever wrote that manual…1 don't know how to pronounce the name, so I won't…but, this person knew what he was doing. You see, there were no real directions on how to run your life. The writer simply assumed that whoever was reading the map or manual already knew they were robots. Robots are already pre-programmed to survive. The blueprint for survival is right there inside each of us encoded by the genetic intelligence of DNA. But…here's the clincher. DNA doesn't really care *how* you do it, just as long as you *survive,* get it? The goal of DNA is immortality and the way we've been doing it so far has been through the reproduction bias…we make new fleshy robots. So, once that's clear, our options become more obvious. We can choose *how* to survive. Freedom is really just a matter of style, wouldn't you say?

CD: Very interesting…so what did this manual tell you?

KM: Without going into too many details, it told me about the nature of Intelligence and how there are different functions of Intelligence…eight of them to be precise…as a system for Intelligence increase. These functions followed an evolution from the most basic, simple way to survive to the most wayout, expanded…uh, simplex ways to survive.

Robots who know they're robots will have no problem in realizing that all these functions already exist as circuits in their Central Nervous System and that each robot experiences each circuit differently. One man's heaven is another's hell, y'know. With each individual, different circuits are more active than others. Some circuits have been over-amped and need repair, others simply need adjustment. The manual tells you what the circuits are, what problems they face and how to facilitate the essential adjustment for optimum operational capacity. It works. There's a hell of a lot more, Chip but I think its just too much information for a single interview. Robots should just get the manual. Start with Book One, *Angel Tech*...that's basic training.

CD: Quite. How has your life changed since becoming a karma.

KM (interrupting): Radically, Chip. There are no words.

CD (peeved): Yes, but...if you were to attempt to describe...

KM: Why not... Third Gear needs adjustment anyway. OK, the... description. The responsibility is awesome. The process of reclaiming one's old, discarded self from the shelf of a meaningless life is no small task. It's basically a creative endeavor. One of the ways I knew my life was a mess was its "soupiness." It was all glued together, hodge-podge with no distinction at all. I couldn't tell one part of myself from another and so I really had nothing to say, yet I felt like I had so much inside me I could burst. I just didn't have the energy or articulation to communicate myself. I mean, I don't think everybody starts out like this but I did. My soupiness...uh, fuzziness...just served as the ideal kind of putty to be shaped by...the artist. Everybody's an artist: And my life became my first art project. I went into retreat and brainstormed about how I wanted to create myself. I set up research topics to learn more about where I really stood with different aspects of my existence. The maps in *ANGEL TECH* provided a format. My work was to evolve through each grade and graduate in the manner best suited to my personal style. I suppose that's what "enlightenment" means to me. Funny thing, enlightenment... there's really no place to go because no matter where you go, here you are! (laughing) Seriously though, the biggest way my life has changed is that I'm no longer concerned with being just one type of person. Sixth Grade Psychic Intelligence changed all that. I just don't get caught up in being anything, so I end up being able to do more. I've stopped trying to change the world, too. I mean, why should I change the world when I can change myself? One more thing. I'm not as judgmental as I used to be. Judgmental people are so-o-o boring...just dismal...

CD: Right. They certainly are. You say you don't want to change the world, only yourself...why do you want people to read this book? Isn't that a bit hypocritical?

KM: You're such a literalist, Chip. Not everybody is going to understand or even want to understand what I'm saying. The awakening robots will take to it right away, I think. Those individuals are already changing themselves. This book simply presents a guideline to accelerate the transformation. It teaches the value of "quick decay" rather than "slow death" if you catch my gist. Besides, I'm more of a quick change artist anyway and I hate unnecessary suffering. I just don't have time to stay miserable or hang out with martyrs.

CD: I can see your point. So, in wrapping it up, is there anything else you'd like to share with the readers...uh, robots?

KM: Yes, there is. In all seriousness, there's a lot of anti-life influence going around in the mass media. The messages we get everyday from television, radio, newspapers and everybody's brother are so crossed and confused that if you don't start thinking for yourselves, you'll be woven into the social fabric of a great dying beast. For many of us, it's far too late. For the rest of us, I say: Stay Hungry, Let It Rot and Don't Get Lost In The Sauce. Remember, children have nightmares to wake up.

CD: That seems a bit cryptic, doesn't it? Won't you elaborate?

KM: Not a chance, Chip. It's as clear as a bell.

CD: Well, maybe to you it is. What about the millions who...

KM (interrupts): Goodnight Chet.

CD (upset): That's Chip. (suddenly laughs) Oh, I get it! Good Night, David.

Within each gear, there alternates a current sustaining its revolution. This current expresses its charge negatively or positively depending upon the karma being experienced. Positive/negative is not synonymous with good/bad but the essential polarity of manifestation…as in electricity, both are needed to generate power. There is a way to read these alternating patterns of positive and negatively charged karma in…

THE KARMIC CODE

Two alternating patterns have been detected as a means to read and decipher the "karmic code"… **1) Excitement & 2) Resistance.**

Excitements are "positively charged" and develop into attachments, bondings and obsessions. These are areas of direct, intuitive contact with Life Energies. Resistances are "negatively charged" areas of judgment, avoidance and fear. Whatever is judged as being "wrong" and "not OK" the way it is, is a resistance. Whatever is resisted soon develops into patterns of habitual avoidance. Many times, resistance stems from an attachment to an idea or belief *about* Life Energies which consequently inhibit direct, intuitive contact with Life itself. Just so it won't seem too simple, excitements and resistances take turns being each other. We become what we resist.

The Karmic **Code** expresses **fundamental** insight **into** the **way** we **define** ourselves. Between our excitements and resistances, we attract situations, persons and lessons geared to elucidate our karma or "destiny". By becoming more familiar with our own code, it is possible to understand what turns us on and what we are running from. The shape of our destiny can be altered, if needed, by first reading the karmic code. This demands a scathing self-honesty and an encompassing self-acceptance. This course studies the process of reading the code towards its adjustment based in a personal style and preference of survival in the first four grades. **(SECRET MESSAGE #666:** *There is no Energy Shortage, only Energy Blockage. Remove the Block and Life takes care of itself. The nicest things happen by themselves.)*

SANCTIFICATION OF THE KARMIC CODE

The first homework assignment in Karmic Mechanics is learning the lesson of NO JUDGMENT. What this means simply is when you hold court make sure everyone is there. (Defense/Offense/Jury/Judge/ETC.) It remains virtually impossible to relate to resistance and excitement if we are being judgmental in the moment. The objective is: How to Let Excitement and Resistance (our own AND others) Be Ok the Way It Is. This helps minimize the mechanical tendencies of resisting resistance and judging excitement and versa visa. The resistance of resistance, in particular, may be the source of that psychic tension which enforces muscular armoring. (See *The Murder of Christ,* by Wilhelm Reich; *Wilhelm Reich In Hell,* by Robert Anton Wilson; and *Undoing Yourself with Energized Meditation* by Christopher S. Hyatt, the last by Falcon Press.) The graduation of Intelligence depends on how open and vulnerable we are to the education at hand…our excitements and resistances, for example. Excitement tells us what turns us on. Judging it simply lowers our over-all energy level by disconnecting us from our source of life. (Pleasure Anxiety). Sometimes, during intense self-denial, we reconnect to the excitement of others for vicarious thrills. (Safe Pleasure). This is akin to portraying an "extra" in somebody else's "B" Movie.

†What IS Sacred?†

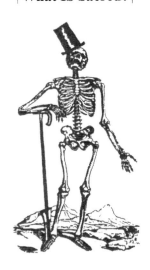

Life is sacred to the living and a threat to the dead.

To sanctify is to make sacred. Sanctification of the Karmic Code implies the act of regarding resistance and excitement as sacred. More specifically, it means relating to resistance as energy itself. Resistance may not feel energetic but that is the illusion Life casts in its frozen state. From this perspective, resistance is negatively charged, frozen energy. It is not different from Life. As an alternative to resisting resistance, try *blending* with it. For further instructions, *don't hold your breath.* As for excitement, an alternative to resisting or judging it is: *Let it Shake You...tremble...quiver and sigh.*

As you explore your own Karmic Code throughout the first four levels, BREATHE, BLEND and TREMBLE with it. How else can we find out about our dogmas without letting the cat out of the bag? Self-knowledge remains preliminary to self-transcendence. Now Thyself.

6   LOVERS

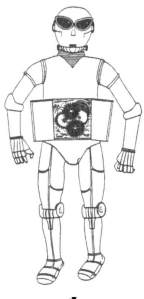

1
PHYSICAL SURVIVAL

A – PASSIVITY

B – SAFETY

C – NOURISHMENT

FIRST GEAR

Gear One develops with establishing physical safety in times of threat. Its momentum is slowed down with any messages negating safety of the organism and it is accelerated with signals affirming physical survival. First Gear processes *fear,* both mechanical and innate responses to danger. The robot naturally contracts to a security threat (All Systems Alert!) Fear can be processed by: 1) Accepting and giving it expression *and* 2) Responding creatively by restoring safety yourself. You don't have to wait for anybody to make you feel safe. You have the choice of reclaiming your body: Become your own parent and protect yourself.

Security isn't a goal when seen in relationship to the process of Initiation: *Be Safe Enough To Take Risks.* Emotional, Conceptual, and Social safety depend upon the prototype model of physical Safety. If the basic reality of safety has not been programmed into Gear One, then it is quite possible that a basic distrust and fear remain. Graduation can only occur with the thorough Absorption, Organization and Communication of our Physical Safety. The absorption of safety depends entirely upon how vulnerable we can be.

!SAFETY FIRST!

Any setting providing a **womb-like feeling** or environment is one way to feel safe enough to relax control. This can occur alone or with a "trusted other." First Grade Homework is with locating how we let go and *trust.* Trust means that there is a possibility of us not being violated, hurt or killed in this moment.

ALTERNATIVE MOM

First Gear is mobilized through an underlying sense of trust and physical safety, initially felt as the bonding between Mother and Infant. To the degree this basic sense of trust was not imprinted, an imprint of distrust and survival anxiety emerges. It is possible to (re) stabilize basic trust through alternatives other than trying to recover it from our actual genetic mothers or by projecting this need on our mates or friends.

Gear One is defined inside the Mother-Infant body/bonding; we learn to oscillate between the roles of Mother and Infant. This dynamic sets up creative opposition for balancing the biological needs of nourishing—

with being nourished—being helpless—and being protective. These are outlooks necessary for understanding Biological or Physical Intelligence.

Two settings providing direct contact with the Infant Within are the 1) Isolation Float Tank and 2) Bio-energetic breathwork or Rebirthing. (Just before the 3rd printing of this work I was informed that *Chakra Therapy* developed by Drs. Regardie and Hyatt should be added to this list.) Float Tanks can be rented at most Health Spas for a nominal fee per hour, the average time for a float. Tanks replicate womb conditions: totally dark and silent, you float freely in heavily salted water heated to 98°F until the sense of floating overcomes the sense of separateness. In the silence, the only sounds heard are your own breathing, heartbeat, blood pumping and whatever the mind is creating. If you consciously agree to relax your desire to control you can yield to a primal sense of trust in being totally supported by the water. The more physically passive and vulnerable you permit yourself to become, the more support you can experience.

Mobilizing First Gear begins as soon as we relax the desire to control, and become impressionable to complete safety in the physically receptive state. The deeper the vulnerability, the deeper the potential for imprint.

Unlike the Isolation Tank experience, the process of Rebirthing cannot be effectively conveyed in words and so, for a dearer definition, consult a practicing expert. However, the basic principles are simple and easy to explain but are not recommended for practice without a "certified" Rebirther to assist you. In our normal everyday breathing you'll discover a certain discontinuity with inhaling and exhaling. For example: We tend to hold our breath at irregular intervals as certain inhales will be more shallow than others. The process of Rebirthing, however, supports a consistent breathing pattern wherein the breath becomes "connected." There is no gap between inhale and exhale. This may sound like hyperventilation but it's not. Instead, it is the process of inhaling until we can no longer inhale, then releasing the breath into its natural exhale. The exhale becomes an unforced reflex to inhaling.

The evolution of connected breathing gathers momentum and eventually charges the organism with "prana" or life force. (Read *Undoing Yourself with Energized Meditation and Other Devices,* Falcon Press, and Wilhelm Reich's work on Orgone and Bio-Energetics.) The body rejuvenates with more energy than it's accustomed and can even react by contracting...the hands and fingers may curl...the face may come to a point of tension. This is because the body's natural reaction to being energized is to sometimes get more tense, thus leading to a deeper relaxation. If and when these contractions happen it is suggested that you trust your instincts: 1) Stop the process or 2) Deepen your commitment to your physiological state by following through. If you choose the latter, you will enter into new levels of profound relaxation and self-trust. If you choose the former, you'll have another chance next time around.

SAFETY FIRST

Once safety is absorbed, it can be organized so that it's there when you need it. Organizing safety means figuring our how you make yourself safe and then, doing it yourself. Once this process is stabilized, it becomes easier to communicate safety to and with others. Physical safety isn't always best communicated through talking. It can be, simply transmitted or radiated, as a sense of well being. Other bodies pick this up instantly and are put at ease. Communicating physical safety is the same thing as being instinctively confident. Others can feel safe around you because you feel safe with yourself.

One of the more popular, and more subtle, forms of negating physical safety is in a psychological attitude called *Body-Trashing*. Body-trashing is when we think poorly of our bodies. The most powerful form of this is contained in the crux of any doctrine, spiritual and/or otherwise stating a belief about the body as being "bad" or separate from Life, or Spirit. This "imposed" division between Body and Spirit is simply an art form for understanding, unless we begin to believe it is real whereby we develop a "spiritual schizophrenia" with further complications born from a lack of self-communication. The ancient Kabbalah views the body as a denser form of spirit. That is matter is in spirit and spirit is in matter but simply in finer and denser "particles." The Tree of Life is an excellent model to begin viewing your entire universe. It allows you to see differences while at the same time maintaining unity. No single part can ever be the whole. This is what is meant by the Holiness of the body.

When the body's signals are ignored, its devotion to Spirit is excited to speaking louder for attention. With prolonged negligence, the body may start screaming by getting sick or by "accident-prone" behavior. There are no accidents. The body will literally die for you in its all-consuming need to be felt and heard. And if you think you body is "bad" or "not OK," there's less reason to feel it or hear its cries and whispers. If you are not feeling or listening to your own body, it's quite possible you're doing it to *some-body* else's. Spirit needs a body to feel and stay alive on this planet—here and now.

Whose body are you in?
NOW?!

†††

NOW THYSELF

Our physical body is the only part of ourselves that is always in present time. Every other aspect of ourselves is prone to wander from being in the here and now. Reclaiming First Gear means confronting our commitment to being on the planet, physically. Put another way, it is our "being's" commitment to our body. For those of us ready to take the pledge, brace yourselves. Years of self-denial, tension and repressed emotions may need releasing. Some of us may have been operating under the strain of a sophisticated death wish with the best of intentions yet, unwittingly denying ourselves access to our true source of life *in our bodies.* That's the bad news. The good news is that we've probably repressed a lot of pleasure, too and so there are emotional treasures as well as nightmares. As bodies, we feel *real* by feeling ourselves…either through pleasure and/or pain. This is one way our energy stabilizes itself, without which, things get pretty spacey.

   The body's central need is to be felt deeply. As discussed, it does so through pleasure and/or pain. The choice is yours and is really a matter of personal preference. (Is the last word a lie?) The bottom line is that the body must be felt lest it screams as silently or blatantly as necessary. *How* we end up feeling ourselves is up to us. If we grow negligent in meeting this need, we run the risk of exciting the body's awesome devotion and power to call forth cosmic allegiance. The body is a piece of this puzzle we call Universe…it's *your piece*…and if listened to and spoken with, it becomes the doorway to your whole self.

BODY—IMAGES

Body-images held that do not refer to the organism's unique and ever-changing nature are invitations to conflict, drain and disintegration. The organism is alive; our ideas of ourselves must reflect life or struggle against living. One way of initiating Body-Mind rapport (Physical & Conceptual Intelligence) is *keeping one's word.* Say what you mean and mean what you say. Follow through with your actions. Your body is a lie-detector. If a promise is broken the body feels betrayal. This emotion can be projected outwardly and dramatized in relationships. Such a seemingly small negligence can lead to self deception. The credo of *keeping word* is especially potent where physical rewards are concerned. If you promise yourself physical assurance and do not follow through body/self-esteem diminishes. The organism picks up everything.

The physical body is the visible manifestation of the so-called Subconscious Mind. The body is the fingerprint of the soul, a Rorschach of the Self. Nothing can be hidden. The body communicates it all.

To the degree we are able to speak with our body, we are also speaking with the subconscious. This goes for speaking to and with other *bodies* as well. Body/Mind rapport is the same thing as Subconscious/Conscious rapport. There is a certain way of speaking with and to the body. It has to do with a style of communication which recognizes the element of *space* as a value. If messages to the body are too defined or spelled out, the body naturally resists. The organism loves space and knows itself by its movement *in* space. Openness provides room for the body's natural responses as well as defining the life space of the "EGO".

There is an art to speaking with bodies. This is the art of Speaking In Blanks…just enough incompleteness to *evoke* as well as explain.

Another way of courting the body is in the conscious avoidance of generalizations. It can be useful at times to generalize, however, one rule is sticking close to the "hard Data." This prevents the body from falling asleep. Our Body comes alive to any self-reference. If such an experience is immediately transferred to the universal or generic realm of things, the individual is unwittingly negated. If, for example, you use the words "Most People" or "Oneself" or "You" to communicate what is essentially a personal truth, then you are negating yourself as an individual. Taken by itself, this does not make much of a difference until it has become, in time, a habit. A simple shift in semantics can make all the difference in the world in winning your body back again. Instead of saying "most people" try "this is my thought or my feeling." Instead of referring to "oneself", try more self-referring pronouns…like "me, myself and I." Once generalization has set in as a defense, it will take a great conscious effort to pay attention because a part of you has been put to sleep.

BODY WISDOM

Physical Intelligence naturally avoids what is toxic and approaches what is nourishing. It is only by being out of touch with our basic instincts that this natural tendency is reversed; we avoid nourishment and are attracted to the toxic. There is nothing particularly "WRONG" with this until we fail to see the long-term implications of self-destructive tendencies. At times, it may be nourishing to *intoxicate* ourselves and so forth. Body Wisdom means knowing our limits...knowing when to stop and when we've had enough. It is the realization that the body must assimilate, or digest, what has been absorbed before anything else can be taken in.

Physical Intelligence is sharpened through hunger...ask any dancer. There is a saying in Zen which demonstrates this kind of body wisdom: "Eat whey you are hungry, sleep when you are tired and wake up when you stop dreaming." What could be more simple? And yet to understand this basic rule of survival, we have to first learn how to simplify ourselves. Being in touch with our basic needs is, in a way, *staying hungry*. Don't misunderstand...not in a manner suggesting poverty, self-denial or similar torments. It is living life enough On The Edge to KNOW when we are hungry and tired...and then, responding.

Once you move in, it's not a house anymore...it's a home.

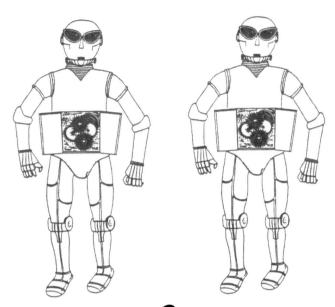

2
EMOTIONAL SURVIVAL

A – SELF-EXPRESSION

B – STATUS

C – PERSONAL POWER

SECOND GEAR

The first four gears of KARMA MECHANICS express "ego-functions" serving the necessary information for the survival of the individual. Once we have learned how to survive as individual egos, perhaps then we might begin approaching our part in groups, nations and worlds with more integrity. Ego is defined hereafter in at least four ways. Physical Survival refers to ego-safety. Emotional Survival is defined in terms of ego-strength. Conceptual Survival is in charge of ego-concepts, or "maps" and Fourth Gear Social Survival develops with ego-bonding and networking. As an aging Buddhist once said, "Once you understand ego, you pretty much understand it all." There's no easy way out. We are called upon to grapple directly with the territory itself. Once understood, it is possible to see beyond our self-imposed limitations but first, we must take a good, hard look and even wrestle with Beauty and the Beast. It is imperative to never forget that as long as we have bodies we have egos and desires. The assimilation of this simple truth permits us to proceed with our graduation.

Our emotions are put into action by meeting territorial needs. More complex than Physical Gear One, Emotional Gear Two concerns itself with stabilizing ego-strength through Personal Freedom, Status and Political Awareness. Its basic driving force is territorial in that it defines emotions as territorial signals: Emotions get excited whenever one's sense of self, or territory, is diminished and/or augmented. *How* one defines oneself is an expression of personal freedom. Self-definition is the basis of ego-strength. It is accessed whenever Status, Power and Winning are defined on one's own terms.

Status is simply knowing your particular position in any given situation and knowing where the power is. Everybody is special and important. Status is the style by which this condition is realized and then, shared. To catalyze its action, find out *how* you personally attract importance and how you wish self-emphasis. Define your status and what makes you special. Everybody gets status in different ways: from helping others…to…winning a beauty contest…to…getting published and so forth. The bottom line with status is: What would you like to be known for, or for that matter, famous or infamous for? Exercise One is knowing how to receive recognition. Exercise Two is discovering the area in which you'd prefer this recognition.

Our definition of "power" governs our attitudes towards powerful people and determines the power structures we attract into our lives. Power is here to stay. It is a function of our Intelligence as survivors on this planet. The evolution of power has shown us its myriad forms throughout the ages...from our dominion over others to our self dominion. The state of our personal power is ready to evolve when we are ready to define it. In KARMA MECHANICS, we will focus with the kind of power that suggests a greater self-dominion, rather than power over others. By evolving our sense of status (by defining it) it becomes more obvious just what our real territory is. (We own whatever is most personal to us.) Personal power cannot be taken away from us. However, it can be and often is drained away by our own ignorance of its nature. This is a trial-and-error and a trial-and-success process identifying what is most personal to us and surrounding ourselves with choices made from personal needs and preferences. We tap into our power by becoming more aware of our current motives and intentions and, then following through with their expression.

AUTONOMY

Our personal freedom is sometimes defined by the manner in which we respond to invasion, violation and emotional challenge. It takes a certain power to express ourselves in the midst of adversity. It we don't stand up for ourselves in a challenging situation, it is easier to lapse into the common emotional trap of being a "victim." Victims do not exist unless we have defined one or two other role players: "saviors" and/or "persecutors," both of whom need victims to stay alive. This holy trinity of emotional game playing can be creatively destroyed by simply choosing to save ourselves and/or providing our own punishment by playing the game intentionally. Emotions can be expressed in a playful spirit by remembering, it's just a game.

Winning is important to the self-esteem nurturing our autonomy. There are a lot of ways to win but perhaps the most direct is finding the freedom we have to express ourselves. Personal freedom gives the necessary Permission to act outside of the socially accepted norms and standards of behaving. It offers us the chance to see how we really feel about things instead of following the ideas and reactions of those around us. Perhaps most significant is the quality of flexibility it provides, enabling our social Personas to become more emotionally integrated than before.

COMPETITION

Winning is as essential to Emotional Survival as food is to our physical hunger...the question remains: Are you a Winner and how do you define "winning"? As referred to earlier, KARMA MECHANICS will investigate power as self-dominion, rather than dominion over others. It is in this same spirit that we approach competition. The big difference between competing with oneself and with others is that you get to set the performance standards with the former. This is where the real power is. Meeting your own standards and even bypassing them...*self-approval ignites self-empowerment.* A good way to drain your personal power is engaging in any activity which has the effect of exciting your disapproval. The awareness of this mechanism makes it possible to see where you are seeking empowerment from. What exactly merits your approval?

    There are basically two types of winning: 1) Where you get ahead and 2) Where everyone gets ahead. Since the second type of winning already includes the first type inherently, that is where we begin. Sometimes it's not possible for all concerned to get their individual way, however, this doesn't have to be an impediment. There is an area in every emotional situation that expresses "the mutual." It is not readily apparent at times due to the pressing needs of individuals in conflict. Nevertheless, the mutual can emerge if those individuals involved become politically aware and create a policy based in mutuality. This is a very simple agreement demanding absolute commitment and integrity to work. It states:

WHATEVER IS NOT MUTUAL IS RELEASED.

This means that whenever people want different things, they agree to just drop them in favor of whatever remains mutual to all concerned. As difficult as this may sound, it actually gets easier with practice.

POLITICS

Gear Two processes anger. When our personal space is violated, it's only natural to push the intrusion out, unless Second Gear is a bit rusty and "back-up" Gear One processes fear instead. Emotional Survival functions when we stand up for ourselves, reclaim our space and carry on. The crux of our Emotional Intelligence are the values, beliefs, and convictions we identify with. Being out of touch with these is a good way to get stuck in power struggles. (Remember, Graduation depends upon how thoroughly Intelligence is absorbed, organized and communicated throughout each Grade.) Knowing what we believe in makes it a little more difficult to feel emotionally invaded. There's just less vacancy for intruders to set up camp.

Power struggles can occur when we are insecure about our own position and don't know where people stand. When we are unsure of our boundaries (how far we can tread around others without stepping on them and vice-versa), insecurity is the norm. It's awkward walking through No Man's Land, but how else do we find out unless we take the risk? As Kids we learned various emotional strategies for checking people out. We found out if people were friendly or if they were prone to hit us or if they were submissive to our whims. We learned tactics to get our way and to avoid being dominated. Reclaiming Second Gear means looking for these very tactics in our everyday interactions and becoming aware of the dominance-submission games we are playing. These can express themselves in a number of different forms: Tyrant/Martyr, Parent/Child, Boss/Worker, etc....all of them revolving around a "one up, one down" political relationship based in mutual oppression. Our alternative is finding the point of mutual autonomy between ourselves... where people are allowed the personal freedom of being themselves.

Status Report

MAKE AN IMPRESSION.

A CHANCE FOR REAL POWER

MORE COMPETITIVE

All The Fire, Fury And Passion

THIS MUCH POWER

Winners
STRATEGY

SUPER SPECIAL

THE PASSIONS AND POWER PLAYS HEAT UP! TENSION

TAKING UP THE CHALLENGE

BOUNDARY
Control
Now.

BE ALARMED!

A·C·T
Passionately

A Triumph

THRILLS

CONQUERING

SPECIAL Alliance

special CAMOUFLAGE

The
natural
struggle

feel Important

FEEL... advance in support.

WE THINK YOU'RE VERY SPECIAL.

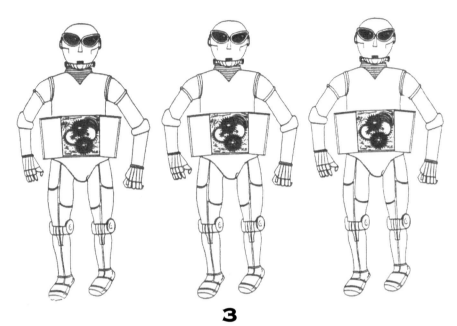

3
CONCEPTUAL SURVIVAL

A – PAY ATTENTION

B – MAKING MAPS

C – ARTICULATION

GEAR THREE

Third Gear Conceptual Survival activates with our capacity to absorb, organize and communicate concepts our mind uses to define what is real. Symbolic research includes the skills of Problem Solving, Map-Making, Articulation and the Power of Naming. Our purpose is with learning how to use these tools for maintaining our sanity and comprehension of our universe...the manner by which we individually experience realities. The crucial point rests with understanding our intellect's appropriate position in relation to the Whole Self. As was introduced at the beginning of this book, the intellect's forte is To Figure Things Out.

One of the smartest things intellect can do is to figure out more effective ways to survive with the least effort...this is called Using Your Head. Conceptual Survival depends upon how responsible we can be for our own peace of mind. We can not be at peace as long as emotional and physical survival issues are pending. In fact, we can not even begin to discover its real function until physical and emotional problems are solved. Once we figure this out, perspective and clarity are restored and we will not have to frequent others with a higher symbolic intelligence to recall our serenity.

One method of developing mental clarity is in not striving for it. The more we resist confusion, the more confused we're likely to get. Confusion can be a natural result of too much unassimilated information. The mind can process this information O.D. by simply dreaming, either by going to sleep or daydreaming. Another way of "downloading" input is to take in a deep and meaningless movie or go on a short vacation. In fact, any activity will do as long as it doesn't require much thinking. Confusion is a conceptual survival signal.

"*The apparent*
        randomness by which *Universe*
    reveals
    itself **is**
but a signal from a still higher sense of intrinsic order."

An Ancient Confusionist Proverb

The real reality is there, but everything you KNOW about "it" is in your mind and yours to do with as you like...conceptualization is an art and you are the artist. Your ideas about anything constitute your "reality maps" or how you've defined and described it. These maps most likely include definitions from the local culture, mass media, schools, parents, friends and possibly, yourself. You learn to make your own maps when it's time to think for yourself. Once you recognize the difference between the map and the territory, i.e., your ideas about something and the thing itself, then it is possible to increase your Conceptual Intelligence by being aware of your thoughts as…thoughts. Since the "mind" is a rather slippery entity to define, look to your thoughts and dreams as a way of understanding your mind. Whosoever understands metaphor, then governs the mind.

Another way to increase Conceptual Intelligence is by making maps as fast as you absorb information. You're constantly taking in information. If you don't find ways to organize and process all the information, this data will tend to get backed up and cause you mental constipation. Learn to process information more slowly until the previous experience is digested. How you interpret your information and put it to work is your map-making process. If you haven't discovered a way to start this process, it will become easier for you to: 1) Live in the past 2) Grow stupid and 3) Become a dogmatic, little bigot. What's interesting about making maps is that you get to find out how you think, talk and write. The amazing thing about knowing how you think, talk and write is this: You change your reality by adjusting the way you think, talk and write *about* it. The illusion is that reality changes. The reality is that only your maps do.

Conceptual Intelligence is also the ability to pay attention. Direct focus increases the chances that what you have learned can be easily accessed. This ability to pay attention becomes especially useful when we are unable to believe the very thing that is happening to us. Yet, unless we can register what is occurring with ourselves, we will not have any reason to articulate our inner truths. Another technique, called Going Through Changes, has a way of unjarring the attention when it has become stuck in the mysterious inertias. It goes like this and takes discipline:

Pick yourself up and throw it into activities and situations opposite in nature to what you are accustomed to. Act "out-of-character"…read a magazine you normally wouldn't…strike up a conversation with someone unexpectedly…activate your own changes.

KO

revolution

Revolution is going through enough changes
to Produce the clarity necessary for seeing what
is possible in the ever-molting Now.

THE LIFE OF MEANING

Conceptual Intelligence is symbolic by nature, requiring a sense of meaning to function. That capacity enables us to organize signals received into meaningful bits of information which can be called our "conceptual framework" or psychology. This symbolic skill of translating signals into useful information emerges as we come to think of ourselves more as *interpreters,* rather than "creators." Our interpretative ability is only precise as our definition of what is "meaningful" and to the degree that we are consciously aware of our assumptions. Articulation demands a certain depth of self-knowledge regarding values. What is important? Without this link, the communication of our ideas becomes, at best, vague and at worst, standardized.

    The spectrum of meaning vacillates between two extreme degrees of significance: Life is either 1) Too Meaningful to talk about and/or 2) Too Meaningless to bother with. If your values become too closely focused into either of these two "red zones," your capacity for communication will deteriorate along with the overall degree of your Conceptual Intelligence. This is one way normal people inadvertently become Air-Heads. To bypass this mental dilemma, what is required is a certain thought adjustment. To enhance the elasticity of your thinking, refrain from thinking in black and white. Things are not necessarily one way or another, they might be both simultaneously, depending upon which angle you are looking from. Black and white thinking works off an "either/or" basis. To integrate more shades of grey and color into the picture, change "either/or" to "and/or/?". Life is not necessarily a True-False Answer Test. (Aristotle died, didn't he?) It might just be a Multiple Choice Question or a lot more.

DISCORDIAN INTELLIGENCE TEST*

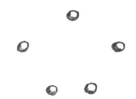

1) Do these five pebbles form a pentagon?
2) If crisscrossed, do the pebbles form a star?
3) Are they randomly placed without intended order?

DISCORDIA by Greg Hill).
Answer: Pentagons, stars & disorder are all your own creations...it's up to you. (Adapted From PRINCIPIA

Our thinking is only as flexible as our minds are open to incorporating the Unknown as a value. The Unknown, hereafter referred to as *Factor X,* is a symbol to help us refer to a Concept-Free Zone...one which we have no preconceptions about. Integrating Factor X into our psychology enables us to operate in an open-ended system...one which can change and adjust itself to the incessant stream of new information arriving each moment. In relation to the Unknown, the term "information" takes on new meaning. With Factor X as part of our conceptual framework, information becomes *the unpredictability of a message.* This means that the more unpredictable a message, the more information there is in it.

Factor X makes it possible for new information, not necessarily in agreement with previous concepts and beliefs, to be received and reviewed. One particularly humbling method of including Factor X in our thinking is through the task of Confessing Ignorance. When we are not "in the know" it is suggested practice to say so. Rather than feigning knowledge, the magical words I DON'T KNOW suffice to complete the experience. The honesty and courage it takes to confess ignorance renders our real knowledge as accessible as the light of day. It's also a terrific way to introduce our conscious mind to subconscious depths, until there is no division at all but only deeper levels of consciousness.

THE ART OF THINKING PRECISELY

Whatever can be named, can thereafter be identified and articulated...though we run the risk of closing our minds to what we define and "know." Once we are "in the know" about something or someone, we suffer the misconception of thinking there is nothing left to learn. This is a natural tendency of imprecise thinking...of not having established Factor X as an ongoing conceptual value. Once established, Factor X nourishes conceptual development by minimizing our need to: 1) Find ONE ANSWER or DEFINITION 2) Have IT ALL FIGURED OUT 3) Dominate the organism. It does this by tuning our conscious mind into the unknown. This relationship initiates the cutting edge necessary for the Art of Thinking Precisely.

Precision cuts through the nonsense to extract the essence. The magical act of extracting essences by thinking, writing and speaking perhaps came from an Olde English word for "magic", *grammarye.* Magic, on the other sleight of hand, might simply be the illusion cast by a technology more advanced than we are presently accustomed. The technique behind thinking precisely can be demonstrated with the words WHY and HOW. WHY explains and HOW evokes. WHY gives us the reason and HOW provides the method and action. In our own "grammarye", where can we discriminate between explanation and evocation? To explain is to answer the WHY question. To evoke is to think, write or speak in such a manner as to trigger *the experience of the energy or process in question.* Where explaining might kill the spirit invoked in an attempt to comprehend, evocation conjures the very spirit forth to *be moved by it.* The Art of Thinking Precisely is learning to select those words which honor *THE EXPERIENCE OF THE ENERGY ITSELF.* In the end, it doesn't matter what we "know" as much as how we can proffer THE EXPERIENCE OF THE ENERGY.

TOO NEW INTELLIGENCE TESTS

TEST NUMBER ONE Contains six levels of Intelligence, all of which apply potentially to every individual no matter what their "IQ". The first level is called:

1) *Stupid:* This is where you are passively taking everything in without associating, interpreting or thinking about it.
2) *Bright:* This is where you begin seeing the associations and relationships of whatever you are taking in.
3) *Smart:* After seeing the associations between things, this is where you begin to predict outcomes by combining those associations in such a way as to get desired results. Here we have "figured it out." (Most people stay here.)
4) *Silly:* When you are bored enough with being "smart" it is possible to be silly. This is where you start seeing the relationships between apparently incongruous elements in your inner and outer environments in such a way as to be utterly delighted.
5) *Brilliant:* Whereupon you begin combining incongruous juxtapositions towards unpredictable yet illuminating outcomes without necessarily knowing why or needing to know.

6) *Simple:* Taking in, understanding and communicating what is obvious to all.

Intelligence TEST #2 is more subjectively based than TEST #1, in that it depends entirely upon your capacity to register your own experience. It goes like this:

If your world feels like it's getting:
1) Smaller and slower; 2) More grim and less fun; 3) Less sexy and more dull; 4) Impersonal and scary; 5) Petty and predictable;
THEN, there's a good chance your overall level of Intelligence is...

F a l l i n g

However, if your world is feeling:
1) Brighter and exciting; 2) Funnier, instructive & creative; 3) Sexier and more attractive; 4) Personal, loving and warm; 5) Expanded, free and open-ended;
THEN, your Intelligence level is...

R i s i n g

CAN WE TALK?

YOU WILL LEARN

SANITY

AT VERY REASONABLE

language on your own!

OLD
MAPS
AND

New facts

Afraid of ideas?

THE SOLUTION!

PRECISION

Advanced Thinking

Financial planning

THINK & GROW RICH

IF AT FIRST YOU DON'T SUCCEED, FIX IT.

"Learning is discovering what you already know."

Think Again.

THINK

BRIGHT

FRAME IMAGE

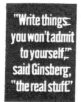

我們

REASON

THINKS LIKE YOU

Words to the Wise

CAN WE TALK?

THE MOST USEFUL IDEAS ARE OFTEN
REMARKABLY SIMPLE.

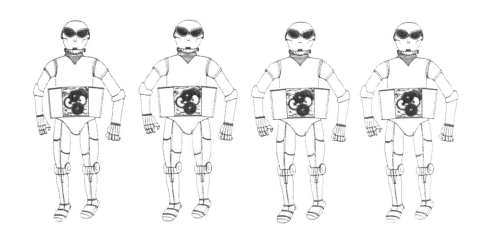

4
SOCIAL SURVIVAL

A – ADOLESCENCE

B – ADULTHOOD

C – COLLECTIVE

GEAR FOUR

Fourth Gear Social Intelligence is defined through the manner by which we relate with others. Gear Four is incorporative by nature, combining and assimilating information from the previous three gears in order to function. After registering enough physical safety, emotional strength and conceptual skill, it's only natural to reach out and share with others. On the other hand, it's difficult to socialize if certain survival needs are not met first. This sometimes projects a quality of "neediness" impeding spontaneous social interaction. By emphasizing our individual integrity first, it is possible to deepen our capacity for giving. Imbalances in the previous three gears often show up as the quality of our socio-sexual life and/or lack of it.

The personality is the necessary self-reference for integrating Social Intelligence. As the incorporative function of the Robot, we review the previous references necessary for integrating the first three functions of Intelligence: 1) First Gear is THE BODY. 2) Second Gear are BELIEFS. 3) Third Gear, THE INTELLECT. As the Robot develops, a certain style or approach evolves and eventually its "signature" pervasively instills every activity. This individual style unfolds as it's permitted. Due to certain inhibiting factors, by which socialization thrives, the individual style or personality is under constant challenge and pressure to conform and repress itself. Without a strong personality, however, it becomes difficult to maintain meaningful person-to-person relationships. In its extreme tendencies, a kind of "social idiocy" takes over. The key to increasing our Social Intelligence, then, is in our ability to develop and deepen individual integrity as a basis for playing with others.

Socially, there are three major phases of personality development: 1) Big Kids (or Adolescents) 2) Adults and 3) The Process of
Collectivization. Though there are a number of different ways to
describe degrees of social involvement, they have been often referred to
as Strangers, Acquaintances, Friends, Lovers, Family and Extended
Family Organizations. The Big Kid phase, hereafter referred to as
Adolescence, is essentially self-indulgent, egotistical and narcissistic due
to its wild and experimental nature. This also seems to apply to any adolescent entity, be it a group, corporation, nation or spiritual movement.
Adolescents either don't know enough to establish themselves as Adults
and/or don't want to know. Characterized by high-flux, adolescent
phases often appear "socially irresponsible" to others attempting to
stabilize themselves in the next evolutionary development of Adulthood.

Adults can be recognized by their social response-ability and seriousness around the issue of linear, sequential and scheduled time.
Having lived longer, Adults become increasingly aware of the time limit
placed by Mr. Death upon their lives. In fact, the most important thing
we can know as Adults is that: *We Are Going To Die.* As our sense of
time deepens, so does our desperation to finding meaningful contact and
purpose with other human beings. This search brings many Adults
together to initiate the genetic process of Collectivization. This expresses
itself in the genetic and extended family, friends, church groups and even
secret societies. When this process gathers momentum in our lives, it
often excites our need for identifying with Something Bigger Than Oneself for a greater sense of security, power, knowledge and social acceptance in the face of our own helpless feelings around death. Sometimes,
Adults join groups and become lifelong members in an attempt to guar-
antee the survival rewards of security, status, knowledge and social
acceptance that a particular group provides its members. Often these
groups are religious cults providing solace to those unable to reward
themselves on their own. In time, the personalities of individual group
members can tend to dissipate their unique and singular characteristics in
favor of the more standardized, homogenous blend of that collective's
lowest common denominator.

SOCIAL SECURITY

Social Security means Knowing Who Your Friends Are. From Adolescence to Collectivization, our social circles are influenced by and require adjustment to our personal transformation. Occasionally, when Individual Intelligence accelerates, certain people will fail to fit our social criteria for friendship. In fact, as Intelligence increases, we may acquire a taste for being more selective about who we want as friends. For example: Someone, who was the best of friends at one time, gradually or suddenly, drops out of our lives...*not* because somebody did Something Wrong but perhaps from conflicting values. This can happen whenever our own true feelings become so vividly obvious to us that anyone not in direct resonance with them may simply stop *moving* us, dwindling a rapport based on what was once true but no longer alive. It is a strange yet spiritual fact that certain people become friends for the purpose of ushering us to our True Self but once realized, can not remain with us because they were only there to help us arrive.

Periods of high flux often serve to clarify who our real friends are and who was only there for the ride. Personality changes usually require an adjustment in self-image. We learn to think of ourselves in different ways in order to integrate new information on who we actually are. If members of our social circles are unwilling to also change their minds about us...a natural discrepancy ensues, wherein we must choose between adapting to their image of us or our own. The business of reclaiming Fourth Gear begins with finding out whose image we are living for and then, deciding what kind of person we want to be. Social evolution occurs by defining for ourselves what friendship means. If friendship is only based in emotional support, ego-stroking or personal attraction, it falls apart whenever these conditions are withdrawn. Perhaps, a true friend is someone who, somehow, encourages us to be completely ourselves and occasionally challenges our "act" in order to touch our hearts.

("Opposition is Friendship.")
William Blake

Adolescence is approached two ways: Genetically and Consciously. Genetically, everybody goes through the Hormonal Havoc marking this rite of passage. There really is no choice. We learn by running through the gauntlet. Some of us work to bypass Terminal Adulthood by prolonging adolescence. It's possible to remain young-at-heart and never really grow up, while knowing how to play the Adult Games required to survive in Adult Society. This is called "neoteny" or Conscious Adolescence, and is genetically innate to only two creatures on Planet Earth...Humans and Dolphins.

Neoteny is catalyzed through a careful, non-judgmental study of adolescent characteristics and their acceptance and integration in a creative lifestyle. The spirit of experimentation so crucial to Adolescence necessitates a certain daring. *No daring is fatal.* What's deadly is our FEAR of: *Making Mistakes,* Taking Risks, and *Being Awkward.* This is because all three are essential to relating with uncertainty. Neoteny is dependent upon improvisatory skills...of quick, in-the-moment adjustments to new information. Refer to *mistakes* as "God Leaks." When they're made, we see that Life is what happens when we're busy making other plans. The fear of mistakes can be subdued by including them. The secret to *taking risks* is being just safe enough to do so and not too safe to feel threatened. *Being awkward* becomes an art form of considerable beauty when allowed its natural expression through the body. Its genuine vulnerability endears. Its groping, searching spirit brings truth to the moment it beholds.

One way Adolescents are initiated into Adulthood is through the process of Domestication. Like Adolescence itself, this process unfolds as an inevitable, genetic prerequisite for social evolution. Also, like Adolescence, it can be approached consciously or as a robot for DNA. When we are ready to style our own domestic advance, we are more free to bypass the generic models passed down by DNA as our Ancestral Gestalt...that group-mind made up of generations of our genetic heritage.

One symptom of domestication is its inhibiting reaction to the chaotic growth of Adolescence. In a broad sense, to domesticate means to "spiritualize"...or tame, cultivate and refine. It's not unlike tending to a garden wildly overgrown with weeds. There is an art to trimming the hedge...to weeding the garden and harvesting the crop. This art requires a fine balance. Too much refinement kills the wild, sacred spirit, as too much wildness obscures our responsibility to "finish what Nature has started," so, that we might enjoy her riches. So it is with domestication. If we become too comfortable, we fall asleep and if we're not comfortable enough, anxiety will prevent us from settling down into ourselves to enjoy the gifts of an organized social life. The trick is in the balance and the nerve to do it your own way. The alternative is to float downstream in the genetic river of ancestral currents.

12   HANGED MAN

THE TRUTH ABOUT SEX

Adolescents anticipate their first sexual experience so much because that is when their sexual reality imprints itself. During the first genital embrace with another, the body learns to associate its sexuality with the conditions surrounding this event. For example: If the qualities of danger, uncertainty or pain prevailed, then a pattern was set up to need these conditions in order to be turned on sexually. If the first imprint was safe, loving and fulfilling, then these require replicating before getting tuned on. It is in this way that each person's sexual reality is different and beyond the judgment of others. The classic way to erase the old imprint and initiate a new one is in being celibate for about three months or more and then engaging sexually only under preferred conditions: Whatever Turns You On and Gets You Hot. Without erasing an old imprint, its pattern will repeat itself throughout a number of lovers until a new imprint replaces it. As with any kind of re-imprinting, the more vulnerable you are, the deeper you will be impressed.

THE URGE TO BELONG

One social impulse expresses the urge to belong and because it does, we are required to select the entity we wish to belong to. The options are rather abundant in that we can belong to ourself, another, a family, team, church, religion, corporation, a society, government, a country, a planet, galaxy and/or Universe as we know it. However, in order to survive socially, it remains imperative that we belong somewhere. When we discover the entity we wish to belong with, we learn its Code of Acceptance and what it takes to be included as part of that entity. The code expresses itself as a pattern of "virtuous behavior" wherein virtue is defined as what is needed to become and remain a "good person," i.e., a member of that entity or group. Learning this social code is a process of Growing Up and becoming an Adult. Once accepted as part of the entity we wish to belong to, we learn what it takes to be a "bad person" i.e., an outcaste and/or non-member. Bad persons violate the Code of Acceptance and are judged accordingly and punished through rejection, persecution and/or banishment depending upon the severity of the violation in question. Sometimes, in order to belong to something, you have to divide yourself from others who don't belong to the same thing.

COLLECTIVIZATION

Collectivization begins with sacrificing individual differences for the morality of a particular collective over one's sense of "right and wrong." Sometimes this includes devoting one's life to the collective: speaking their language and conforming to the rules of conduct they set as incentive for advancement. The particular morality defined by the collective instills a judgmental attitude to contrary doctrines and behaviors. This tendency becomes acute with collectives claiming spiritual authority. These are the Elitist Cults, many of which know enough psychic technology to impress those naive enough to forget that spiritual truth starts within. *The individual's submersion into collective uniformity is a valuable lesson in Social Studies.* Certain individuals will always feel resistance and pressure while conforming. Some may require this kind of "shaping from the outside" to find out who they really are. Some of us are like raw coal, needing tremendous outer pressure before we can crystallize into our Diamond Self. Others generate enough inner pressure so as not to feel obliged to conform to external sources. These are the "oddballs," unable to fit the mold of any collectively defined morality… those rare individuals who have chosen a greater solitude and, as a result, continue to run against the grain of collectively defined truths, while forging their paths to the beat of different drummers.

Mechanical PROBLEMS

Graduate Study

MECHANICAL PROBLEMS
AN INTRODUCTION

Karmic Mechanics is Undergraduate Study. It delves deeper into the practical application of the first four functions of Intelligence as presented briefly in Grades One Through Four. The next level of understanding requires active participation rather than mere conceptual recognition. The degree by which we can re-interpret these four functions of Intelligence within our lives and live out our own definitions, is the degree we'll be able to move through the most difficult, densest and grueling prerequisite to Graduation: **MECHANICAL PROBLEMS, Graduate Study. MECHANICAL PROBLEMS is just that and explores the "pathological realities" of robots run amok. A thorough comprehension of robot problems is mandatory to sustain ourselves throughout the high velocity living of High School, where anything that can go wrong, usually does. So, it is through the course of KARMA MECHANICS** that the stage is set for creative responses to robots in crisis. When something breaks, fix it. If it can be fixed, there's no need to worry. If it cannot be fixed, still, no need to worry. (At this point Read *Undoing Yourself with Energized Meditation and Other Devices*. This book addresses the Illusion of Un-Fix-ability.)

THE ORIENTATION

As with the breakdown of any machine, mechanical problems can be detected and figured out by the competent mechanic. There are a number of causes for robot malfunction and this section of *Angel Tech* is dedicated to the clarification of these sources, so the appropriate adjustments and repairs can be made by you, the user. The first thing to remember is: *Be Kind To The Robot.* Most malfunctions are associated with faulty or outdated programming, which, of course, is the user's responsibility. The robot simply follows orders and only takes command when nobody else wants to. Robots are responsive to the firm yet benevolent commands issued forth from the Soul In Control. The robot is here to help and only gets in the way when it is refused the help it needs when it goes...out of control. People on this planet domesticate animals for pets. Souls domesticate robots as pets. How would like to train yours?

There are four major areas of robot malfunction, referred to here by their code names: 1) Confusion Alert 2) Pretty Vacant 3) Broken Record and 4) Short Circuit. All four areas prevail throughout each of the first Four Gears, enabling instant access to immediate investigation. These prementioned code names designate specific areas of mechanical collapse. For optimum operational procedure, please memorize and acquaint yourselves with their workings:

CONFUSION ALERT

The basic disorientation occurring when an *idea of reality* contradicts and/or resists the living experience of that reality itself. Once conflict ensues, there can be an energy drain in the gear(s) involved. "*Is reality distorting your ideations?*"

PRETTY VACANT

To the degree a particular gear remains unclaimed, there exists a fundamental *inertia* around that function of survival...diminishing its innate intelligence. Origins to be scanned: outdated parental programs, fear of existing, irresponsibility...robots whose gears are vacated often hook up to other robots to feel themselves and meet these survival priorities unclaimed in themselves, *"Is There Anybody Home?"*

BROKEN RECORD

When one gear becomes *over-emphasized,* immobilization often sets in and the robot "spins out" in a non-stop fashion of ineffective surviving. Origins include an over-development of one gear at the cost of others, an inability to *organize* excessive information pertaining to the gear in question and/or the establishment of one gear as a "point of worship" wherein a religion develops around one function of survival. *"Is your dogma becoming your karma?"*

SHORT CIRCUIT

This happens when a survival gear can no longer operate as a support function for its overtone as a result of a sudden blast and/or overwhelming influx of High School information. First Gear supports Fifth Grade, Second Gear supports Sixth Grade, Third Gear supports Seventh Grade and Fourth Gear supports Eighth Grade. Causes of "over-amping" or short circuit often include Premature "enlightenment" without previous stabilization of survival priorities, information *overdose* (forgetting to include assimilation time), the need to *redefine* the nature of the gear to include more information and/or energy from its overtone, and an inability or unwillingness to *speak with the robot.* Short circuits happen when the ground wire is loose, disconnected and/or inadequate to handle the amount of charge coming through the wire. The robot is the wire. The charge is How Much Life We Can Take. Ground The Robot. *"Earth to robot, Earth to Robot...do you read me!"*

All four major areas of robot malfunction often overlap, providing an intrinsic cross-reference system of scanning. After getting used to adjusting one's own karma, the competent karma mechanic soon develops enough skill to survive any situation whatsoever. By the process of self-communication (talk to the robot), enough rapport can be developed to eventually get the robot to work for you. As the karma mechanic learns to listen and tune into his/her own survival signals when they come up, the perception to *read others* emerges as a potential healing aid. The process of integrity is crucial to healing, as all healing is actually self-healing. After healing oneself, it is possible to catalyze this process in another due to the real knowledge gained by actual work on oneself. Every robot heals at a different pace and style of recovery based in it's programs. If somebody does not want to be healed, they won't. Belief plays a powerful part in the concentration of positive emotion...

those feelings which *affirm* one's being. To the degree one is able to affirm one's own being, is the degree one may affirm another, as we are all equal in being alone. Healing is simply any activity capable of quickening and deepening this affirmation.

HEALING THE ROBOT

As we learn continual responses to our survival signals, it soon becomes apparent that the robot is our friend as well as our pet. Once the function of the ego is understood, "it" can be integrated. No more will we have to fight, resist and condemn the ego when it has found its rightful place as our faithful companion. Once its needs are met and its definition more or less understood, ego becomes more obvious, hence, easier to read, direct and instruct. It is in this gentle approach that the karma mechanic begins his/her initiation as a spiritual warrior because in the spiritual realm, the only conquest left is that of the self.

8 | STRENGTH | ☉

1

PHYSICAL

FIRST GEAR

CONFUSION ALERT

Physical disorientation often occurs when body-images are out of sync with body realities. If the organism can not be accepted for *what it is,* it cannot provide the Soul with the essential grounding necessary for its worldly manifestation. The body needs to feel accepted and safe before it willingly works for us. Otherwise, a tremendous effort of force and will is necessary to direct its activities. This process of willfully forcing the body to do things creates physical tension and eventually drains physical energy. The body naturally resists any advances coming from a source that does not recognize its (the body's) innate wisdom. Who wouldn't?

The body is the source of physical intelligence and must be recognized, accepted and loved for itself before an effective body-image can be developed. For example: If you think you are overweight and condemn yourself for being "fat," most likely you will remain that way. On the other hand, if you accept the *shape of your body* (no matter what shape is held dear in your mind), your very acceptance of *what is* serves to transform the situation. Another example: If your body is sick and you fight being sick, you may be able to hold off for awhile but eventually the momentum of your resistance begs for your collapse. The body collapses because it is externalizing the collapse of a body-image that has stopped working. Physical collapse is a survival signal to be read towards the adjustment of First Gear.

Only after the body is accepted for what it is, is there enough internal affinity to initiate self-communication. As Karma Mechanics, we realize the importance of an experimental spirit in what we do because the real education often arrives via trial and error. Most of what is of real value often occurs in the guise of mistakes, failures and accidents. This is especially true with First Gear. Physical Intelligence is biological and because it is, it moves in its own ways. Mistakes, failures and accidents occur when we are not in tune with biological reality enough to sustain a direct relationship with Life Itself.

A—VOID-DANCE

A basic fear of self-definition, or existence, contributes to the struggle of reclaiming First Gear. Fear of existence is synonymous with a fear of not existing…the fear of being nothing. There is nothing wrong with being afraid of reality… *We Are Nothing.* Our modern culture is designed to keep us from facing nothingness, so that we have to really work at it. If our parents avoided nothingness, it is likely that they taught it to us, as well. When nothingness has been judged as being wrong and "not OK" the way it is, it's only natural to spend our lives avoiding the void. When this avoidance program ceases to function, due to the insurmountable evidence of new information, we collapse or get depressed until we change the program. This change expresses itself as a shift from avoiding nothingness to relating with nothingness to finally being nothingness. It is possible to say that when we are not caught up in being anything or anybody, we are simply being…ourselves.

INSTRUCTION: SITTING MEDITATION

There is no goal in sitting meditation, no-where to go and nothing to do. Due to its utter simplicity, this method can be quite difficult to master. To aid in the actual practice a few guidelines are offered:

1) Sit in a position that is comfortable and with spine erect.
2) Watch your breathing. Keep your eyes open or half shut but not shut.
3) Remain *motionless.* First for 10 minutes, then 20, then 40…
4) Every time you detect a thought, say, "Thinking." Remain consistent.
5) Sustain awareness of all previous four guidelines, simultaneously.

□□□□□□□□□□□□□□□□□□□□□

Q. What did one Zen Master say to another?

A. Nothing

"...THE HORROR...THE HORROR..."

In addition to fearing nothingness, the fear of being "pegged" or typed by others (society, mom & dad, friends) remains a guiding light to those of us remaining ambiguous. Especially prevalent amidst "artists and intellectuals," the need for personal ambiguity and indirectness often obscure the development necessary for objective art...that kind which is received in the manner intended by the artist. Part of this "anti-ego" trend emerged from the 1960's Hippie Era which spawned doctrines of Erasing Personal History, Anti-establishmentarianisms and other Ego-killing Meditation practices, not to mention the Fantastic Pharmaceutical Explosion. All these had their place in history but the ego, like our body, remains necessary for planetary survival, personal relationships and artistic expression. Without self-commitment, our ego boundaries dissolve without ever having had the chance to develop first. The only obvious purpose to developing a sense of self (ego) is to eventually have a self to give others, the world...god. It's the instrument and without it, we can't expect to be played. Without tuning it, we can't expect to make music.

One solution to the fear of existence is the practice of Making Statements. (Only that which exists is subject to change.) Being direct and definite in self-expression helps; so does watching babies. Babies are Masters of Expression. The direct expression of our *fears* and *needs to be taken care of* brings us a little closer to reclaiming Physical Intelligence, as do our needs to *feel hungry* and *take care of others and ourselves.* As an artist, if you are too Fatally Hip to be defined, you will never become accessible enough to receive the recognition necessary to feel appreciated. As an intellectual, if you are too existential to fully exist, you may need to attract a mother to double as a mistress, lover and/or mate, to help you out. This level of existence is indeed terrifying, even shocking...but that's how it starts. Besides, children have nightmares in order to wake up.

So called "accident prone" behavior can be a result of losing touch with biological reality...the body. Life will not be ignored. If we are not conscious enough of its living pulses, Universe delivers still another message from the NO COINCIDENCES DEPT. to remind us. One type of message comes through the format of the Mac Truck Delivery Service, wherein its point is Presented with such direct impact as to leave the recipient dangling on the Precipice of uncertain survival. Not everybody is dense enough to require this type of delivery yet it's always there for those that do.

Perhaps the most severe form of the Confusion Alert comes as the idea that the body is an "inferior or lower" self, suspected of the most heinous intentions. These kinds of body-images perpetrate the belief in a "split" "between the body and the spirit. This singular illusion may, indeed, be responsible for provoking and sustaining the state of spiritual amnesia so prevalent today. People started buying this illusion in a big away around the 18th Century, as the Age of Reason came about to excite logical processes, tick-tock technology and science. Around this same time more intuitive and mythic methods of transferring knowledge (Fairie Tales, Geomancy, Alchemy, etc.) were shunned and negated as not being quite "scientific" enough. So, knowledge began fragmenting as the human psyche started its intellectualization process towards the Industrial Age. Currently the Industrial Age is undergoing its mechanical collapse giving way to the Information-Atomic Age with the miraculous onslaught of computers, global networking and the re-integration of more intuitive correlative sciences. Still, it is First Gear that is most severely impacted and upset by over-intellectualization of issues best left to body wisdom. We are caught between eras and are learning to make the best of it(?)

Any spiritual doctrine denying the body and its free expression also creates a basic confusion around body-images, hence, indirectly enslaving members to that particular religion. Organized religion has been, in addition to a path of salvation, a means of social control throughout history. Sects, from the Hindus and their "psychic caste system" of regarding psychic ability with Holy Status to modern day Evangelism and its mythic afterlife of Heaven And Hell, all support a basic conflict in the primitive mind about the body. The body is seen as anything from "evil" to an impediment on the path of enlightenment, something one must overcome and come to grips with. It is this very "grip" that we have on ourselves that is begging to be released.

There has been such a tremendous era of self-negation, that our need for self-affirmation has grown so great as to require elaborate systems of thought and belief to justify its existence. Pay close attention to the heritage of your spiritual orientation (what were you brought up believing?)...*without judging it.* By believing the body to be "bad" or "not OK," church members are asked to join the religion in order to meet their needs for self-affirmation...to remain "good" or "holy" in the eyes of the minister or rabbi and the dogma of that church. There's nothing especially wrong with this because most people resist Life enough to need a religion or church. The alternative, of course, is the self-empowerment of loving ourselves completely...of living "religiously." SCAN: Any ideas of the body being "unspiritual." **Instruction: Adjust body-image to include the spiritual...i.e., the body is spiritual and an expression of spirit.**

Even though one may not agree with the religion one was brought up with, it is useless to think we can rid ourselves of its influence by resisting it: on the contrary, our early spiritual orientation provides a useful foundation for immediate development. (**See** *Zen Without Zen Masters,* Camden Benares, Falcon Press.)

Our first contact with "God", blessed by his HOLY Unknowable Name, was most likely the floating, blurry faces of our parents as we struggled to peer through infant eyes. These giant faces were somehow responsible for feeding us, comforting us and keeping us alive. They were "outside" of us, too, and as we grew older they continued being gods, demigods and/or demons depending upon the parents involved. We did what we were told and marveled at their worlds. Then, somewhere along the line, we were introduced to another notion of God...something to take the pressure off Mom and Dad. This other notion of God, often non-human and invisible, became the next step in our spiritual evolution...the recognition of an Intelligence greater than our own.

Many people will stop here and rest content with an organized religion. A few others will choose the long journey inward to find

God...before religion...before Mom and Dad. This is why our spiritual upbringing is important. It marks a reference or detour along the way, without which one could stay lost or worse yet, keep travelling out and away from oneself to find God. Every religion also carries an essential seed of truth which can be extracted, transplanted and nourished.

BRING YOUR BODY WITH YOU

Spiritual &/or religious methods can be tested for their biological validity by asking the question: "Can I take my body with me?" This question imposes the paradox of physical death and rightly so. During our time on the planet, we "fallen angels" are here to restore ourselves as beings of light. True spiritual discipline entails the development of a "body of light" or soul-consciousness, so that when substantiated, we may transcend death and claim a piece of eternity. The development of our "light body" depends entirely upon our relationship to the initiations we pass through in the school of Life. First Grade provides the foundation for all that follows. First Grade Graduation does not mean leaving physical Intelligence behind. On the contrary, we are now ready to take our body with us. The physical body, as metaphysics states, is *the* substantial portion of the rest of us and not separate." The body remains the boundary or the crucible wherein the alchemical opus of our Life Work takes place. Instruction: BRING YOUR BODY WITH YOU.

PRETTY VACANT

First Gear inertia usually expresses itself as an overall inability to get our **"physical survival act" together.** Wherein the previous area (CONFUSION ALERT) concerned itself with structural issues. First Gear Robot Malfunction preoccupies itself with more functional problems. The conflict often occurs when we are Pretty Vacant and expresses symptoms of: 1) Fear 2) Depression 3) Low Energy States and, of course, 4) Inertia.

These are all symptoms of a physical program operating out of control. This is not to exclude these states from the spectrum of human living because they are all quite human indeed. They are out of control when *dominating* the life of the individual. Many times, the individual is on "automatic pilot" with physical survival issues because they are not running on their own program but that of their parents. Until this situation is recognized, the old parental program will continue to determine security needs and just how they are supposed to be met.

The process of becoming a Mother to oneself often follows the disillusioning realization, or enlightenment, that there is really nobody else around to do this. Depression may follow helplessness when we expect somebody to come by and take care of us, especially when nobody does...or somebody does arrive but doesn't do it the "right way." Another factor to this *inertia* is the growing disappointment of feeling unappreciated. Eventually, the momentum of these negative emotions effect an immobilization...an inability to move. The real danger is Getting Used To Not Moving. Immobilization can have its own satisfying comfort called "laziness" which is another resistance to change. The first adjustment necessary to release inertia comes with a conscious choice to use comfort instead of making it a goal. This ignites the self-appreciation for turning First Gear.

Until Motherhood is reclaimed, we are controlled by Mother types who keep beating us at this game, including our genetic Mothers. The secret of being a Mother is starting small. Nourish and take care of houseplants, then, when ready...the garden. This will tune us into the purely spiritual expression of Mothering. When ready to graduate, get an aquarium and feed the fish. If prepared to mother small mammals, hamsters do well...then cats and dogs. By this time, there will have been enough actual practice for the rest of ourselves to catch on. If all of this sounds just too "maternal" to do, feel free to continue projecting "Mother" unwittingly onto your friends and lovers until it's time to get it together.

One way we depend on others (or Physical Safety is by "grounding" through them. This means we use others to feel safe to live on the planet. It's not necessarily "bad" unless it's draining somebody and/or it's done indirectly...not out in the open. If this is a personal need, it's time to admit it. If it's not and we want to change our ways...simply *be aware of it.* (BE KIND BUT FIRM TO YOUR ROBOT.)

Another malfunction in the Pretty Vacant series stems from outdated programs of self-nourishment; a dietary overhaul and/or adjustment is called for when we can no longer eat the foods we were brought up with. The High Starch-Sugar-Fat-Protein Plan some of us grew up with no longer suffices as nourishment for the new individuals we are becoming. As we adjust our self-images to synchronize with more of who we actually are, an inevitable sensitivity ensues. This sensitivity develops its own food preferences. If we fail to recognize it, sooner or later we find out by getting sick or breaking out; the awakening body has its ways of alerting us. When the old food programs begin collapsing, they do so because we are transforming and are in need of a new menu. It is during this vulnerable phase of crisis that a "gap" emerges in our knowledge about food. At this "gap time," a new menu may be designed and applied. As a result of each individual's having such unique needs, and with so many books announcing contradicting messages around nutrition, no particular diet is condoned. We can adjust the amount and type of Life Force in the food we eat to match the amount of Life Force in ourselves.

The most alive or biogenic foods are the ones that are still *alive,* **like sprouts from seeds and beans, uncooked and raw.** The next most alive or bioactive foods are fruits and vegetables in their ripe, mature and naturally sweetened stages, which also includes uncooked but unsprouted seed, bean and grain. Biostatic foods (foods which initiate aging in us) are all cooked foods not using refined sugars, flours and/or preservatives. Biocidic (life-deteriorating) foods include refined sugars and flours, fats and preservatives. That's the basic breakdown. For more information, contact The International Biogenic Society, Apartado 372, Cartago, Costa Rica, Central America which will send you brochures on the Essene Way of Living. In order to determine your biological constitution, visit several nutritionists, iridologists and/or naturopathic health practitioners for examinations, muscle testing and dietary diagnosis. Go with one that feels the best, least sudden and most gentle. Realize you are raising the level of your Physical Intelligence and starting to Own Your Body. Go slow—feel it out—trust your instincts—let your body decide.

✪✪✪✪✪✪✪✪✪✪✪✪✪✪✪

BROKEN RECORD

One result of over-emphasizing Physical Survival is an obsession with security issues. Obsession is often a mechanical reaction to the shock of trauma, so that the object of obsession serves as a temporary ego-stabilizer. Trauma can be defined as any situation beyond our control, comprehension and assimilation. In the event of trauma, shock temporarily disconnects us from our usual ways of feeling and being secure. In seeing this, it is easier to understand the object of fixation in its appropriate place as the symptom of a previous shock or a conditioned response to being out of control. Fixation is the *ricochet* effect of undigested shock.

When physical needs are not met directly enough, security will become the preoccupation until these needs are recognized for what they are and fulfilled. Ignorance of the specific nature of one's security needs can catalyze a frenzied, hysterical search for substitutes when the actual needs are not faced. Everybody's basic needs for security are the same: FOOD, SHELTER, SELF-PRESERVATION, etc. but the quality, quantity and preferred styles differ for us all. Until our needs in this area are faced and met, we'll suffer physically with anxiety, nervousness and hyper-sensitivity. Most importantly, perhaps, is that we'll miss out on the most important survival information of all…that of BEING A SURVIVOR.

BIOLOGICAL REPAIR

The most direct way of assimilating, or organizing, an excess input of survival information is through the physical rest of sleep. Sleep is that period of physiological repair, during which the cells of the body undergo subtle healing processes. Here, the human cell is charged with life energies enabling the integration of new information to flow freely. In the deeper, more profound states of sleep, the ego (personal consciousness) completely merges with the I AM universal life spirit, thus, releasing all our latent powers of organization into action. Recognizing the true function of sleep (as body-consciousness organizing itself) helps us see sleep in its appropriate place. Afternoon naps may be very beneficial during times of intense physiological assimilation, as can be the Art of Sleeping Late.

Those of us who live for security as a way of life, philosophy and/or religion run the risk of trying to stop an ever-changing world. Worshipping security upsets basic physical well-being. Due to the ever-changing nature of the organism itself, any excessive emphasis on enforcing order simply compels more disorder and chaos. Worshipping security is a good way to stay very busy making sure nothing changes. It will also tend to keep your energy at an all-time low until you're able to communicate the reality of safety, shelter and nourishment. If you're in a phase wherein you feel "nothing is enough"…(that you are not enough the way you are) then there is a fundamental biological ignorance working against you. On the basic biological level...*LIFE IS ENOUGH.* Ironically, being caught in Gear One develops into a constant negation of personal autonomy due to a passive identification with "everything." This is called being LOST IN THE SAUCE. When we are Lost In The Sauce, we have lost our ability to differentiate from the organic heritage of our biological origins. We can begin to distinguish ourselves by recognizing the Abundance of Life As It Is and stop floating helplessly waiting for somebody else to take care of us. (Is God not good enough?)

WHO'S GROUNDING WHOM?

When Gear One goes on Broken Record, if it's time to check the limits and boundaries of our own survival information and/or energy. Most of us have a *limited supply* of personal survival energy. Some of us, through grace and expanded capacities, have more than enough and can share it by grounding others...(being responsible for their safety and survival). Others among us have barely enough to stay on the planet and must work extra hard to remain here in one piece. At either end, living involves the risk of getting stuck "in survival." During these times of intensity, there is an alternative to reacting out of fear, panic and/or desperation. It's called *GROUNDING* and it happens anytime we consciously stabilize our own energy in times of crisis.

Stabilizing First Gear is *PLANETARY BONDING* and refers to the process of entering a Concept-Free Zone in order to become receptive to global support. The Earth, as was pointed out earlier, is a vastly compassionate and intelligent entity who has chosen to incarnate as a planet. We are children of this entity...products of gravity and the result of planetary unfolding. Put another way: The Planet Is Not In Need of Healing Or Saving...*we are.* Step One is learning how to receive from & send signals to this entity called Planet Earth. By passing through the Concept-Free Zone, we gain access to The Realm of the Senses. Our first step may be taken now, by learning to stabilize our own *INTEGRITY CONDUITS.* Practice this first while sitting, then learn to apply it *wherever needed,* especially as an alternative response to panic in times of intensity.

THE INTEGRITY CONDUIT

1) Sit, relaxed but spine straight with feet flat on the ground.
2) Eyes closed, center yourself in the way you are accustomed to do so.

3) Let the base of your spine be heavy, anchoring you to the ground.

4) Open up the base of your spine, so it's open-ended and heavy. Open up your arches, as well at this time. Watch your breathing process.

5) Begin absorbing Earth Energy up through your arches and spine, letting it move whichever way it desires, once in your body. Don't control it.

6) Let yourself be vulnerable to the influence of the Earth Energy. If it feels "dense," then, *be* dense.

7) Watch your breathing again. Begin connecting your inhale with the absorption of Earth Energy…inhale Earth Energy into your body. While exhaling, circulate the Earth Energy throughout your entire body. Inhale it in, circulate it by exhaling. Keep repeating…

8) Regulate the intake of Earth Energy by: a) Breathing deeper and expanding the size of your opening to increase the flow and/or b) Breathing shallow and contracting the size of your opening to decrease the flow.

9) Sustain the energy level you feel comfortable with. Move towards the sense of being a "bump on the planet" (hereafter, referred to as Bump Consciousness). Feel the immense support and strength of the planet. You and the planet are one. Be with this until you feel complete.

10) (Optional): Resonate a sound which matches the frequency and/or quality of the Earth Energy. It doesn't matter how it sounds, as long as the sound emerges from the energy itself. Let the sound change with the energy and let your body be vulnerable to its currents.

In concluding, open your eyes and register any change in perception and/or state of being. If with others, talk about what happened.

By learning to stabilize your own energy, it is possible to stabilize others. In times of acceleration, whether it be personal, interpersonal and/or planetary, it is reassuring to know how to respond creatively. If someone becomes irrational around you, just stabilize your own energy *first* before attempting to ground them. Then, you will minimize the tendencies for their volatile state to upset yours. By stabilizing your own integrity conduit through Bump Consciousness, you have already begun to stabilize theirs through osmosis. You begin serving as a Universal Ground this way and like any "ground wire," you function as a release valve for excess electricity or emotional charge. This works best when you've managed to stabilize your integrity conduit first, though. Remember...SAFETY FIRST.

The Universal Ground is a spiritual function where one person bridges another to the planet for stabilization. Some of us do this all the time without knowing it, from both sides: being grounded by another and grounding another. The intent here is to approach it consciously. A good way to practice is with a group of three or more individuals. The following method is called a *GROUNDING CIRCLE* and is training for the practice of becoming a Universal Ground for others when necessary.

GROUNDING CIRCLE

1) Each individual stabilizes their own Integrity Conduit towards realizing Bump Consciousness while sitting in a group circle.
2) When the Earth Energy is dense, or "real" enough, each individual resonates a sound by matching the frequency or quality vocally.
3) After completing the prementioned "sonic resonance," individuals return to the connected process of breathing: inhale/exhale: absorbing/ circulating Earth Energy. In silence...
4) When the energy is strong enough, individuals exhale it out their arms and hands. Then, the right palm faces down and the left palm faces up. The hands of each individual connect...the group holds hands while the energy circulates amidst them via hand-to-hand contact... left palm up, right palm down.
5) Then, after feeling complete, *a gap* is created so the hands are no longer touching physically but still circulating Earth Energy in the group circle via the gap. Recognize the difference in this.
6) Experiment with both gap *and* touching hands to determine which is most appropriate. Experiment.
7) When done, individuals withdraw hands and return to contact their own personal relation to the planet via Bump Consciousness...having a sense of the other individuals as "bumps"...a circle of bumps.
8) Open your eyes and talk about what happened. If possible, minimize philosophy, politics and/or socializing until the Grounding Circle is over. Focus the talking on what actually happened. This will help introduce our Conceptual Intelligence to Planetary Bonding in a way that is both integrating and instructive.

FASTEN YOUR SEAT BELTS

The actual practice of Universal Ground in a one-to-one context begins with asking permission from the person requiring stabilization for it to happen. It's almost impossible to help somebody until they acquiesce to helping themselves first. Once this is underway, it's a relatively simple technique incorporating elements of Integrity Conduit and Grounding Circle methods combined. If possible, have the "groundee" sit in a chair with both feet flat on the ground. Explain to this person that you are going to stabilize your own energies first before stabilizing theirs. You can suggest they attempt to "center" themselves by: 1) Feeling the weight of their body 2) Becoming aware of the base of their spine as open-ended and heavy and/or 3) Absorbing Earth Energy through their arches. In short, inform them of the Integrity Conduit.

UNIVERSAL GROUNDING

1) Stabilize your own Integrity Conduit at least two feet away from the person you are working to stabilize. Vocalize if necessary.
2) When dense enough (become as solid as a rock for this), start circulating the energy out the arms/hands via exhaling…without touching anybody.
3) When you feel solid enough and are circulating freely, place your right palm against the base of the person's spine, gentle and firm. Circulate the Earth Energy through your own body, then out your right hand and into his/her base of spine. Direct this energy down into the planet, forming a vertical stream from the spine's base downward.
4) When you are ready, "get out of the way" and become a channel for Earth Energy. (This may shake you or cause trembling or jerking. Not to worry, even jet-liners have bumpy take-offs sometimes.) Let the Earth Energy work for you and through you, as you continue directing the energy into the spine's base and vertically down into the planet. Do this until trembling stops and stabilization ensues. You can let go when the energy "cruises" or evens out.
5) Repeat Steps #3 & #4 but apply it to the person's feet, so you are in front of them on the ground.

Stabilize Integrity Conduit   Circulate the Energy Out   Up Into You, Down Into Hir

Become a Channel   Don't Forget Their Feet   Talk About What Happened

When you feel complete, separate yourself and re-establish your Integrity Conduit at least two feet away from the person. When working with another in this way, there is often an energetic acceleration catalyzed in the process. Become aware of whatever intensity develops and stabilize yourself accordingly. After this, speak with the person about what happened for you and ask the same from him/her. The more a "normal" type of mood is set with this work, the easier and more accessible it remains. It's just another way for people to help each other out and, *in.*

SHORT CIRCUIT

Short Circuit, or "over-amping," on the Physical Level is when we absorb more sensory input than we can contain. The first cause to be scanned is where we have gotten *Too High.* First Gear is the support function for its overtone in Fifth Grade Sensory Intelligence. Some symptoms of First Gear Short Circuit are: spaceyness, forgetfulness, scattered, ungrounded-ness, disregard for others' moral codes, loss of integrity and sense of personal diminishment. There is nothing intrinsically "wrong" with exhibiting any of these effects until they start negating the necessary integrity for surviving on this planet with others. Our personal power is restored with the first recognition of these conditions and actions taken to rewire, re-ground and re-integrate the new sensory information.

A fundamental dispersion follows any truly rapturous state and teaches us the restraint necessary for understanding. This principle is most eloquently framed in the *I Ching's* hexagrams #58 through #61, from (58 TWEE) *pleasure* to (59 HWEN) *dispersion* to (60 KHIEH) *restraint* to (61 KHUNG-FIH) *understanding.* This particular cycle within the Book of Changes articulates a highly creative response to the Short Circuit.

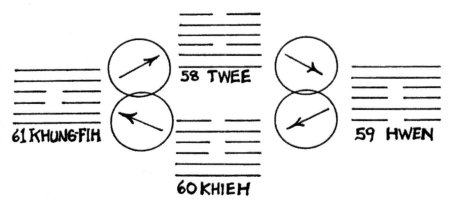

PLEASURE

The basic criteria for Fifth Grade Intelligence...losing our minds and coming to our senses to fully experience each unfolding moment for what it is without projecting meaning, judgment or comparison. This is the "zen" state of living in the present through our five senses and enjoying its free-floating direction as a reward in itself, as there is nowhere to go, nothing to achieve and nobody to be. The surrender to absolute pleasure in the moment releases endorphins in the brain and a sense of rapture and ecstasy throughout each cell in the body. Pleasure begins the complete, harmonious merging with Oneself as a source of energy unto itself which can be shared easiest with others resonating at a similar level within themselves. This sharing is "charismatic" (See *CHARISMA TRAINING in Fifth Grade*) and is reserved for self-realizing stars.

DISPERSION

Dispersion results from the release of physiological energy after total immersion in pleasure. Rapture is the brilliant union of our personal consciousness with universal spirit in the body. It marks a moment of Embodiment, as well as "ego-death"...in that the experience of Self is always a *defeat* for the ego. Dispersion is the dissolution of the crystallization occurring when ego and Self fuse together in momentary, rapturous embrace. It is natural that a "darkening of the light" follow, as what comes together alchemically, also must come apart. Conscious dispersion is the Art of Falling Apart.

RESTRAINT

Restraint is simply the discipline of knowing when to stop and when you've had enough. Dispersion is clearly the destructive force working hand-in-hand with the creative. Restraint is the wisdom of pulling back to oneself...one's center...after sufficient dispersion communicates the need to do this. Without this kind of insight, self-destruction would tend to dominate our reasons for living. The practice of exercising restraint with dispersion strengthens the self-appreciation essential for integrity. Integrity is the great fortifier and grounds us enough to permit more pleasure.

UNDERSTANDING

Understanding is the innate comprehension of our inner union with Self, God, etc., and the clarity which permits us to see this in others. True understanding is never forced. Rather than a tried effort, it will tend to "dawn upon us" when it occurs, as something we've known all along but only now realized. An understanding of this 4-phase cycle of pleasure-dispersion-restraint-understanding simply restores our sense of what we already know for ourselves from experience. This understanding doesn't necessarily come about until *after* exercising restraint, without which, our lives would end with dispersion. And...it would never begin without our surrender to absolute pleasure.

Somatic over-amping can also diminish our sense of physical coordination and concentration...ask any pothead. Intense sensory awareness, ironically enough, can blow us "out of our bodies" until this new information is organized and put to work. One of the most basic ways to organize somatic input is learning the Art of Slow Motion... moving slowly *while increasing awareness.* If we are creative enough, it's easy to do this on one's own. lust locate your threshold for slow motion movement...how slow can you move without losing your consciousness of each moment? Practice this until it's easy. Test your coordination, concentration and agility by moving slower while increasing your moment-to-moment awareness. If you need a stronger sense of structure, locate a competent instructor of the "soft" Martial Arts like Tai Chi Chuan and/or Aikido, both of which demand more awareness while moving slower.

If physical survival priorities are not met (Food, Shelter and Security), it becomes more difficult to integrate Fifth Grade education. The basic rule of thumb here is: *GET YOUR ACT TOGETHER BEFORE GETTING HIGH.* Stabilize survival priorities before even thinking about disconnecting from them to float fancy-free in the void. It's our responsibility as spiritual warriors to order and arrange our world in such a way as to reflect the void, so we have somewhere to return from our "extra-terrestrial" excursions. This is called Coming Home To A Clean House. Order your world so it accommodates your Creature Comforts and you'll discover the Art of Flying with Both Feet on the Ground.

How do you catch a beautiful bird without killing it?

By becoming the sky . . .

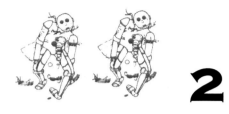

2

EMOTIONAL

SECOND GEAR

CONFUSION ALERT

Emotional Intelligence moves Second Gear in ways that are often irrational, unpredictable and cathartic. Emotions are not meant to be figured out. Gear Two disorientation can result from having ideas *about* our feelings that stop us from feeling them. On the whole, concepts don't really belong in Second Gear because when emotions are rationalized, they are repressed. This condition has been referred to as Having One's Head Up One's Ass. It furthers no one to stop feeling. Of course, there are exceptions…like being in so much emotional shock that one can only put off feeling for later. However, that, too must be re-felt before emotional survival is a reality.

    Synchronizing ideas to emotional realities means accepting them on their own terms. Emotions follow their own rules. If they are judged or criticized just because they are not understood, it's time to call a Confusion Alert. The first adjustment is learning No Judgment in relation to emotions. When emotions are allowed to flow freely, they fulfill their intent by expressing themselves. Another source of ideas which confuse our emotions are those self-images inhibiting and denying our personal freedom. This kind of self-denial keeps us emotionally immobilized until we breakthrough by coming out and being ourselves more. So, whenever you're ready, express those feelings you've been holding onto. If you've forgotten what it's like, here are a few examples:

joy fear contentment rage fascination envy longing sorrow disgust excited terror wonder disdain sympathy defeated triumphant embarrassed devotion inspired cynical grouchy

shy awkward panic naive flirtatious rebellious surprised condescending grief lecherous charmed courage delighted lonely worry whimsy boredom despair respect ecstasy complacency confidence doubt jealousy eager awe ambivalence amused urgency greed solemn enchanted

PRETTY VACANT

Leaving our emotions unclaimed is accepting invitations for a collision course with The Cosmic Wimp-Out. Gear Two is pushed by our convictions. Without strong feelings about what we believe in, we are but rudderless boats LOST IN THE SAUCE and unable to take charge by initiating direction. When Second Gear is Pretty Vacant, an emotional inertia develops…all the unexpressed love, fear and rage gradually devolve into the slimy sludge of emotional mush. Here, in this poisonous soup, our decision-making mechanism disintegrates from sheer lack of conviction. There are a number of ways to enter The Cosmic Wimp-Out that stem from two basic convictions about life-in-general: 1) Pointlessness and 2) The Depth Charge. *Pointlessness* is that particular emotional bias claiming an "indifference" to life-in-general because: 1) It's all the same, anyway 2) Life is a joke at best 3) Entropy will get us in the end, so why bother? 4) Or any other existential treatise emphasizing the meaningless.

The Depth Charge is a way of describing the conviction that every moment is fraught with cosmic significance. This starts the other path towards The Cosmic Wimp-Out. As you have probably already noticed, Life possesses a very slippery and wiggly characteristic in that it keeps on changing, growing and evolving. When we get caught on a Depth Charge, it becomes more difficult to remain in the present due to our attachment to the depth and intense significance of a particular moment. Besides, things can only remain so serious up to a point, wherein through grace alone, it turns silly. Hence…if something is True, then it is also Funny. If it's Funny, Laugh. (Are you deep enough to be shallow?)

Without an emotional bias, it becomes a struggle to stand one's own ground amidst other contradictory convictions and beliefs. When we grow afraid of claiming an emotional bias, it often originates as a fear of "getting stuck" or "growing too fixed." Yet without a bias, emotional survival is almost impossible.

Convictions cause convicts, yet the greatest urge for freedom pounds in the heart of the prisoner. Take away all limitations, boundaries and pressure...and you eliminate the need for freedom by replacing it with the need for First Grade shelter. Our emotional bias and convictions provide enough self-reference to shelter us from being too affected and shaped by others. *Define yourself or be defined.* Our greatest personal freedom is with being ourselves, as we wish to be defined. This has also been called "strength of character." It depends upon a strong belief in oneself. Besides, without conviction, who's going to believe you?

PARENTAL PROGRAMS

Parental programs around emotions manifest as three basic orientations, each breeding a distinct emotional style: 1) Attack 2) Repression and 3) Open. The Attack style roots itself in an atmosphere where emotional closeness is constantly required to prove family love. When family members grow so close to each other emotionally that communication *fails,* then greater displays of emotion are required. Communication, by its very nature, demands space between individuals to occur. Once that gap closes up completely, individuality and recognition become extinct, hence, forcing individuals to try even harder to prove their love. This kind of emotional attack breeds a smothering style of affection and often, with the more intense emotional displays, a kind of emotional "dodging" as a way to avoid getting hit, emotionally, by others. One way this dodging manifests is in an evasive, indirect style of expressing oneself...a tendency towards not feeling safe enough to be direct for fear of getting hit.

In an emotionally repressed family climate, members learn to be loved in symbolic ways...like receiving respect, admiration and approval for achievements. This orientation emerges through acceptance of emotional distance among families members because "love goes without saying." Instead of direct emotional displays to prove family love, the fulfillment of virtues and laws defined by the Mother and Father become the criteria for acceptance. A repressed orientation tends to breed a detached manner of expressing oneself...one's emotions may not be taken as seriously as the previously described orientation. Also, there may be an emphasis on self-love and gaining recognition through overt status. The direct expression of emotional closeness may have to sublimate through artistic, symbolic and/or humanitarian ideals and activities.

The open orientation to expressing emotions is found in those family structures wherein an agreement is made to permit mutual emotional expression. This particular approach tends to neutralize the roles of Mother and Father as being "law-makers" in exchange for a kind of democratic anarchy where all members are equal from the start. This is a departure from the traditional nuclear family unit in that hierarchy has been cancelled and replaced by mutually encouraged "holarchy." An open orientation will tend to breed greater emotional honesty. These three styles are, by no means, exclusive but co-exist in different states of potential in every family. None of the three are "bad" or "good"; they're simply ways to help the Karma Mechanic read the emotional code of Second Gear. If one particular orientation tended to dominate your upbringing, perhaps you'd like to adjust your karma by trying another style of expressing yourself. It is also a way to remind you how each of the Four Gears influence each other.

HYSTERICAL PASSIVITY

Emotional laziness expresses itself as a lack of "response-ability" to living. This is the passive mask so prevalent amidst the Pretty Vacant. Once the laziness crystallizes, the mask gets stuck on and the emotions grow hysterical beneath the passivity. This is especially common with highly "reasonable and rational" types of people, who, grace permitting, are ever so often subject to complete irrational outbursts. Until those among us can *become reasonable enough to be emotional,* we will have to continue these periodical bouts of insanity. And, hopefully not at too much of a cost to ourselves and others.

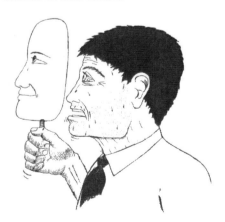

BROKEN RECORD

Our emotions go on Broken Record where we make something so important it obscures our relationship to the whole. Emotional obsession usually follows an emotional shock or trauma. For example: a person whose marriage fails (trauma) becomes a true believer towards a cause and absorbs himself (obsession) in a group or business (object of obsession) to manifest its cause. The object of obsession keeps the person blind to the actual source of the obsession, in this example the emotional shock of divorce. In any event, a strong attachment to the object of obsession develops as a way to re-stabilize the ego and perhaps, to restructure the personality itself as the initial shock is re-integrated.

Being stuck in Second Gear also happens when we over-emphasize the importance of our emotions. This kind of immobility tends to occur when we expect others to take our emotions as seriously as we do ourselves and...they don't. As stated earlier, emotions are "territorial signals" conferring the enhancement and/or diminishment of our personal sense of status and power. People get emotional by feeling a greater and/or lessening sense of themselves. In a collective situation, the most emotional person dominates everybody else. In order to survive emotionally, others must *react* to the dominant person or be dominated or...leave the room, physically or emotionally. Emotional game-playing can develop into the Soap Opera Antics for people who use power tactics to get their way by dominating the scene. The only way to deal with emotional games, besides leaving the room, is challenging the game with a stronger counter-game. Until one's autonomy, ego-strength and status are defined and realized on one's own terms, emotional entrapment and non-stop game-playing continue. Where there's nothing to prove or defend...freedom reigns.

The world's problems will be solved the day everybody stops taking themselves so seriously and according to Dr. Hyatt when each person contains his own sense of authority without having to steal or diminish someone else's. Negative emotions only have the power we give them. They become negative by the sheer condensation of belief that makes something more important than anything else. *ADJUSTMENT: Lighten Up and Laugh More Often.* Laughter is the most direct route to God; it fills our heads with light. Good belly laughs massage and stimulate the digestive tract and diaphragm, helping us "stomach" our more difficult experiences.

Hey, kids!   **Look here!**

Are you in the need of
PSYCHIC and SPIRITUAL HELP?
THE
GRADUATE SCHOOL
of
M E T A P H Y S I C A L
SEWER AND DRAIN SERVICE
Presents

LOWERING YOUR KUNDALINI ENERGY
(An Endarkment Workshop)
Featuring FRED MERTZ-BODHISATTVA

EXPERIENCE AN INSTANT LOWERING OF YOUR KUNDALINI!
In this workshop we will share each other's Voids, Abysses and Emptinesses.
INSINCERITY: SHARPEN YOU POWERS OF DECEPTION AND PERFECT YOUR ABILITY TO APPEAR TO BE LISTENING WHEN YOU'RE ACTUALLY NOT!
FOR ONE-HALF HOUR EACH DAY WE WILL FEEL SORRY FOR OURSELVES, AND FOR ANOTHER WE WILL COMPLAIN SEPARATELY AND IN GROUPS!
LEARN TO CLOSE YOUR THIRD EYE!
THE RIGID BLOCK EXERCISE- Maximizing tension and inducing it in others.
FRAGMENTATION THERAPY: LETTING GO OF OUR OBSESSIONS WITH "WHOLENESS"
LEARN HOW TO GET OFF CENTER AND STAY THERE!
Each day of the workshop we will experience "skeleton out of the closet hour" and "welcome to my nightmare" in which you will discover specific techniques for frightening friends and relatives.
HOW TO INVADE ANOTHER'S SPACE!!
For one hour daily we will collectively "bark" the word TRUTH in order to come to a realization of its relative nature.
TEXT: I'm OK, You're NOT!
Fred Mertz-Bodhisattva experienced the lowering of his Kundalini during the Nixon administration and has since served as Tentrick Consultant to the Boy Scouts of America.

Break out
of the
CYCLE

The results are a New You
who has experienced more living
in one week than you thought
possible in a lifetime

FREE BEER CHUCKROAST Hypnosis

The Legacy of Fred Mertz-Bodhisattva

Fred Mertz, as many of us already know, was the fat man in the background from the old I LOVE LUCY television show, you know...Ethel's husband? This humble "fat man in the background" bore more than a mere cursory resemblance to the Buddha himself... and...has shown distinct signs of being a premature New Age Avatar, transmitting his compassion over the neuro-electronic medium of television. Recently, privileged viewers have received his transmission through the reruns, where such sophisticated techniques as Senseless Bickering, Scathing Indifference, Bad Timing, Advanced Balding and the Five Secrets of Stinginess have been revealed. Truly, a more vivid demonstration of our own fixations has never before been portrayed with such guileless intensity as through this giant of American Spirituality. For more information, look for the TV GUIDE Study Groups and Kundalini Cowering Intensives in your neighborhood...or just catch Fred on the reruns!

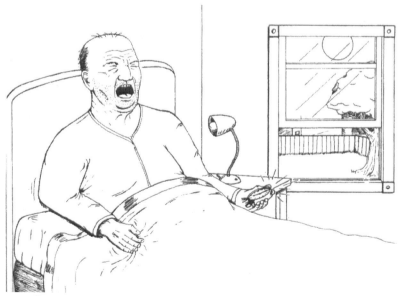

"No matter Where I Go, Here I AM..."

Fred Mertz on the morning of his endarkenment

EMOTIONAL O.D.

Too many unprocessed, unfelt emotions have a way of immobilizing our capacity for self-expression. This is especially true where the emotions we are absorbing are *not* our own. Some of us are endowed with the ability to feel the emotions of others before feeling our own, so that our own reactions follow the reactions of others. The creative side of this ability is knowing where people are at, emotionally, without having to talk with them about it. This knowledge makes it easier to recognize irrational behavior, hence, offering the opportunity to respond consciously. The destructive side of this kind of sensitivity comes from not having a strong enough sense of one's personal boundaries to stop getting sucked into somebody else's emotional field. The ADJUSTMENT: Learn the difference between *SYMPATHY* (being others) and *EMPATHY* (being yourself while letting others be). Empathy is mutual recognition honoring the integrity of all concerned, wherein Sympathy is matching another's emotional state without necessarily claiming one's own emotions in the process.

The secret to developing a sense of personal boundaries rests within our capacity to permit emotional differences. Emotional responses are unique to each person…one man's heaven is another woman's hell and so on. To live with people who respond differently than we do, a certain amount of solitude is necessary. If we are afraid of our essential *aloneness,* it's easier to define ourselves in terms of how other people feel, instead of how we feel. Our emotions are uniquely our own. They form the basis for self-definition and whether or not we can relate with others *honestly.* As with any process involving integrity, the more we find out where we are at emotionally, the better we'll be able to read other people's emotions *without becoming them.* When we are feeling ourselves, there is less need to project our emotions onto others, i.e., feeling their emotions because we're unwilling to feel our own.

Two ways to get stuck in our emotions are obsessions to: 1) LOSE and 2) WIN…as a goal, both orientations lodge Second Gear into Broken Record mode, portrayed as the Non-Stop Ego. Both winning and losing are highly charged emotional polarities or opposite sides of the same game. In order to transcend the Game of Loss and Gain, it's crucial to understand how winning and losing are both appropriate and when they're not depending upon their context. In order to comprehend the context, we look towards our Orientation to Success for more information.

How success is defined determines the degree of its manifestation. One element of success is what will be referred to here as our Havingness Level...our capacity to have and own whatever comes to us from success. If we define success in terms of how much we acquire, then failure will come with losing it. Even though this orientation to success appears to "win," it actually loses by its *fear of losing*. The fear of failure is probably the best way we can keep losing. This fear is the basis for the Loser's Script and keeps its Author "on top of it" through constant worry, threat and insecurity. The easiest way to re-write the Loser's Script is to wait for the next failure and *then, fail*. The Loser's Script attracts failure, so we won't have to wait long for the next loss.

Sometimes, we have to lose in order to win. A sixties Folk Rock icon once said, "There's no success like failure and failure's no success at all." Failure can be successful if it serves to collapse the Loser's Script to create space for Winners. Winners are those of us who can afford to lose once in awhile because we are risk-takers and, sometimes things fall through. Without the fear of failure looming in our guts, there are simply more possibilities to choose from. The Winner's Script leaves room for failure, losing and loss because in doing so, it finds out what wasn't meant to work and what was. Sometimes, defeat can taste sweet after the pressure of a non-stop winning streak. We're bound to make a mistake somewhere and thank God...we're human.

THE COSMIC COPS

Freedom turns to frustration when it's defined as Always Getting Your Own Way. As experience will reveal, freedom isn't necessarily doing whatever you want to do, whenever and wherever you want to do it. Through the constant fulfillment of one's own personal desires, there develops the emotional stagnation of Too Much Self-Emphasis. Warning Signs include Dominating Tendencies, Arrogance, Personal Isolation and the Alienation of Others. When you become Too Big For Your Bridges, they collapse beneath you and you lose ground. When you become Too Full, the Universe sends a messenger from the No Coincidences Dept. to initiate the Process of Emptying through Ego-deflation Tactics. If you "stick out" too much, Life has a way of shaving away the excess. It is in this way that the Cosmic Cops arrive and arrest your development by making your self-imposed limitations more obvious to you. This adjustment can be made by the competent Karma Mechanic instead, so that the *Cosmic Cops* are not alerted.

SCANNING INSTRUCTIONS

---

1) Learn to write Reality Checks...REALITY CHECKS NEVER BOUNCE.
2) Recognize the symptoms of being Too Full Of Yourself.
3) Listen to those closest to you...there may be a tendency to control those you are attached to. Tune into their feelings.
4) Detect any diminishment in your capacity to listen to others.
5) Make Your Heart As Big As Your Ego by remaining Grateful.

   P.S. (Gratitude is The Gracious Leveler)

SHORT CIRCUIT

Graduation into Sixth Grade Psychic Intelligence is nothing short of a neuro-electrical explosion, illuminating our consciousness to the relative quality of Life in all its glorious multiplicity...in short, an invitation for the emotional ego to step aside or be "disintegrated." Relativity can be described as a particular perspective permitting an *EQUALITY OF VALUE* to everything perceived. This is a "transpersonal" outlook, in that it sees beyond the judgment of: Good and Evil, Right and Wrong and, perhaps, most importantly...the emotional bias. Sixth Grade Psychic Intelligence reveals the qualitative, multi-dimensional nature of reality, i.e., something is true according to the particular Central Nervous System that perceives it to be so. Truth, in other words, rests in the third eye of the beholder. Until our emotional bias is integrated in this light, Emotional Short Circuits remain inevitable in the face of accelerated psychic energies.

Emotional bias, by definition, is opinionated. It's defined according to its attachment to seeing and interpreting things in a *certain way. A* relative perspective, on the other hand, sees the equal value of every bias presented. The necessary integration of these apparently opposing views is the understanding needed to fix a Second Gear Short Circuit. Read the last sentence again. One of the misconceptions common to individuals presently entering Sixth Grade (hereafter called "Baby Psychics") is the apparent need to deify the "transpersonal" while condemning and trying to do away with their emotional, opinionated self. This naive, yet well-intended, attempt at annihilating the ego in order to achieve "enlightenment" only crystallizes a more repressed and dogmatic bias than before. It's true...we tend to become what we resist.

One way to stabilize Psychic Intelligence is through realizing its innate connection with emotional growth. If we wish to sustain our emotional integrity and minimize getting Blown Away, then it becomes important to *develop a personal response to the psychic experience.* Integrity, here, functions as an overall stabilizer...fortifying our "psychic boundaries" so we may learn to stand our ground as Beings of Light, Auras or whatever we wish to call The Psychic Self. Once your emotional bias is accepted for what it is, it is then possible to stabilize Psychic Intelligence. This kind of self-establishment is soulful. It expresses a desire to be somebody and in your way. By being yourself more, you'll eventually be able to get beyond yourself to relate from Soul-Consciousness...or heart to heart. It's impossible, however, to give of yourself without a strong ego, that very confidence which affords giving. This is the crux of emotional survival...knowing that no matter *what happens,* you'll always return home to your basic self.

EMOTIONAL BIAS

The Performing Arts, notably Theatre and Dance, provide a provocative arena to challenge the soul's development, expression and need for discipline. As performers, we are called upon to give dramatic expression to facets and dimensions of human nature, using ourselves alone as instruments for creation. We learn to stay true to the particular bias, or integrity, of an action, character, dance or ritual until we're comfortable enough with it to project the illusion of our authority. The Magic of Performance becomes obvious when our illusion is convincing enough to transfix the audience. The professional performer *knows* it is an illusion and thereby, is able to leave the stage after performing to return to his/her own bias. This kind of knowledge assures continuity in the medium of performing arts, where it remains crucial to keep the show *alive and fresh,* as well as diminishing the rut of always playing yourself. The stronger the bias, the self-identity, the less need there is to cling to it, thus enabling other points of view to emerge. This is one example of the inextricable interplay between the relative and personal bias.

(A deafening round of thunderous applause.)

To be or not to be, that is the question. The answer is in *when* to be and *what* not to be. Reality Selection is a function of Psychic Intelligence. It offers the perceiver the distinct option of Changing Channels and fine tuning the most appropriate station for accurate readings of a particular situation. Without a basic sense of emotional integrity, however, you'll be changing channels forever. With a bias, you can stop and even turn off the TV.

Another way Baby Psychics short circuit their emotions is by idealizing the notion of being a "clear channel."

(!Achtung!!! — Is Reality Distorting Your Ideals?)

Nobody is a "clear Channel." Even highly trained Trance Mediums, those folks who leave their body and invite spirits to come in and speak through their vocal circuitry, have a semantic-moral bias which shapes the communication style for the spirit in question. Our bias is *the* circuitry rendering psychic information palpable and useful to our lives *on the planet.* The more definite the bias, the more specific the translation can be. It's up to us to accept our bias and co-create it through our personal responses. If our bias has become so repressed as to be almost completely unknown to us, perhaps we can discover it by the way we project it onto those outer authority figures spouting spiritual dogmas reflective of our inner immobility.

The truth will set you free but first it may make you miserable.

THE DEVIL .

The secret, of course, is in knowing your own bias well enough, to convey the illusion of your authority with others. It's an illusion because true authority rests within the innate Intelligence of each individual. Our bias bridges the innate with the obvious: it lets us recognize the bias of others, thus, helps us respect their integrity and distinction amidst the rest. We *resonate* with others, be it friends or so-called "clear channels" because we somehow *get along* with their bias. We don't have to agree with it, necessarily, but we must be able to bear its manifestation before us.

JUICE JUNKIES

Trancework and other psychic-type absorption requires a certain inner stillness and physical passivity to catalyze the "psycho-active" state. Psychic experience can be seductive. The Training involved for the practice of reading auras alone demands fine-tuning the Central Nervous System (no drugs, alcohol, etc.) to scan energy vortexes for information. There is always the possibility of getting too close to these sources and getting sucked in. This is not meant to sound like an episode from The Twilight Zone, however, a realistic assessment of occupational hazards is in store. During the earlier phases of psychic development, it's often popular for Baby Psychics to indulge in the self-intoxicating effect of Brain Pleasure. This is a necessary phase not unlike the one in which adolescents first discover beer, pot or LSD. It's even somewhat necessary to get lost in the "high" as a way to develop *psychic self-reference.* In this psychic infatuation phase, Baby Psychics fall in love with the energy rush, thus become Juice Junkies.

When Juice Junkies are finished "becoming the energy"...they can start the long and difficult discipline of "reading the energy," towards developing clairvoyance. This is major transition point. To comprehend it more thoroughly, is to understand the Juice Junkie phase as appropriate preparation, i.e., "the Fool" prepares to become "the Magician." As with any foolish phase, there is a tendency to become carried away, overwhelmed and even "transported" off-center to the Gates of Delirium itself. This is why Teachers are necessary at some time for more reckless jesters. Another foolish style consists of becoming too impressionable, "sensitive" and/or spacey to maintain physical and emotional survival priorities. This has been pegged YINNING OUT, deriving its title from the Chinese symbols of YIN (feminine) and YANG (masculine) polarities of existence. When there is an over-emphasis of YIN, especially for men (whose bodies are Yang), individuals move through various degrees of Terminal Mellowness and Fatal Flakiness until either their immune systems break down or Cosmos sends them a shocking message from the No Coincidences Dept. recalling a certain finite body.

The adjustment required to rebuild an Emotional Short Circuit comes in the balance between psychic-time and playtime. Every hour of inner-oriented, psychic practice necessitates equal time (an hour) of outer-oriented pleasure. This polarizes obsessive tendencies when Baby Psychics get too caught up in being "psychic." Exercise One is knowing which is inner-oriented and which is *not*. What is not is: Dancing, Socializing, Bowling, Gardening, Exercise, Most Sports, Jogging… anything done as a physical activity in itself and it's follow-through, in a spirit of play. The prementioned areas obviously lend themselves to inner-orientation (practically anything does) but they are outer-emphasized here for the sake of balance. Activities that are inherently more outer-and-inner related are: Sex, Psychotherapy, Reading Books, Eating, Watching Movies, Falling In Love, etc whatever excites a simultaneous inner/outer response. It's a matter of personal style and preference but definitely Mandatory Research for a balanced approach to psychic development.

Psychic-time and Playtime activities stimulate the release of specific brain chemicals, thus, changing Reality As We Know It. The practice of conscious psychic work excites the pineal gland in the midbrain, releasing the neuro-transmitter chemical *serotonin.* In moderate "doses," this drug increases our sensitivity to light…in its excess, hallucinations and severe fragmentation of thought. Those already initiated to the use of LSD can, perhaps, understand the difference between a small dose and a large one. LSD and serotonin are molecular twins. LSD could not effect the brain if it didn't fool the brain (at its synapses) into thinking it was serotonin. In moderation, from a disciplined psychic training period, serotonin increases our capacity for *light absorption* enabling the psychic to "see" auras, chakras and other autonomous energy forms. Too much serotonin is what you find in the dissected brains of clinically diagnosed schizophrenics…the hallucinations, distortions and the rest of it, all from being "too psychic." The purpose of psychic discipline is to regulate the serotonin level *without ingesting drugs,* so as to turn it *off,* as well as on. Pleasure turns it off, especially emotional satisfaction. Absolute pleasure is what triggers the release of the pituitary gland's *endorphins,* which are the molecular twin to opium, which could not effect us without the former. The endorphins aid in polarizing the serotonin. Pleasure and emotional satisfaction are "trance-dispersion" devices. Emotional and sexual growth is fundamental to clairvoyant development. It's also why it's so important for psychics to know what *satisfies.* (See *FIRST GEAR Short Circuit* for "excess pleasure.")

Emotional balance means redefining "happiness" in terms of our capacity for feeling, rather than the desire to be up, smiling and perpetually radiant. Twentieth Century psychologists have invented names like Depression, Anxiety, Hysteria, Mania and Neurosis to fool unsuspecting people into believing there is something "wrong" with them, thus motivating a visit to the Shrink. Human emotions are a natural occurrence and run the gamut. They are not wrong and most importantly, not "sick." What is, perhaps, "sick" might be our inability to feel our emotions, follow them through and come out the other side and richer for it. Emotional commitment, that peculiar capacity for being "happy" wherever we *are,* nourishes emotional health and balance. If the opposite of commitment is, let's say, apathy, then it starts Right Where You Are Sitting Now…in being the best apathy you can be until it's time to move on.

Emotional response-ability restores the kind of understanding necessary for minimizing a short circuit from being "too psychic." Relativistic consciousness can be emotionally immobilizing in that there are too many options and possibilities to feel strongly about any one of them. Psychics can be very low-key people in this way, unless emotional balance has been reset and their passions renewed. The emotional self is often "sublimated" through psychic development and this, sometimes, is seen as the highest virtue, especially by the Olde School Psychics and Spiritualists who still can't figure out where to put the ego. So, the tendency is to sublimate and "spiritualize" until we become selfless servants of divine light. This wouldn't be so bad if we didn't need so much love and emotional attention, alas, like most children and creative persons, we do.

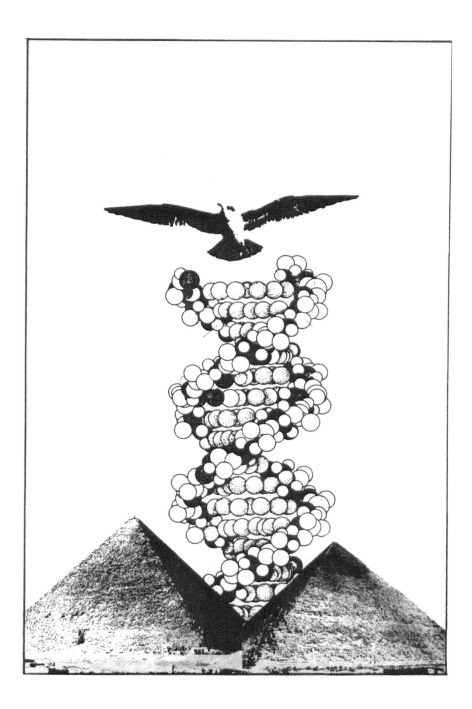

3

CONCEPTUAL

THIRD GEAR

CONFUSION ALERT

Conceptual Confusion shows up when our ideas about ideas, thoughts & concepts fail to coincide with their true symbolic nature and purpose. The nature of Conceptual Reality is *symbolic,* in that concepts represent and reflect rather than create reality…unless we're referring to conceptual reality itself. One example is when we are identified with our thoughts and are unable to discriminate who we *are* from what we *know.* When we are too close to our thoughts, it is difficult to articulate. A certain detachment from thinking is necessary to create the space for a playful intellect. Creative thought is excited when we realize the possibility that thoughts don't belong to anyone. Concepts are autonomous images traveling freely from one mind to the next. Our ability to concentrate on a singular concept keeps it in our mind until we're ready to let it go. It may be a popular misconception to believe we: 1) Create our own concepts 2) Own them and 3) Can forbid their use to others. This is simply a naive notion about the true nature of Thought. (Copyright Laws withstanding.)

The function of Thought is not so much "creative" as it is "interpretive." Mentally, we are Translators…processing conceptual input through our psychological filters to give us an idea about what the hell is going on. Due to these filtering mechanisms, it is never really possible to report more truth than we can experience through our Central Nervous System and our interpretation of same. However, if we are aware of our conceptual limitations, we may begin to understand its shape and propensity towards language. We may begin a more eloquent attempt at communicating the Purpose of Conceptual Intelligence, which is simply to Get The Picture others are sending you and to make sure others are getting yours. As a Translator, there is literally no time to "create" when you are busy speaking somebody's language, especially your own. Interpretive skill depends on becoming familiar with our own filters, so we may learn to tune into those of others.

Attachment, or identification, with one particular concept over another is fundamental to knowing Where Your Head Is At. To the degree we forget that our identification is with a concept, we can be said to be Stuck On A Picture...which is a good way of slowly closing our mind and, eventually, going crazy. (Remember, Nobody Owns A Concept.) Think of concepts and, for that matter language, as a code. Codes need to be deciphered before releasing their goods. These goods are like arrows pointing you somewhere else, within yourself or down the block to buy a beer from the supermarket. The point being...even when the concept is understood, it still refers us somewhere else. (For more information, re-read *The Royal Trap* in the INTRODUCTION.)

PRETTY VACANT

To the degree intellect remains unclaimed, we will look to others for our conceptual maps to navigate our lives. This kind of mental inertia stems from an inability to think for ourselves and come to our own conclusions. People who are Pretty Vacant in the mind often hook up to mates and others of a greater conceptual sophistication as an attempt to recover their wholeness. Sometimes this works and other times it does not when it becomes obvious *whose mind is controlling whose.* The kind of discipline it takes to liberate ourselves psychologically requires a total commitment many of us remain quite unfamiliar with. It has to do with taking time to organize your thoughts. Everything we *know* requires organization before it's freed up for: expression, communication and practical application. It's a matter of digesting before elimination can take place. Before you can digest however, you've got to have guts enough to think for yourself (pun intended).

REMEMBER TO REMEMBER

One method of organizing your concepts is by recalling everything that happened during the day, right before going to sleep at night. Verbally, express the events from the time you first woke up that day. Speak through them, one by one, until you remember each one. As you follow through in this, notice which events demand your attention the most and come back to them when you're finished going through them all. Then, return to those events requiring more thought from yourself so that you might be able to understand and digest it easier. Leisurely, spend your last lingering moments processing these events so when it's time to sleep, you can let go knowing your dreams will take care of whatever you could not. The important thing here, is to take the time to organize your thoughts *about* those events requiring your attention. **This will get you into the habit of having a say and developing a point of view about your own life.**

Sometimes, our conceptual laziness dictates itself from outdated parental programs reminding us that we are "not smart enough" or "not smart unless we go to college" Etc. If we secretly think that we are *not smart,* our minds will probably remain Pretty Vacant until this attitude changes. When we don't take the time to set our own standards and definitions for Intelligence, there's a good possibility we're driving Last Year's Model, the one given to us by our parents. No Blame, our parents may have excellent taste but if we desire a strong sense of direction in our lives, we have to make our own maps.

Our personal psychology reflects how well we know ourselves, how willing we are to know another, and be known by others. If we are to design our own maps, it doesn't matter right away so much if we are understood by others. Priority One is understanding ourselves. Our responsibility is to Make Sense of Things. If they don't make sense to others at first, we must persist. It is only through this kind of absolute dedication that it is possible to penetrate our personal vision and surface to a more objective, universal understanding. *("The fool that persists in his folly becomes wise."* — William Blake)

BROKEN RECORD

When Conceptual Intelligence over-emphasizes, we become priests and clergy in the Church of Reason. This does not necessarily mean we are "reasonable" or even prone to rational, logical behavior and decision-making. It simply implies we are *stuck in our heads* and do not have control over our thought process enough to bypass thinking. If there is a ravenous intellect starved for knowledge, it is our responsibility to feed the beast. If our mind is bloated with facts, it is up to us to initiate the time to assimilate its *Information Overdose.* Such a condition can make it almost impossible for the other three gears to function effectively, unless time is allotted for digestion. This can mean getting away from whatever source of knowledge is keeping you on Broken Record, conceptually.

Another way to exit the Storehouse of Swarming Knowledge is through Humor and Nonsense. Nonsense is a conceptual reality relative to the point of view it starts with. Nonsense expresses one's limit or threshold of knowledge...the Outer Limits. When one can no longer take any more information, things can get pretty silly and nonsensical, unless there's some way to make sense of it all. If there isn't, one is left confounded, perplexed and potentially disturbed until one sees the humor of it all. Humor is what keeps knowledgeable types of people from going crazy...or Knowing Too Much For Their Own Good. The funny thing about nonsense is that we can always be sure that when we use it as a measurement on something, from another point of view it applies to us. Isn't that silly?

CRAZY FAITH

Another way intellect goes on Broken Record is in response to the Fear of Going Crazy. Anybody with their mind on Broken Record is already a little nuts or "mental." No Blame, madness is common in crowds and rare with individuals. The Fear of Going Crazy is what makes people crazy. Sometimes, it may be quite appropriate to pass through a "crazy phase" in one's life just to let the chaos run its course and evolve a form true enough for us to live by. However, it takes a great deal of courage to run Willy Nilly on the faith that a sense of direction will emerge right when we need it the most. In fact. Faith may be the only known antidote for the Fear of Going Crazy.

9 | HERMIT

*'Yesterday they called it coincidence; today — it's synchronicity
but tomorrow they'll call it — skill.'*

SHORT CIRCUIT

**Whether one is terminally Sane or Insane, what ultimately matters is
that it doesn't (matter).** Only the paranoid is disturbed by the insignifi-
cance of the Universe, while mystics celebrate the equality by which all
things are related. The fear of the paranoid stems from an unwillingness
to become one with the Universe, or God, through the terror of losing
oneself or thinking one is the only God around. The joy of the mystic, on

the other hand, comes with realizing the illusion of our self-created separateness, thereby, consciously having a choice as to how to participate as
a piece of a greater whole...seeing God in every other piece. This kind of
choice becomes more obvious as we open up to the mandalic consciousness of Seventh Grade Mythic Intelligence, which requires our service
before we can actualize our part in the Grand Blueprint of Planetary
Awareness.

**When our Conceptual Minds are "blown away" by the vast pano-
rama of Mythic Intelligence, it's up to us to re-stabilize our psychology by integrating the new outlook.** The Mythic reveals the related-
ness-of-all-living-things...much like the DNA codes the language of
universal life. To the degree our concepts (of the world & ourselves) are
obliterated by the impact of universal truths, we are obliged to adjust our
thinking to include their reality, if only to put our minds at peace. If we
attempt to ignore what we know to be true, we'll find out how long we
can live a lie and maybe even suffer in the paranoid tradition of thinking
the Universe to be an evil, threatening place to be...missing out, of
course, on the Incredible Benevolence of Synchronicity. Who knows?
Life may just be a Positive Conspiracy bent on putting us in the right
place at the right time every living, breathing moment of the day. It just
takes a certain kind of perspective to see this. Realizing this can put our
"analyzer" on hold, our interpretive mind on "ga-ga" and our hearts on
breathless.

**An antidote to this "ga-ga" syndrome can be found in the practice
of Silent Witness.** The Mythic is only awesome to the conceptual
because the latter insists upon comparing itself to the former. This is only
as natural as children being overwhelmed by their parents power. Just as
DNA designed the Central Nervous System, so does Mythic Intelligence
create the Conceptual Mind. Who wouldn't be terrified by looking into
the face of God? Besides, the intellect can only function in an attitude of
comparison and in the face of Mythic Unity, it must include itself or...go
paranoid.

So, in the face of God, people go crazy or go sane depending upon
how ready they are to *include* themselves. If the intellect is going to
include itself, it will have to surrender its tendency to Figure Things Out
until it knows more. We can do this by referring to another function of
the intellect, namely, its capacity for just *paying attention* or portraying
the Silent Witness. It is in this manner that our minds may begin serving
the expression of Mythic Intelligence through its *articulation.* And it

does so as a servant until it knows enough to be included as part of the Mythic Identity itself. In the role of servant, the intellect is ennobled in its rightful place as Translator...a scribe to the King. If it chooses to serve, it must dedicate its life to the clarifying, refining and tempering process of translating spiritual messages. If it's not ready to serve and gets confused into thinking it's God, then, we produce a Hitler, Attila or Napoleon needing to dramatize its own spiritual catastrophe as an obsession to rule the world.

GUERRILLA ONTOLOGY

Art is the communication of spirituality through symbols. When faced with the undeniable depth of our Mythic Origins, there comes a time when we must develop our own *ontology*...our theories about God, Reality, etc. The word "theory" stems from "theo" meaning God, hence our theories are our *ideas about God.* Since from the Mythic perspective, *everything is God,* our ontology determines our participation as a piece of God. We can also choose which theories from other sources are influencing the manner by which we participate: 1) *Gorilla Ontology* and/or 2) *Guerrilla Ontology.* Gorilla Ontology are those theories of God generated and sustained by our so-called civilized masses. They include the Fundamentalist, Creationist and any other "ist" ideologies most popular with the majority and involve various methods of social control, primitive wish fulfillment and herd instinct strategies. Guerrilla Ontology are those methods by which innovative individuals manage to bypass the influence of the previously mentioned Monkey Business.

Whosoever understands the metaphor also controls the mind. Metaphors are symbols, emblems and buzzwords which trigger a chain reaction of associations in our minds. Depending upon the symbol or buzzword, an entire language can be accessed and set in motion. Metaphors are the "keys to unlocking our minds" in this way. Learning to use them as reference points helps in the ongoing conceptual challenge of Not Getting Stuck on a Picture by mistaking it for the reality it's describing. Guerrilla ontologists learn to become very picky about the particular words used to talk about things. Our names for example, are mantras shaping what we come to know as real. Words transform bodies...as the Central Nervous System controls the Physical Body, so do the symbols it uses influence the cellular organism.

"It's the real thing, in the back of your mind, what you're hoping to find, it's the real thing...Coke is!"   — Popular Gorilla Ontology tactic

MODERN SHAMANISM

Traditionally, every culture has produced exceptional individuals capable of entering the Mythic Realm with the purpose of returning to humanity and sharing their impact through various "powers" of healing, seeing and teaching...these are the "shamans" and "medicine men/women." Each culture has also developed their own psychic technology or "medicine," usually passed down through the generations orally, in order to perpetuate their shamanic traditions. Paying all due respect to the world's shamanic traditions, we shall *not* refer to them any longer but instead explore our own position in relation to the time and place we live in as "modern shamans." Just as any fool can be psychic, any man can be God but this does not make us Shamans. The real test to our shamanic tendencies is *not* in our ability to enter the Mythic but in *how* we return to our humanity and *what* we do with our powers. It is in this light that we return now to the arena of Guerrilla Ontology.

Guerrilla Ontology is a response to the kind of "psychic warfare" modern shamans engage in when they are trying to seduce each other (and the masses) into believing their reality map is the most important one around. As we are beginning to understand, whosoever understands the map, controls the territory. During those times when we are still recovering from the shock of Mythic Intelligence, we have only to read the maps of other shamans to get a temporary grip on ourselves. However, we are controlled by the ideology of those who have Been There before us and have found ways to think, write and talk about the experience. These are our Influences and they sometimes determine the style by which we start designing our own Mythic concepts, or Ontology. To ground the short-circuited conceptual mind, we might begin by scripting our own myths to live by *or* live by the myths of others. It is time to start scripting, casting, directing and starring in the epic of our choice.

"Hollywood is the capital city of the United States and Marilyn Monroe is the White Goddess..."
                                                            — Modern Shamanic Bias

SPACE-FORMING MEDITATION
"How To Make Things Go Away"

Space Forming is a method to help awareness enter a Concept-Free Zone. Before presenting the actual technique, let's explore the nature of space. Contrary to popular belief, space is *not* empty. It's teeming with stuff we'll call "potential energy" or energy which has not become anything yet...but energy it remains. The conceptual task in Space Forming is learning how to give space a *value* equal to the things filling it. This is possible by discovering the habits by which we violate our spatial awareness, both inwardly and outwardly.

Whether we're thinking, painting a picture or rearranging the furniture in our living room, the tendency to fill in the space will violate our spatial awareness. This inclination to "fill in the blanks" reflects a style of thinking prone to resist ignorance, hence, embody it. Read that last sentence again before moving on. If we're in the habit of coming from a point of view emphasizing how much we know, we'll tend to fixate on the *things* in our mind (our thoughts) and miss out on where we are receptive to new information coming in every moment (the space between thoughts). The "knowing" view finds it difficult to confess ignorance unless it's been trained to do so, which is a good idea if we don't know everything. On the other hand, there's our "unknowing" mind, which is the one responsible for Space Forming and Making Things Go Away. It works by Playing It Straight and saying "I don't know" instead of filling in the blank. We don't have to be afraid of ignorance, when we can realize it when it's happening.

Related to filling in the blanks, the fear of being incomplete also violates spatial awareness. Whatever is truly complete is also complete enough to be incomplete. It is by realizing our incompleteness that we can become sensitive to what compliments us and makes us whole. This attitude also helps to develop the Art of Talking in Blanks in order to *evoke* rather than explain our experience. Space creates mystery or rather, it "frames the unknown." As we figure out how to expose life processes instead of spelling them out, we come to honor the formers influence on our consciousness. The task is knowing how to create space in our minds so we can appreciate its presence everywhere.

The process of Space Forming suggests the possibility for a funda-mental transformation in our thinking. Since thoughts are the seeds for action (we do as we think), then it follows that scattered thinking makes for scattered activity...as creative thinking produces creative acting. There is an underlying illusion to thinking in that it appears continuous. Thought after thought, an apparently endless stream of concepts passes through our minds. We can't "stop" thinking. We might ask, "Is there anything the mind is not capable of producing? Is Life nothing more than a dream, a ceaseless torrent of fragmented images in dire need of editing?" We can see the illusion of continuity in our thinking if we learn how to watch our thoughts as they come up. We begin right where we are sitting now.

Sit down somewhere relatively quiet and make yourself comfortable. Center yourself in whatever way you know how so you are more in present time. Watch your breath without changing its rhythms. Then, watch your thoughts as they float up and away from you. Let any image come up. Don't try and stop thinking but invite thoughts to dance before you. Let them do whatever they want to do, just don't get attached. See them as concepts floating and passing away. See them as images happening without your control, coming and going as they please. After a few minutes of this, begin paying attention to the spaces between images. These spaces may be very tiny at first, like minuscule sparks of silence. As you continue focusing on the space between thoughts, you'll discover the illusion of their continuity, as they are quite dearly, **fragmented...coming in pieces.**

The sparks of silence between thoughts are beyond description but we call it "space" or "silence" as a way of instructing our Conceptual Intelligence of reality beyond itself. This silence is not an invention of our thinking mind. It is, however, an expression of who we *are,* as opposed to what we *know.* Who we are is beyond time and space. Thought requires time and space to exist. Time is the movement of thought through space. We don't have to try and stop thinking because that is impossible. One alternative helping us to bypass thinking is simply to pay more attention to the space between thoughts than the thoughts themselves until eventually, there is more space than things inside.

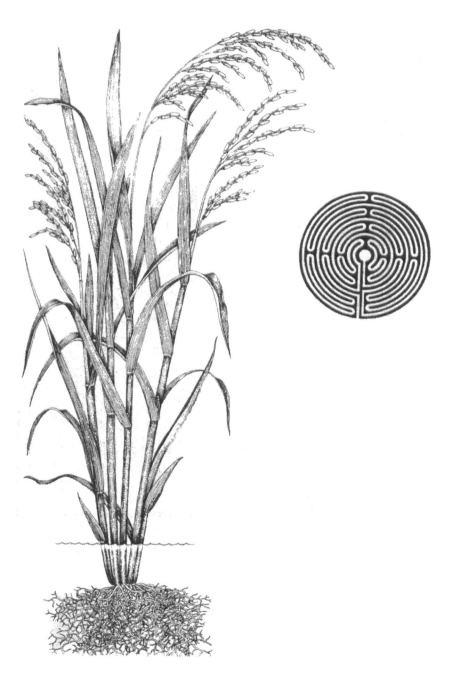

140

4

SOCIAL

FOURTH GEAR

When our social survival is confused, it stems from misplaced ideas about our social life: interaction with ourself, friends, others, groups and "society en masse." A popular method of our social confusion comes with neglecting to update our self-image to coincide with our chronological and internal growth. One example is with individuals still dressing, talking and acting like they're in the 1960's when it's the 21st Century. Another is the middle-aged person affecting adolescent attitudes in relating with others. Perhaps one of the more devastating demonstrations of personal disorientation can be revealed in The Once Famous Person. Here is a person who came into vast public recognition for being a certain persona and who believed themself to *be* this persona, even after fame withered. Then, the inflated ego of The Once Famous Person must suffer its loss by facing reality or continue living in a dream with those willing to go along with it. The common element of all social confusion of this kind is the inability to live in the present and maintain present-time interactions with others…unless those others agree to live in the same Time Warp as the disoriented.

   The sensitive persona is able to adjust itself to the ever-changing demands of the present. Identification with one's persona or public image invariably freezes the features of the face, as well as instilling a certain thickness to its overall texture. Thick faces don't take as well to animation and spontaneous expression as sensitive faces do. The sensitive persona is simply an attitude given to responding moment-to-moment in ways conducive to its expression. Good film actors require sensitive personas to signal a variety of internal conditions and external reactions with a distinct subtlety of their own. The sensitive persona also is capable of portraying multiple roles without necessarily identifying completely with any of them. With this kind of self-image, there is a certain chameleon-like quality…of bending to whatever the environment asks. One does not have to be a film actor to go through personality changes, however, many of our role models reached us this way.

PERSONAL GROWTH

One purpose to personal growth is in discovering the freedom to change our self-image and public image in accordance with the changes the rest of our life is going through. This kind of conscious synchronicity makes it easier to remain in the present by strengthening the ego-function of bonding inner-and-outer selves. Otherwise, we are torn apart and drained by the conflict. Self-torment easily manifests as the Boring Old Martyr syndrome until heroic attempts towards self-liberation are made…like Acting Your Age and Adjusting Your Act to accommodate the needs of your community. If this kind of personal flexibility is not feasible, then change communities and live somewhere else. The advantage to adjustment is that it increases your Social Intelligence by tuning you into the needs of others.

One side-effect of social development is severing relations with other persons who have not gotten around to letting us go through our changes. Changing one's mind about oneself is difficult enough but when you ask others to change their minds about you, it is then you find out who your real friends are. People get used to thinking about each other in certain ways and grow attached to certain ways of relating. If someone cannot handle the personality change you are going through because you are updating your self-image, then it is their problem unless you make it yours, as well. If people create friendship on the basis of personality alone, then when personalities transform, the relationship requires some adjustment or it dissolves.

Another source of social discord is when we outgrow our present social circles and neglect to withdraw and/or find new ones. Our circle of friends constitutes our Power Elite because this network affirms and supports the person we are or want to become. Once this circle stops doing this for us, it's time to take a few steps back and review our criteria for friendship based in our present-time feelings, responses and social realities. If we don't, it's possible to harm ourselves and others through subliminal resentments, hidden hostilities and other emotional signals announcing the need for more personal space than is presently offered.

POSITIVE THREAT

One impetus for changing social circles comes from loving yourself more than your friends can love themselves and/or you. You can only receive as much love, affection and/or acceptance as you've been able to give yourself. Any more becomes a Positive Threat. When you are loved more than you can love yourself, it's decidedly uncomfortable unless you surrender to a greater self-acceptance. If not, the Positive Threat of Too Much Love shrinks the ego or inflates it. One antidote to this type of Positive Threat is the simple recognition of your social needs…to belong, to *be* accepted, to be loved. This way it becomes more obvious whether or not you must leave one social circle for another… based on how good people feel about themselves. If your present "friends" appear too self-negating for your social comfort, it's time for a breath of fresh air. Self-negation comes in many shades of grey…everything from sheer suicidal attempts to ultra-narcissistic delirium.

Terminally Independent people become the most socially confused when they forget the interactive nature of Social Intelligence. The same goes for Fatally Dependent people, as well, who cannot permit enough personal space to maintain an honest relationship. However, it is the mingling of these two extreme tendencies which bring about the social reality of *interdependence*…whether it is within oneself, with others or in the group mind context. It is in this way that the social impulse expresses itself most directly. Highly social persons are often the most complex, exotic and fascinating due to the constant flux of interactions they require to define themselves and be happy. Personal adjustment becomes a way of life in the Fast Lane.

PRETTY VACANT

Of all the ways to become Pretty Vacant socially, perhaps the most poignant is becoming Faceless. In Fourth Grade, we find out for ourselves just where we stand with the process of collectivization. We are socially Pretty Vacant when we decide to repress and/or sacrifice our autonomy in exchange for collective membership. For some of us, this kind of pressure to conform to group standards is impossible. Others among us may welcome the pressure of conformity in that it gives us definition and the feeling of belonging to something greater than ourselves. However, during this phase of personal surrender, people often re-emerge as more homogenous, standardized and bland versions of themselves. They become Faceless. This also tends to happen whenever the Human Factor is down-played in favor of worshipping principles, knowledge, status, security, money, power, leaders and the rest of it. Socially, people are what we are here for. Until we realize this simple moral truth, we remain…Pretty Vacant.

For the Terminally Dull and Faceless, there's still hope. The Pretty Vacant can bring color to their personalities by Acting Out Of Character. This precarious act entails engaging in those activities contrary to the standards of acceptance set by the governing collective, whether it be family, friends, group or government factions. If Acting Out of Character excites a predictable guilt reaction, congratulations, you are in the grips of Social Control program. The key to dismantling this program is Response Ability. Respond to the guilt and the resentment you feel for being guilty based on someone else's judgment. Rage has been known to animate a few Faceless Phenomena back to life again.

THE PSYCHOPATH

Rebellion, in its extreme, takes a different form of Social Idiocy in the conscience-free habits of the psychopath. A psychopath, defined here, is that person (or aspect of ourselves) who comprehends social moral codes but uses this knowledge to take advantage of people. Many times, psychopaths are highly intelligent in political and conceptual ways yet lack the social vulnerability so necessary for personal development. Also, without a sense of guilt, they find no reason to feel bad or be punished for violating the ethics of others. The ethics of a psychopath simply fail to include other people and so, these tendencies often create isolated, misogynist and misanthropic personalities. Our own psychopathic inclinations surface whenever we enjoy getting ahead without regarding the cost to other people and/or the means by which our objectives are met. The psychopath is not so much Faceless, as many are colorful, flamboyant individuals self-taught in the social graces of charm, charisma and seduction. They are, as a rule, more Soul-less…in the most personal and social manner with others. Our psychopathic tendencies make us Pretty Vacant on the *inside.*

Another way to become Pretty Vacant socially, is by judging the social side of people as too frivolous and shallow to take seriously. Certain Artists, Writers and Serious Thinkers often become Faceless due to their fundamental naiveté as "social critics." These Very Deep People are sometimes so immersed in their creative medium that they never get around to developing themselves as people. It is easy to justify their social ignorance by masking it in cynicism, elitism and the multiple aromas of condescension. The personalities, in this approach, are often highly dogmatic, rigid and even cruel *or* it can swing to the other extreme of being hyper-sensitive, timid and terminally shy. In either way, there is a kind of a "benevolent psychopath" at work unable to take society seriously unless it's through public recognition, political influence to change society and/or being supported financially to keep creating. An adjustment can be made in a number of ways: 1) Create a community project 2) Befriend highly social-types 3) Explore "social or folk art" 4) Research topographical origins of culture 5) Initiate an Artists' Organization 6) Confess your depth by becoming deep enough to be shallow 7) Go to more parties.

SOCIAL CODES

Social bonding begins within the family and then, extends out to friends, groups and society en masse. The first bonding experience is between Mother and Infant. As we grow up, this initial bonding refers us to how we relate with women. If there is a lot of "karmic charge" around Mother, then, we work through our social karma with women until our relationship with Mom is more neutralized. The same goes with our Paternal relationship, and because we live in a Patriarchal Society at this time, its reflection in our relationship with authority figures in general. To the degree we resist authority, we create the karma to become authority figures ourselves. We become what we resist. The precarious point of balance dances with our ability to be *radical enough* to be conservative. The same also applies to the Maternal…to the degree we resist our Mother, is the degree by which our karma is to become nurturers. That is to say, *if* we seek to polarize the karmic charge and liberate ourselves from outdated parental programs, we learn how to re-claim ourselves on all levels.

The "social victim" is one who is unable to find an identity outside a group context because he/she is caught up in needing acceptance and/or ejection from the group to be free. One way to bypass the need to be attached and/or banished from a collective is through a form of self-discipline called Intentional Suffering. This is an arduous yet rewarding process of defining a personal morality: a set of principles to live by based on the realization of your highest ideals regarding The Model Human. Adhering to this code, one becomes the best person one is capable of being. When this code is violated from within, you take responsibility for your own punishment. This starts intentional suffering. Do this privately. The less dependent you become on others' approval for your morality, the less you are influenced by their opinions, rejections and reactions. Whatever your morality, permit it to others as you love yourself. This will help you forgive yourself and others for mistakes made. Gifts are for-giving. Lastly, by defining virtue in your own terms, proceed silently, lest you confuse your virtue for public justice and judge the human beings around you.

BROKEN RECORD

Fourth Gear spins out on Broken Record more from the fear of loneliness than perhaps, anything else. This resistance to standing on one's own two feet might be a judgment on loneliness as not being OK as part of Life. Indeed, this fear is conditioned into us from birth, possibly as a form of social control. If we ever got over it, we might just find our true source of power, creativity and authority within ourselves. The Herd Instinct is nurtured by the fear of loneliness. However, without our loneliness, we have no place to begin the evolution of our personhood. A look at the pain, sorrow and longing of loneliness will let us feel a heart that has not yet been completely broken…a mind which has not yet been utterly disillusioned. Why is it important to have our hearts broken and our heads disillusioned? Before any answers are presented, it's suggested practice to ponder these questions for ourselves.

BROKEN HEART THERAPY

Broken Hearts aren't much fun and Disillusioned Heads tend to ache but between the both of them, there's a good chance of getting off Broken Record. If a heart "breaks" maybe something wasn't real in the first place and reality was distorting our ideals. If a mind gets confused, perhaps it wasn't that clear to start with. When it gets used to writing reality checks on its own, the conceptual mind will soon realize a most amazing thing: REALITY CHECKS NEVER BOUNCE. With every heartbreak and disillusionment, we get a little closer to our "true selves" and the less we need to repeat our errors. We'll discover the heart that doesn't break and the mind that sees through itself. Our disappointments are actually spiritual victories telling us *when* we're off the track and many times, *how* to get back on.

Social addiction to a collective indicates group karma to work through. Here are the "group people"...those defined in terms of the collective they belong to. The karma of a group mind can survive many incarnations and present-day members may be completing tasks left undone in previous lifetimes. In any event, some people require the context of a group mind to fulfill their destiny. Some need groups as a springboard for the manifestation of their own individual dreams, while others simply cannot motivate without a group behind them. In either case, there is a tendency for group people to be "other-starters" and "outer-oriented" as they learn about their resistance to being alone by *working in conjunction with o*thers. Left alone, they may not be as productive, creative and free. For those who feel ready to dissipate the connection with their group mind, there are ways to set yourself free.

One way to release yourself from a group mind is through the willing participation of every other member to ceremonially grant acceptance (with no judgment) of your desire to leave. If this is not possible, then it is up to you to decipher and read the specific nature of your karmic debt to your group, as a whole and with individual members. Once understood, proceed to pay your debts as directly and simply as you can. The karmic code of the group mind consists of those excitements and resistances which bind you as a member to that group (to work them out).

A MESSAGE FROM YOUR SPONSORS

To assist those who are either considering joining a "spiritual group" or "religious cult"...or...considering leaving one, the following guidelines are offered:

CULT EVALUATION GUIDELINES

(On a scale of 1–5, with 5 being an *absolute yes* and 1 an *absolute no,* check off the underlying areas of evaluation.)

1) AUTHORITY   degree by which the group and/or
_____   leader(s) claim ultimate knowledge
                        about the nature of reality.

2) POWER   degree by which group &/or leader(s)
_____   offer power & status as a result of join-
                        ing the group as a member.

3) MONEY   degree by which your finances are
_____   involved to support your membership in
                        this group and its leader(s).

4) POLITICS _____	degree of internal hierarchy or distance between new members and leader(s)... pressures for attaining position.
5) INDOCTRINATION _____	degree by which members must follow the group's morality and ethical code over their own; also the degree of dogma and philosophical rigidity.
6) CENSORSHIP _____	degree of control leaders exercise over members' style of communicating; degree of inhibition towards outside ideas about the group, its dogmas and leaders.
7) FEAR _____	degree of concern over real or imagined enemies; also degree by which humor is forbidden in relation to group dogma, etc.

THE INNOCENCE OF GUILT

One way of immobilizing social survival is spinning our wheels from the guilt of an overbearing conscience. Guilt, as we know, is the negative emotion signaling violation...of Doing Something Wrong to ourselves and/or others. We feel guilty in two ways: 1) Like a robot and 2) Like an animal. Robot guilt is a conditioned response felt *after* Doing Something Wrong. Animal guilt is an organic response sensed *before* Doing Something Wrong. Understanding the difference between the Mechanical and the Alive, in this way, is a social revelation.

Conditioned robot guilt is a reaction to a moral program accepted as a basis to tell Right from Wrong. These programs have their own reward and punishment systems...we feel good for doing the Right Thing and we feel bad for doing the Wrong Thing. When this program fails to recognize and include the organism's innate sense of Right and Wrong, then we are subject to its ignorance. The organism instinctively senses Right from Wrong by its innate aversion to invasion, violation and potential extinction, as well as to the negation of the integrity of others. If we are out of touch with the organism's "moral impulse," then it becomes more difficult to recognize its signals. Without this recognition, we'll have to settle for the pre-set program's moral criteria. A creative alternative is in designing/defining the moral program ourselves by basing it in our animal reality.

Animal guilt is the direct, intuitive knowledge that something is "wrong" before it actually occurs. It acts much like a kind of emotional radar and demonstrates the basic self-respect of life protecting itself... whether it's someone else's life or our own. The next time we feel guilt before something "wrong" happens, we'll understand its wisdom by the time we're given to change our mind before actually participating in our diminishment. The trouble with robot guilt is that it changes into resentment because the organism simply detests having to feel guilt automatically. The resentment turns into an emotional kind of mush, immobilizing our capacity for direct response and obscuring our sensitivity to our natural radar. It takes a few personal examples and a great deal of attention to begin detecting the distinction between our mechanical and living selves.

SHORT CIRCUIT

The nature of Eighth Grade Spiritual Intelligence is highly interactive, unpredictable and beyond conceptual comprehension...only a strong Personality could endure the intensity of its High Uncertainty Zones. The Process of tempering ourselves towards developing this kind of strength often guides us through a series of defeats, as any true spiritual work tends to. This is because moments of complete spiritual exposure have a humbling effect on the personalities involved. Ego experiences anything larger than itself as the threat of death. From this perspective, it is plain to see that within every personal catastrophe, there's spiritual triumph. Once we have a greater understanding of spiritual intent, it is possible to become an instrument for its expression.

Spiritual intent is nothing less than self-penetration. We are all moving closer towards God-Creator...evolving at different paces but moving en masse to the Source. Self-penetration is the spiritual activity of becoming vulnerable to being impressed, penetrated and even broken by the force of life within us. This is something to the effect of being rolfed by God. (For the uninformed, "rolfing" is severe, deep tissue bodywork). The result is an everlasting-sensitivity to anything alive.

Socially speaking, a Short Circuit emerges with a loss of personal integrity as a result of complete encompassment in the spiritual experience. This is akin to capsizing in a rowboat out in the middle of the Pacific Ocean. With Third Gear Short Circuits, we responded to

Mythic Intelligence by forming our own cosmology to maintain sanity in the face of a greater reality. From Fourth Gear, there is nothing we can hold onto, conceptually, because we are asked to *participate* in the transmutation of our personality. Social response-ability starts with becoming the kind of person you want to be. Without this kind of integration, severe personality disorders can ensue. So-called Insane Asylums are filled with Fourth Gear Short Circuits lacking the information to integrate their devastating spiritual experiences.

CIRCLE OF HUMANITY

There comes a time in everyone's life when another kind of family emerges which is neither genetically related or people you've met before...(hereafter referred to as your Circle of Humanity). Many times when our Social Survival is on Short Circuit, we meet certain individuals who show up almost as if by sheer coincidence to help us in our personal evolution. These people are social messengers from the No Coincidences Dept. arriving to provide solace, friendship and reassurance while we are engaged in a high state of social flux...between friends, lovers, spouses, etc. As we shift from one persona to the next, between one social circle and the next, these social messengers provide meaningful transitions and often become soulful friends, whose bonds traverse time and space. We may only see them occasionally or once in a great while or whenever our lives are in the midst or turbulence and transition. They always show up at the right time and the right place...our Circle of Humanity.

The Circle of Humanity may have evolved over the centuries through reincarnations and each member of these circles may indeed be neurons in a vast Central Nervous System covering aeons of time and space. One can sense another member of one's circle by the profound *recognition and safety,* one feels in their presence. It is as if we knew them before but logically attest to never having met them in this lifetime. Another indication of being in the presence of fellow circle members is the quality of *silence and beingness* that is shared. It's almost as if you've known each other a long time and have already passed through the phases of personal expectation, heartbreak and disillusionment that usually mark the beginning of many relationships. There is a feeling of not having to prove anything or become anybody. There is a shared peace of mind.

**Our Circle of Humanity may or may not involve a particular
spiritual and/or religious orientation.** Circle members are spiritual
friends. Here are people we can say anything to and with whom we listen
very closely to. Our circles can provide the structure by which we begin
integrating our spiritual experiences through their relationship to the
circle itself. Circles sometimes belong to a religious affiliation but don't
have to. The primary intent is learning to understand how we respond to
the spiritual. Many of us will be unable and/or unwilling to integrate
spiritual information on our own so, we turn to religion for solutions.
Historically, religions and their churches have provided solace for the
spiritually bereft. This, however, has not gone by without its price. By
joining a religion, sect or church, we sacrifice a certain spiritual autonomy: our own personal response to the experience unhindered by the
effect of outside authority. Those of us who actually do respond either
end up going against the grain of socialized religion and/or invent our
own religion. People still resisting the most personal type of spiritual
response-ability, will always be welcome in the church of their choice.

**The truly mystical experience carries with it the complete disper-
sion of personal boundaries.** Spiritual reality is all-pervasive; personal
identity dissolves and becomes part of That Which Is Everything. The
profound sense of Being Nothing and existing *in* non-existence is as
close to the Source as we're going to get. Yet, if we're planning a two-
way ticket, we'll be returning to society searching for our place as people
in our *human form.* Due to the magnitude of the truly spiritual, this can
be quite a difficult task to perform. Modern society really has not place

carved out for people like this. Primitive cultures made them into shamans and medicine people. Our alternative as Modern Primitives is with custom-designing our own personality, its place in society and the vocation we aspire towards to pay the rent. We may have to do this without the confirmation of others. In fact, the need for confirmation may be our last obstacle to self-empowerment.

The ego, especially its social and self-image functions, becomes indigenous to spiritual integration. A strong sense of self, i.e., a strong ego, is fundamental to embracing the paradoxical qualities by which the spiritual flourishes. Paradox, as used here, is a device for permitting the co-existence of two or more contrary forces within one's being...without apparent discord, division or conflict. (To fly higher, plant your feet firmly in the ground.) When we have the nerve to personify Spirit, perhaps we are ready for the spiritual path. When our ego has been exploded into pieces, it's up to us to re-arrange these pieces into another puzzle. No matter how many puzzles we make, it's still a puzzle...a mystery to be lived and not a problem to be figured out. Who are you?

A "spiritual person" is one who lives consciously in the midst of great uncertainty, mystery and singularity because she/he is willing to embody it. This might be something like being the main character in a novel you are writing about a person who is wandering through a novel that is writing itself. If we are willing to "be written" then we are able "to write." If we are willing to be shaped, then we are ready to shape. When we are ready to be created, then and only then are we prepared to create. Who do you want to be?

CHAPEL PERILOUS

"Chapel Perilous, like the mysterious entity called 'I', cannot be located in the space-time continuum; it is weightless, odorless, tasteless and undetectable by ordinary instruments. Indeed, like the Ego, once you are inside it, there doesn't seem to be any way to ever get out again, until you suddenly discover that it has been brought into existence by thought and does not exist outside thought."

From COSMIC TRIGGER
by Robert Anton Wilson

CHAPEL PERILOUS

Chapel Perilous is a name given to that place where "souls" go after leaving their robot bodies...while these bodies are still alive and walking the planets surface. Numerous are the reasons for the leaving the body, each constituting a "sermon" in CHAPEL PERILOUS. Some of these Sermons are included here and others, for lack of memory, are not and must be deciphered for yourself. The Sermons of CHAPEL PERILOUS provide the lessons by which each individual soul learns how to get back to their body. Due to the highly ambiguous and elusive nature of the CHAPEL's terrain, its revolving door is often tricky to find. As one famous survivor said to himself after hearing the CHAPEL doors slamming closed behind him, "Once you're out, you either become stone paranoid or an agnostic." He turned agnostic. *(Twilight Zone* theme music, please...)

> *"To get out of the Chapel alive, become as still as death..."*
> From a conversation overheard between two frightened souls

The word chapel implies "a place of worship, usually smaller and more intimate than a church or cathedral" and perilous means "fraught with peril or danger"; CHAPEL PERILOUS refers to a place where danger is worshipped. Danger explodes in a kaleidoscope of shocks...haunting, petrifying, beautiful, dreary, euphoric, mechanical and alive. It is this phenomena of **shock** that most often sends the soul catapulting out of the body and into the oblivion of CHAPEL PERILOUS, where it gropes aimlessly for its other half. Meanwhile, its body continues on automatic pilot...following its generic, genetic orders like any good robot should. (Cut to *Star Trek* episode #23...).

"Captain, it would be illogical to assume that conditions will remain stable indefinitely..."
    — Senior Commanding Officer, Spock...SS ENTERPRISE

Shock, as defined here, is that effect initiated by a source beyond our control which suddenly alters our sense of ourselves and the world around us. Shocks arrive in a variety of impacts, ranging from the mild to the severely traumatic. An energetic function of shock is to temporarily *disconnect* us from our usual, habitual and routine ways of doing things...behavior, language, attitude, etc. It often produces a sense of Limbo, floating feelings and an overall "disconnectedness." Depending on how traumatic the shock is, we'll enter into anything from "spaceyness" to the Permanent Vocation of Psychosis. Shock temporarily disconnects the soul from the body and sends it to CHAPEL PERILOUS to learn the lesson of its Sermon. This process of returning to ourselves, our bodies will be referred to as INITIATION.

(Note: The following is in very tiny print for the purpose of your immediate interest.)

Initiation is creative response to the shock of the unknown. Since **shock** disconnects us, how do we reconnect and where do we begin? One creative way to respond to shock is by reconnecting ourselves to new habits and routines which increase our intelligence and make us happy. During the phase of our disconnection, we are perhaps most vulnerable to impressions and suggestions from ourselves and others. It is during this time that new directions may be initiated and crystallized when the "gap of our death" eventually closes down again and we stabilize. The contrary is true, as well, but perhaps in a more detrimental way...ask any acidhead. LSD opens this gap and we enter "peak imprint time." If we're naive to this effect and don't reconnect ourselves creatively, we lapse back even deeper into our previous habitual patterns...like them or not. CHAPEL PERILOUS is where we end up if we don't like them because souls don't take well to bodies in pain. They just up and leave the robots to their own resources. Ask any body.

Every Sermon in CHAPEL PERILOUS addresses itself to the soul's need to completely commit itself to living through the body...each Sermon differs, as each soul needs to hear this in its own way. The congregation of CHAPEL PERILOUS is made up of Lost Souls who all wait for the Priest to read their particular sermon so they may leave the terrible redundancy of remaining in church. The following sermons are vaguely recalled but specifically remembered during one very long night in CHAPEL PERILOUS. They were presented to a congregation of lost, disembodied souls...

(As presented by The Priest to the Congregation)

Ominos, dominoes, ear nose and eyes know...nobody knows! Welcome to CHAPEL PERILOUS, Ladies, Gentlemen and O Merciful Others! Many of you have been here before and by the look on some of your faces, some of you have never left. For those of you who have just recently fallen through our trap door, welcome! And, worry not...because no matter where you go, HERE YOU ARE! Before moving on to our Ceremonials, we want to thank all you lovable lost souls for finding your way to the CHAPEL May you find your way home someday. .OM. .The following sermon, EXHAUSTION, will be taken from the Book of Uterus, Chapter 5 Page 23 of the Secret Doctrine of the HOLY Assholia. from subterranean Labyrinths, we bring you direct from the mouths of kamikazes mermaids and broken toy soldiers...the continuing saga of your disappearance.

INTRODUCTORY SERMON —— EXHAUSTION

GREETINGS...it has already dawned upon you, no doubt, that you are here due to certain exhaustions. It is, by no means, an easy task to live through a human form...especially during such a critical era as they are now embarking on in their Turn-of-the Century Matrix. Indeed, their genetic evolution has begun to accelerate at mutant rate, bringing with it all the mandatory pressures and adjustments. It is precisely these pressures and adjustments which require our utmost attention, commitment and endurance. For they hold the key to our understanding, without which, we could not return and your poor bodies would be destined to continue flailing about and ruthlessly bumping into each other. As you can see, the destiny of this beautiful blue planet rests on this understanding...the spiritual information of this sermon is deftly hidden within your own responses around the phenomena of exhaustion. As you have already surmised, the human form is rather limited in its capacity to hold light and contain life energies. It quickly reaches its limit and either collapses or breaks down. Such is the nature of the exhaustion we speak of...and this exhaustion manifests on all possible levels...many of which make up the words to the following sermons in CHAPEL PERILOUS.

As souls, we all have our differing tolerance levels when it comes to human exhaustion. We understand that it is impossible to manifest spiritual intent without the physical human form and yet, when we go to work...the spirit is willing but the flesh is weak. You are here now, in CHAPEL PERILOUS, because you do not understand this completely enough. And, you will remain until you do. The first lesson to understand about exhaustion is this: you don't abandon your bodies when they collapse. The moral response is just the reverse!: increase your commitment to being there without pushing spiritual intent. When bodies break down, it is their way of bowing to us and we must return the gesture and bow back. It is an absolute disgrace to up and leave. We are here now because we have fallen from grace. We will remain until we are moved, at the speed of grace, to return to embody ourselves in the *human form.*

SERMON ONE — OUR KARMIC ANCESTRY

The soul, as we know, travels through numerous incarnations…evolving with each lifetime, century and era, giving birth to the individual we are today. In each of its manifestations, a family is selected to usher the soul into its earthbound adventure. The family is chosen on the basis of what it can provide to furthering the soul's evolution. This, as we also know, is not always to the liking of the soul itself. This is because the soul is drawn down to that family which best expresses its own karma or collection of resistances and excitements. Thus, a soul which abhors violence may be born into a fighting family to learn about violence; taking this simple notion into consideration, the congregation can provide its own examples…

Due to the emotional and genetic foundations by which our Ancestral Heritage is based, it is indeed imperative that we know how its karma is manifest. Many of you are here now because you refuse to live amidst the suffering of your genetic families and so you have deserted your bodies to avoid your karma. As we all know, there is no avoiding karma. Each lifetime has its debt to pay before you are allowed to graduate and evolve. If you have already forgotten, suffering is a mask for growth and a certain degree is required for true development. A decision made to return to your genetic families at this time will help you rectify your mistake through the discipline of intentional suffering.

Once you understand why you were drawn into birth through your particular genetic family, you may proceed with your work. As you know, there are *no accidents* and biological pregnancy is a signal announcing your readiness and availability to the Earth Plane of desire. Learn what you need to know, adjust your karma as need be and prepare to usher in those on the Waiting List by making families of your own. Remember, it is a divine privilege to be born…

SERMON TWO — FATAL ROMANTICS

As you all know, the soul comes into its own consciousness on the Earth plane through various trials and tribulations. Perhaps one of the more popular methods of soul-realization is in the human experience of Falling In Love. As you are aware, the Earth plane is made up of only two sexes, but the humans have more than outdone themselves by finding every possible combination to fulfill the soul's great need for variety. Whatever sexual formula generates the highest karmic "charge" provides the soul with its appropriate arena for actualization through some variation of this previously mentioned experience called Falling In Love. It's apparent that some of this congregation's older souls find this amusing and by the sounds of your laughter, let me remind you that you're all *in the CHAPEL*...and there is much to learn before you are set free.

For the sake of simplicity alone, we shall only refer to one combination of sexual relationship...that of one man and one woman...once we understand the general idea, I'm sure the congregation can use their imaginations to apply these notions to the greater variety. When a man falls in love with a woman, it is quite different from and to a woman falling in love with a man. Before going on, let us be reminded that love is soulfood and without it, there would be no evolution possible. Falling In Love is the initial envelopment of human love and because it is, it marks a dramatic initiation of the human personality into the soul realm. And vice versa. However, as most of us realize, it is the personal realm which suffers the greatest impact in this initiation. Since people are divided up into men and women, we shall now proceed, with how each Fall In Love differently, thus contribute to our perpetual education...

As we now know, each human male is house and home to a more feminine soul...as each human female gives form to a more masculine spirit. It is also known that the greater the soul, the more of its gender is expressed through its opposite human counter-part. For example, a highly creative, human male becomes "feminized" and the highly creative human female "masculinizes"...for these are signs of greater development. As always, there are exceptions to the rule...

This sermon is entitled *FATAL ROMANTICS* for that is what becomes of great souls who "fall in love" with each other. Romance is, indeed, a most perilous phenomena amongst the lovers of humanity. The feminine soul is cast out and projected from its human male form when a man falls in love with a woman. This process is reversed when a woman falls in love with a man. When humans fall in love with the person most closely replicating their own inner self at the time, souls fly out of their bodies with all pandemonium breaking loose. On the spiritual plane, romance is a sacred intersection of astral and material dimensions...an initiation for awakening soul-consciousness in the human form ensues. The fundamental disorientation of Humans Falling In Love is a combination of inter-dimensional collision and a genuine out-of-body experience. It is in this light that some of this congregation are here today...you were released from your bodies, unintentionally, by the human projection mechanism.

Human personalities discover their spiritual nature in many ways, one of which is by throwing their souls away. This is only natural, as hearts grow fonder in absence. The fatal element of romance emerges when humans-in-love realize how much they miss their souls, after throwing them out, while convinced they are missing their human other...the target of their projections. The younger souls of this congregation are, no doubt, most vulnerable to this kind of self-torment. However, it is your very longing...the very fire burning in your hearts that purges the space for your inevitable return. Too ease the suffering of your misguided human forms, teach it to turn within to find its true mate in the alchemical marriage of your union. The female human form learns she is also a masculine spirit, as the masculine human form realizes his internal feminine counterpart. This will dissipate obsession and the exhausting desperation of soulless bodies in heat. It will also render relationship possible to bear.

Once incarnated, there are no divorces until death of the body. Either your marriage is on the rocks, adequate or operating magnificently, but married, you remain. As you are beginning to realize, communication only occurs among equals. And as souls, you and your human form must find your area of mutuality...where both polarities come to agreement. If you refuse, you must continue to struggle with the random madness generated by a conflict of interests so great as to suggest holy blasphemy itself. It is your mutual intersection which fuels the fire of your evolution. Go...

SERMON THREE — THE EGYPTIAN DREAM

It is self-evident, by now, how each individual incarnation carries its own lessons, purpose and destiny. What might not be obvious right away is the accumulated effect the knowledge and power that each lifetime tends to have on the present life. Perhaps, some of this congregation's older souls are just now realizing the implications, responsibilities and solutions to this profound possibility. Why, the depth of feeling and elevated perspective alone can be quite disconcerting to the awakening human consciousness. Even though it's true that we open no mind before its time, we have to realize the significant limitations of the uninitiated. The combined force and information of our astral patchwork design of past incarnations may, indeed, require a much greater sense of selectivity than was previously imagined. Just which past life IS most appropriate to the present? What particular episode provides the most useful information and/or energy for the fulfillment of the present life's destiny? These are questions for this congregation to consider before you can return to your respective human forms...

This Sermon, entitled The Egyptian Dream, refers to a classic example of how Past-Life Memory can flood Present-Time Consciousness. Practically everybody in this congregation has been to Egypt at least once and a few of you, many times over. Egypt is a land common to us all; we know the Nile, the Sphinx and so forth. However, to the Western world of the latter 20th century, Egypt circa 3,000 B.C.E. is a most exotic, magical kingdom of great knowledge and power. A remarkable surge of human identification with this era has unleashed torrents of psionic information from the Akashic Archives. No doubt it is now time for this instruction to be transmitted but I put forth the proclamation of our moral duty as souls to regulate the influx of this information. I am speaking specifically to those of you who have abandoned your human forms because of their confused, deluded and terrified minds.

The danger of the undeveloped mind becomes all too apparent when the mythic and spiritual channels are opened, prematurely, thus immobilizing the human interpretive circuitry. How many of you here have human forms writhing about on the floors of Insane Asylums? How many are prey to the cosmologies of religious cults to justify their psychic and spiritual experiences? How many must resort to dogmatic emotionalism to communicate their truths? Your ethical responsibility is to return and help your bodies become more intelligent. Teach them as if they were your children, as they *are,* and express the denser sides of yourselves. Have patience with their anxiety and ignorance, for without each other—they will grow lonely and you, dear lost souls—will not grow at all—visit their little minds in dreamtime and show them *who you are.* If they are flooded with Egypt, appear as KA—the bird-human symbol for the soul from Egyptian mythology—but appear!

SERMON FOUR — SUICIDE AND FREE WILL

As you've already noticed, the silver cord connecting yourselves to the umbilical region of your human forms was not made to last. A few of you have probably already severed your ties and drift aimlessly like high-flying kites, set free into an electrical thunderstorm. Of course, this was your choice. However, you are also aware of the karmic implications of suicide and because you are, you understand the consequences of doing it again. From the beginning of time, we were introduced to the enormous debt induced by taking our own lives. Its ONLY "spiritual function" is as an evolutionary inhibitor. Suicide is the emergency brake on the genetic roller coaster. It's not meant to be used unless all other resources have been exhausted. As you realize, it requires a great deal of *commitment* to investigate these resources in the first place, without which, suicide becomes an expression of ignorance…of not having the time and energy to see the obvious. For those of you contemplating suicide, there is a terrible humility awaiting you…

As you are starting to understand, the Afterlife is experienced differently by each soul depending upon the beliefs you picked up while living through the human form. I'm sure you can appreciate the humor in this. While we are disembodied, we have as much knowledge of human life as humans do of the disembodied realm…*mercifully little.* This, of course, is part of the immense fascination shared between realms for the other. For example: Humans think death is a very serious, big event where everything changes. Little do most of them realize how big a joke it actually is! For us, this is common knowledge…death changes nothing and it is because of this spiritual truth that suicide *is* suicidal…it doesn't work. We remain ourselves in spite of death. On the other hand, as disembodied souls, we know very little about free will which, as we are beginning to discover, only exists within the human form. In our so-called "spirit realm," we are subservient to cosmic law and this is as normal to us as free will ought to be to human beings…but isn't until we return and claim our human forms to experience the exquisite freedom contained therein…

SERMON FIVE — THE PHILOSOPHER'S DILEMMA

You have, perhaps, witnessed the great philosophical tendency of your human forms. Philosophy is the human way of referring to things mystical. There are as many philosophies as there are minds reading ideas about life. Unfortunately, most of these minds lack the direct, first-hand experience to justify their elaborate ideations in fact. As a result, some of the more discouraged and frustrated of this congregation are here because the minds of your human forms have become stuffed with useless ideas…leaving very little room for your actualization. This error in human understanding is called Thinking Too Much. Humans think too much because they have not yet evolved a more suitable style of responding to shock. It is indeed shock which stops, at least temporarily, the mechanical thinking process but if the mind fails to reconnect in a more intelligent, happy mode, then, back it goes to repeat its meanderings. This vicious cycle is the subject of Sermon Five, The Philosopher's Dilemma.

What I'm about to present may very well be a review for most of the congregation, however, for the sake of the younger souls these words will not go unheard. It is our responsibility as evolving souls to impart to our human existence appropriate spiritual information so that right relationship may occur. Throughout the aeons, it has been discovered that spirituality feels better in the body that out of it. Ask anybody who's been there. As souls develop, their destiny is manifest through intersecting realms...materializing the spirit, while spiritualizing the body. The older the soul, the less distinction is made between the physical and the meta-physical...until their ultimate realization as a unified field blossoms like a wildflower in full bloom.

Therefore, it is the karmic duty of this congregation to define its philosophy according to the intersection of spiritual and material realities. In truth, these realms are completely integrated and it is only through our awakening to this possibility that we become aware of what already is. As long as philosophy is related out of the body, that is where the soul must remain...here, in CHAPEL PERILOUS. When you are ready to include the physical, human form as spiritual, then you may start to live again.

SERMON SIX — HEAVEN AND HELL

As a previous sermon inferred, the experience of Afterlife is seen through the bias of the religious beliefs souls pick up while living through the human form. If your time on Earth is spent following Zen Buddhist doctrines, then Afterlife is the illuminated gate of the void. If Catholicism is your cup of tea, then you have your host of angels and demons and so forth. This is precisely why the world religions can never agree and unite. For that matter, perhaps they're better off that way due to the soul's ravenous appetite for variety.

(great echoings of soulful laughter)

So, it is in the broadest sense that this sermon refers to itself as Heaven and Hell. Once embodied, the soul experiences terrific longing to be reunited with its source in the so-called "spiritual" realm. It will go to great lengths once it is only briefly exposed to its true origins, just to find union with its Creator. Every religious practice has its spiritual disciplines to ignite the sacred fire of this relationship. These practices will put the human form through Hell itself for a glimpse of Heaven. Such is the power of forgetfulness when the soul becomes physical. It will try anything to remember itself, once it starts awakening and often succeeds in just about killing its human form in the interim.

Perhaps the most violent and sudden manner of human spiritual awakening comes through atomic penetration, felt collectively in the recent nuclear explosions and more individually, in the chemical LSD. These events, as you know, have contributed greatly to the present accelerated rate of genetic evolution resulting in the new, improved mutant nervous systems some of this congregation has been privileged to use. However, we must again and again be reminded how exceedingly delicate these human forms are, especially during the turning point of their 21st Century Matrix. It is nothing short of transcendental masturbation the way some of this congregation have conducted themselves. The utter shame of burning out your bodies because of your unbridled spiritual hedonism leaves me with nothing more than disdain for you all. Experiment, if you must, but for Heaven's sake…don't put your human forms through Hell for a one-way ticket to oblivion unless you want a job here. I'm referring primarily to those with extensive chemical history with LSD. Why, the human brain alone is optimally wired to manufacture its own appropriate dose of any mind-altering agent capable of being produced synthetically. LSD and its chemical family, opium and other drugs would have no effect whatsoever if they did not already have their molecular twins sleeping deep inside the human brain.

As for the nuclear explosions, many of this congregation already suspect the worst due to the extraordinary complications which have now beset the world leaders of our human forms. Many of you are here now because you could not live in the terror your body feels when it's convinced it will die any moment. There's just *no room* with that much fear. As you know, the real issue surrounding the nuclear bomb threat is that your human forms are going through the puppet motions of a war in Heaven. This psychic warfare, as you have already discovered, involves the various world cosmologies' depiction of their respective Doomsday Doctrines, all of which refer to the "end of the world" in terms reminiscent of nuclear explosions. The potential for their self-fulfilling prophecy, of course, is somewhat unnerving. Their religious "second coming" may refer to the bright atomic flash of the explosion itself and their idea of "heavenly ascent" may be the release of millions of souls en masse, leaving their burning bodies behind, ascending to oblivion. If you think it's crowded in the CHAPEL now, just wait and see...

The moral of this sermon, dear lost souls, is that Doomsday Has Been Cancelled. You create your heavens and your hells through your ideas about them. They are a very effective polarity that the mind has concocted. If you have forgotten the mastery by which the mind dreams its worlds, then you are here because you took these dreams for truth. Of course, they have their "truth", but let us remind ourselves again and again...we are in the CHAPEL because we have lost touch with that area the mind is incapable of conjuring. Why, even the Chapel itself is a product of thought, and if the congregation can not be free of thought, they shall remain to the sermon which liberates their souls...one man's heaven is another's hell. Fortunate are those who are not seduced by either...

SERMON SEVEN — THE CRUCIFIXION

As you are beginning to realize, all true initiation is preceded by a certain kind of surrender. It is of a certain kind because it is determined by our conscious choice and not from the kind of submission to circumstances often associated with surrender. Another word, *sacrifice,* refers to a very similar type of conscious choice. Sacrifice implies "to make sacred." However, a sacrifice does not make anything sacred unless *what* we are giving up is very dear to our hearts and of the utmost personal significance. Many of this congregation are here now because such a sacrifice was called for. Perhaps you were asked to give up what was most precious of all, your very bodies, so you might know how sacred life is. And as we know, all too well, there is no life outside the human form...for it is within a form that we are to find the essential coordinates for living a life. If more of us knew this while we were living but alas, such is the price of our physical amnesia...

One of the most powerful metaphors available to the human form for its spiritual awakening is that of the crucifixion. Unfortunately, as we have come to bear witness, it is also one of the more misunderstood. What this Sermon will hopefully accomplish is the clarification, once and for all, of the true nature and purpose of the crucifixion metaphor.

When the great soul Jesus Christ was crucified on the cross in her human form as a man, she did so to convert her physical death into a metaphor for the rest of humanity. The crucifixion, then, is a spiritual signal. Its cosmic significance continues to influence the populace of the planet…but for all the wrong reasons, due to some rather awkward interpretive attempts. The primary intent behind the crucifixion is astoundingly simple. It has been completely overlooked due to the human forms' immense capacity for fear, guilt and hatred, all of which has complicated and twisted a rather sweet and elegant message. This is not to offend those of this congregation who are still enraptured by its unfathomable depth and meaning…for that is here, too. It's just that the utter simplicity of the soul Christ requires, perhaps, a bit more elucidation…

(Place a photo of your own face in the empty spot provided above in the cross's center.)

Usually when a soul encounters severe human limitations during its various incarnations, it up and leaves…abandoning its human form. It requires many lifetimes of intense karmic retribution for the soul to even start comprehending the purpose of limitation and right relationship to its immobilizing effects. The function of human limitations are in their articulation of the time-space coordinates essential for manifesting spiritual intent. As you have surmised, one can only know oneself through those acts which *distinguish* oneself, thus, the purpose of limitation is in its capacity to express distinction. It is only that which is distinctly itself that can actually transform and transcend its limits. As Elementary School has taught us so well, karma is what we attract through our limitations. We are not here to lose our shape, or limitations, but to understand the wisdom of shape-shifting. We are shape-shifters in search of our coordinates...

There is only one true way of distinguishing oneself and that is to surrender to one's true limitations. This, like anything alive, is fraught with peril as there are no guarantees. Precisely, what this implies is, when this congregation realizes its area of acute limitation and immobility, the right relationship begins the moment you surrender and "die" to your predicament. You are all crucified to the cross of your human forms. The grace of your evolution requires you to give in completely to every limitation until your entire being commits itself to penetrating its human form. There can be no holding back and no hesitation. The direction is through the center and out the other side, courageously, with all three eyes open.

The great soul Jesus set an example through her dramatic enactment of this spiritual ritual. She did so, so that others would not have to have it done quite so literally. She transcended her limited human male form by resurrecting after *complete surrender.* It is in this way that the initiation of resurrection comes to pass, as every true death precedes rebirth. The key, dear lost souls, is in the commitment of following your death through to its inevitable resurrection...on every level...the message remains: consistency and the conscious choice to surrender. You are here because you have forgotten this. You may leave when you remember...

You Are Now Leaving

HIGH SCHOOL
(GRADES 5–8)

Ladies, Gentlemen and Flying Rabbits!!! Do you spend your days doing absolutely nothing? Is it difficult to get out of bed in the morning? Are you depressed? Do you think too much? Do you forget who you are and where you are going? And...do you feel politically pointless? Are you sorry?

If you answered YES to any one of these questions...YOU ARE NOT ALONE. Masses of millions answer YES. If you answered YES, you are probably showing symptoms of a sinister plague upon us now! Why, it drifts through the very air as you are now breathing! But wait... do not hold your breath. I repeat...DO NOT HOLD YOUR BREATH! The Curse of Greyface wants YOU to hold your breath. Cast the curse aside! OPEN YOUR MOUTHS AND BREATHE! OPEN YOUR MOUTHS AND ...SHOUT FOR...

BUDDHA BUTTER ! ! !

Yes, Buddha Butter...tastes like butter but it's not!

Spreads easy, it's so clean you can't even see it!!!

"We bet every bit of Buddha Butter is better beaten butter, buddy."

CLASSIFIED INFORMATION

5

SENSORY INTELLIGENCE

A RAPTURE — B RITUAL — C CHARISMA

SENSORY INTELLIGENCE PREVIEW

WHERE INTELLIGENCE ORIGINATES
THE BODY — 5 SENSES AND SKIN

In Fifth Grade, the body is a source of pleasure, grace and charismatic sharing. The spatial direction is HERE, the time is NOW. BEING HERE NOW is how we enter Sensory Intelligence. Revelations follow our love of beauty, fun and kinetic joy…love of movement for its own sake. Our participation starts with complete openness to our senses in present time.

ITS QUALITIES AND ATTRIBUTES
FLUID, BUOYANT AND FLOATING

The quality is discovered through the body's natural, direct response to itself and the immediate environment…bypassing thought, preconception and projected meanings. Through direct sense perception, an esthetic sense develops as to what is "beautiful" and what is not. The sensory absorption of BEING HERE NOW strengthens spatial awareness, while diminishing the linear sense of time…everything turns NOW. Tendencies towards a rapturous, fancy-free floating attitude develops where existence is good enough the way it is. When Sensory Intelligence is shared between people, charisma shines forth.

FUNCTIONS OF SENSORY INTELLIGENCE
HAVE FUN, MAKE LOVE AND SHARE BEAUTY

Fun is its own reward. It also serves to *disconnect* us from Fourth Grade Judgment, Third Grade meaning, Second Grade politics and First Grade security issues. Fifth Grade sexuality is not orgasm-oriented but a medium for prolonging pleasure, beauty and more fun. The art of effectively sharing fun, beauty and love is charismatic. It serves to awaken Sensory Intelligence in others. Fifth Grade also provides the necessary homework to encourage somatic resiliency for safe, creative psychic work in Sixth Grade. Sensory Intelligence is integrated through Ritual technology.

RAPTURE: THE ART OF BEING HIGH

Relax. Breathe. Relax, again. You don't have to figure anything out. Fifth Grade begins right where you are. There is no reason for rapture to exist...it is deep and meaningless. There's nowhere to go to find it. It can happen anywhere and anytime...while you are sitting, walking or rolling around on the floor. You can't make it happen but it does happen to you...it goes like that. The ticket is HERE and the entrance is NOW. HERE AND NOW is all you ever need to know. *Instructions:* Let Life Happen. Stop Planning. (Life is a Happening Thing) Let it happen around you, inside you, over and around you, again. Open yourself to the moment-to-moment awareness of your breathing, living organism. The organism opened to Life flows with Sensory Intelligence. The flow of life is intelligent. Trusting this flow is your Fifth Grade Homework.

Fifth Graders learn to Stop Talking About Life. We also learn the skill of Getting Out of the Way. Get out of the way and Life happens. It is unutterably simple. Rapture is what happens when we get out of the way and we are suddenly carried by the grace of more life. Rapture deepens if we surrender to Life in a state of grace. Rapture is the direct expression of being at one with Life...ourselves. This is a very happy place to be. It may feel like home...or heaven...or as *if your body is inside you.* The curious phenomena about Rapture is that once we're there, there's no place to go! No goals, no future, no problem! However, because Sensory Intelligence is just one of eight levels, we learn about not making it a goal either. This helps us come and go whenever we require our next immersion in total sensory envelopment. Until then, we are invited to stay as long as we like...or whenever our survival tells us otherwise.

The skill of Getting Out of the Way can be practiced through an approach called Obstacle Orientation. This means we learn how to recognize an impediment when we see one. Once we can detect a blockage to the flow of life energy, we simply move it away and let Life happen. Since it is somewhat impossible to experience Rapture when we are blocked, we will now dedicate a certain amount of time to understanding the nature of these blocks. As stated earlier, we cannot make rapture happen. We can, though, remove what stops us from our natural state of oneness with ourselves.

OBSTACLE ORIENTATION

All blocks to the flow of Life are related to *resistance,* defined here as that feeling of something going "wrong." Resistance is not "bad" (why resist resistance?) but simply an energetic condensation which stops the overall flow to some degree. Resistance is our way of signaling a violation; once again, where "something feels wrong" within ourselves and/or our environment. Resistances are the obstacles which create inertia to the life energies in our bodies, thus, generating various degrees of tension. Ironically, our capacity for resistance and tension is often identical with our capacity for containing and transmitting life energies. The key is in how conscious we can become of tension as energy and our ability to relax, regulate and regenerate our tensions.

A popular emotional resistance among our freshman Fifth Graders is *status:* making a big deal of the experience. It's fun to get high, and sometimes it's easy to make it a status symbol by getting caught up in the "energetic charge" of the somatic high. This is one way to over-emphasize Sensory Intelligence and eventually block it up by getting in the way and exaggerating its significance. Pleasure Cults and Ecstatic Religions are for Bliss Ninnies. Rapture and joy as THE goal in life often leads to dispersion, laziness and dissolution (See *1st Gear Mechanical Problems*.) As usual, we must find out for ourselves...

SYMBOLIC RESISTANCE

Our resistance takes on a symbolic or conceptual form with our search for meaning in Fifth Grade. Life is too deep to be meaningful in Fifth Grade. This is partially because Sensory Intelligence is post-symbolic and beyond words, description and categorization. At best, words can refer us to and evoke the presence of our senses. The language of the senses is kinetic: Movement, Dance and Mime form its symbols of gesture, posture and attitude. The evocation of sounds conveying the delighted animal abound in our sighs, whispers, blissful whimpers, bubbling laughter and whatever touches and permeates our senses. Sounds and the act of listening are two of the most direct ways to access Sensory Intelligence...as we shall now hear.

LISTENING

This is a simple meditation which can be begun anywhere, so feel free to initiate this process in a variety of environments, many times over.

Close your eyes. Listen, moment-to-moment, to the sounds of your immediate environment. Listen to how your mind may make sense of the sounds: naming, categorizing and figuring them out. Now, give yourself permission to simply listen to the sounds as different energies. You can do this by *not* associating meaning to any of these sounds and just let the sounds come sweeping through you as currents of sonic energy. Let these sonic forces have their way and go where they may within, around, under and over you. If they like, let them merge forces with other sounds to produce new levels and overtones of sonic resonance. Your sensory task is this: How much can you give yourself over to this experience and let it envelop and encompass you...until you are at one with the sounds?

✿✿✿✿✿✿✿✿✿✿✿✿✿✿✿

The creative state of Sensory Intelligence necessitates a certain kind of internal dependence: We create when we are alone. The word, *alone,* comes from combining *all* and *one.* When we are at one with ourself, it is then Possible to become instrumental for the process of creation.

SOCIAL RESISTANCE

Social resistance to Fifth Grade is often expressed as value judgments and are not at all uncommon. With so much Rapture, Bliss and Pleasure floating around, it's highly likely that our conditioned moral and ethical codes start acting up. Accelerated joy and happiness can be a "positive threat" to the *unliving* parts of ourselves and others. Sometimes, judgment acts as a kind of Social Security Release Valve when life gets too happy. Everybody moves at their own pace. When value judgments come up, they serve to lower the overall energy level as somebody is uneasy and requires the safety of slowing down. As was stated from the start, *we are not the program.* When something feels "wrong," we learn to look to the program we're running on instead of condemning ourselves, unnecessarily. Besides, as competent Karma Mechanics, we know that a resistance is a signal requiring our attention for our next adjustment.

More often than not, Fifth Graders go through a totally spacey, disoriented and "untogether" period just to learn about internal dependence and letting go of social responsibility. During this phase, they may get a lot of judgmental flack from "envious" Fourth Graders who aren't comfortable with having as much fun. This is why Fifth Grade Homework entails the task of giving oneself permission to become completely selfish, just so we can follow through and graduate without other peoples' judgments, opinions and fears. In Fifth Grade we can be justifiably self-centered because we know we'll have more to share later.

HAPPY DISCONNECTED

The first homework assignment in FIFTH GRADE is in finding your own way of surrendering to absolute pleasure. Pleasure comes in many flavors, and because it does, there is no one prescribed way. Sensory Intelligence does, however, exhibit certain characteristics innate to itself like: Fun, Beauty, Love, Sensuality, Fluidity, Floating Sensations and feeling Happy Disconnected. This is because the nature of Rapture in its initial "absorption phase" is totally self-centered and unconcerned with social response-ability. Its focus is entirely dependent upon the "inner self" (not the "outer social self") for its source of energy, information and direction. Sensory Intelligence is *internally dependent* in a similar way that First Grade Physical Intelligence is *externally* dependent.

Internal dependence requires a certain degree of self-empowerment. Internal dependence is in direct opposition to our conditioned, social needs for approval, acceptance and permission to be ourselves. From a sensory perspective, our need for outer confirmation occasionally poses as The Last Obstacle to self-empowerment. One way to bypass this obstacle and/or move it from the path before us, is to begin claiming the parental function of *granting permission* to be ourselves. As children, many of us were constantly trained to get permission from mom or dad before doing certain things...especially if these things made us stronger, smarter and more secure in ourselves as individuals. Parents just want to be sure their children are safe and when kids go out and test themselves in new, exciting adventures...*they have to get permission first.* Sensory Intelligence is a Funhouse. Give yourself permission to be here and now.

Another justification for absolute pleasure, unbridled hedonism and delirious rapture is that it feels good. Those of us daring enough to lose our minds and come to our senses will naturally discover their own way of integrating pleasure (to access it anytime) and eventually, return to the world of social response-ability as charismatic agents of Sensory Intelligence Incorporated.

POSITIVE THREAT

One of the social "side-effects" Sensory Intelligence Agents face is the possibility of becoming moving targets for moral judgments hurled by resentful Fourth Graders...comments like: "You arrogant, self-centered asshole..." and "You're nothing but a narcissistic, self-indulgent space-cadet..." and so forth. When you cease to need social approval for the act of being yourself in public, you are potentially a "social threat." This is because you are no longer under anybody's control socially speaking. There are two basic types of social threat: 1) Negative Threats & 2) Positive Threats. The former include psychopaths and those whose social attitude is of the "fuck you" variety. The latter include those charismatic personalities catalyzing Sensory Intelligence in the people they make contact with, directly and/or indirectly.

The preliminary, baby-phase of Sensory Intelligence is bound to cultivate a certain arrogance in us...not the kind that makes us feel morally superior to others but the sense of being privileged or "chosen" to be included among The Living. Life just isn't the same after Rapture. The old Social rewards aren't as satisfying and leave much to be desired. This is only natural and yet, it continues to contribute to the script of the on-going Human Saga of What Are We Living For? In Fifth Grade, we are living for Pleasure, Fun and Beauty. In Fourth Grade, we are living for Social Acceptance. In Third Grade, we worship ideas...in Second Grade, our emotions and in First Grade, security. The original Sun-Worshippers were our first Sensory Intelligence Agents. More recently, during the advent of the 1960's, it was The Hippies who re-stabilized Sensory Intelligence. It didn't last, however, because there was nowhere to go with it. It was as if we were all dressed up with no place to go.

The nature of Sensory Intelligence is very "zen" in that there really is NoWhere To Go because everything is Here and Now. This is kind of like getting "stuck in the present." There's nothing particularly "wrong" with this and everybody ought to try it at least once. For those of us wishing to graduate, it is imperative that we learn how to absorb, organize and communicate Sensory Intelligence (See *Ritual and CHARISMA TRAINING*) so that we might discover...Life After Zen (See *Sixth Grade Psychic Intelligence).* If we don't, we run the risk of remaining in the self-absorption phase of Rapture and must resign ourselves to the perpetual indulgence of our Hippy Ancestors.

LEISURE TIME

The efforts of our Hippy Revolutionaries and Pleasure Agents have expanded two areas of human living: *Leisure Time* and *Sexuality.* Historically, the Ruling Class and Royalty of the civilized world have usually been the only ones to afford Leisure Time, save for the lineage of mystics, hobos and other Goof-off Artists. The rest of the masses were kept in line through various methods of social control (politics, religions, etc.) to keep busy working, paying taxes and, in a word, "surviving."

When a human life revolves around its survival alone, there really is no time and space for post-survival activities like the pursuit of pleasure, art and culture. Only the Royalty and the mystics knew this, with the latter feigning indifference and the former, designating themselves cultural authorities to direct the masses in perpetuating the Great Survival Machine.

Without Leisure Time, Sensory Intelligence has no way to express itself. This is because Sensory Intelligence follows the biological clock and cannot fit into the linear, sequential order of man-made time and schedules. In certain tropical climates which naturally excite Sensory reality, linear time all but disappears. Tropical natives come and go according to their feelings, the sun's position, lunar cycles and so on. There may be no concept or value given to One, Two or Three o'clock. Somatic experience lends itself to a much greater awareness of space and movement through space. Somatic adepts are the original space cadets, arriving fashionably late and instilling the presence of their pleasure wherever they go.

With Leisure Time, our relationship with sexuality has the opportunity to completely shift and transform. Basically, the shift is one from social goal-oriented-orgasm emphasized sex to sensory leisure-oriented-pleasure emphasized sex. The former "socialized" sex reflects the overall compulsion to Get Somewhere, i.e., Going For The Big 'O'…while the latter understands there is no where to go, as everything is Here and Now. In Eastern and Occidental Mysticism, various forms of "tantra" have explored somatic sexuality as *ritual,* the tool by which Sensory Intelligence is organized, thus, easily accessed again. The process of developing our own rituals to stabilize Sensory Intelligence within ourselves is phase number next.

HEDONIC INTEGRATION

Once we are hedonically integrated (having accepted pleasure as a value) we can begin to regulate and control our involuntary, automatic reflexes. It is possible to, at will, disconnect our attachment to the conditioned, robotic response to things and shift into the direct sense perception and response of somatic contact. With enough sensory practice, our access deepens and we learn to Get Out of the Way. (*Technique,* in this context, actually emerges from pleasure.) We have learned that what gets in our way are the many shades of resistance. The technique for bypassing resistance, in general, is aptly named *Non-Resistance.*

Non-Resistance is our capacity to let things be. This technique requires a suspension of judgment and a good deal of personal autonomy. We are as personally free as we can permit the autonomy of others. Non-resistance means readjusting the awareness towards what is "right" instead of what is "wrong" about oneself, others and situations. It's an attitude de-emphasizing the pathology of an event and augmenting its best side. It works this way because it is non-judgmental and it searches for the highest degree of *quality* in whatever is going on. The issue of quality is always sensory. It has no meaning other than the purest expression of its own true nature. For example: We experience the color "red" most directly when the purest expression of its quality comes forth. When "red" is completely "at one with itself," we sense the greatest degree of "red."

Two more ways of detecting resistance and releasing tension are: 1) Stop Trying So Hard and 2) Body-awareness. Trying Too Hard is a self-defeating attitude based on a belief that one is not enough the way one naturally is. We stop trying so hard when we realize there is nothing intrinsically wrong with who we are. And that we are enough the way we are, without having to prove ourselves. Body-awareness can be increased by simply being cognizant of tension in our body, then choosing to relax those muscles which do not require tension to operate. Letting go of arbitrary tension helps restore tension where it's actually needed. Economy of movement ensues and grace soon follows. Relax. Breathe...

SOME SENSORY CATALYSTS

Floating in a boat without an anchor on a calm lake—Floating in an isolation tank for the rapture of it—Receiving a full body massage for pleasure alone—Listening to your favorite somatic music on stereo headphones—Eliminate competition from your life and do things for fun—Be around people that just make you feel good and want to have fun—Remove meaning from your life for one hour, one day...relate simply to the forces of things rather than what you think about them...experience people, nature, environment as qualities & energies—Don't look at your watch or a clock for one hour, one day, etc....and lose complete sense of linear time...

RITUAL

What we will investigate here is the bones of ritual...the stark, inner technology of how they work. A few examples will be presented in an attempt to excite other more personal applications from you, the reader. Before beginning, however, a multiple definition of the word ritual is in store:

1) Taken from the word "root"; tilling the soil for seeding,
2) Any formal practice or custom intent upon maintaining tradition,
3) A repetitive action executed to attain a specific objective,
4) Any activity serving to enhance our sense of self and world,
5) A series of movement forms designed to alter the consciousness of the participant and/or those in immediate proximity,
6) A physical and/or psychic set of instructions enabling the conscious and deliberate evocation of a particular energy,
7) A non-performance medium of meditative action dedicated to defining a scrupulous approach to the sacred,
8) Preparation for grace.

Ritual, as presented hereafter, does not refer to "routine"—those activities diminishing awareness for the purpose of closing the senses. This approach to ritual is distinctly Asocial in that it serves to bypass social interaction to delve deeper into the underlying forces governing personality in general. This technique will be referred to later on as setting up a Rare Area...one untouched by social obligation, personal judgments and intellectual discourse. A network of similar techniques have congealed into a cohesive ritual technology functioning to open external/internal senses for accessing energetic sources *in the body*. The backbone of this technology combines elements of Zen, Dance and Theatre in a*non-performance setting* for the purpose of releasing the pressure to perform. No audience is permitted

Ritual is a Reality Test for checking our capacity for direct contact with whatever state we are in. Through the conscious choice of surrendering to What Is, we come to distinguish The Real from our Concepts of The Real. Ritual, if approached scrupulously, triggers sensory integration...that process responsible for stabilizing our presence. Once integrated, we are ready to share somatic transmission with others (See *CHARISMA TRAINING*.) This ritual discipline works best in the continued commitment of its practice. Until then, forms and functions of Ritual will be introduced to help us Prepare For Grace because in Ritual, preparation is everything. The first ritual task is locating the appropriate location for executing rituals. To simplify, we will refer to indoor spaces for the purpose of containing the energies of our ritual training process. The primary prerequisites for an indoor ritual location are: 1) Open space and 2) No interruptions. This can range from anything from a dance studio to your living room.

A RARE AREA

Setting up a RARE AREA necessitates a specific relationship with the Space Itself in the designated ritual location. This occurs by relating to the Space Itself as a *value*...how do you move through this space to honor it and render it *sacred?* The ritual task of *Sanctifying The Space* is highly personal. The root *Sanctus* means "Holy." Words like sanctuary, sanctum and sanction all refer to the process of ordaining a space as a refuge...free from harm and violation from outside sources. It is up to you to control the setting in such a way that it becomes safe enough to excite your vulnerability. Specifically, what movements, gestures and sounds are capable of blessing the space for the Holy task of Dropping Your Act? If there is a group involved, what motions make it safe for everyone to be there?

Since the group is initially in service to the space itself and responsible for making it sacred, the following habits are best left at the door to help stabilize a Rare Area:

1) Judging others out loud (we are here to work on ourselves).
2) Courtship (we are not here to seduce/charm/attract each other).
3) Philosophizing (this is not an open forum for talking about life).

The Rare Area is sanctioned as a Ritual Training Circle...a place to learn, experience and practice the skills of ritual design. It is the first step toward entering a Concept-Free Zone enabling direct contact with the forces of our being. It is not different than Life Itself but a High Powered amplification lens wherein life processes are experienced more directly and observed. How we relate to the Space Itself determines the quality of time spent there.

TECHNIQUES

Finding A Spot: Once a Rare Area is set up, we may venture to step inside. Within the boundaries of this Ritual area, we start the next task of Finding A Spot. This is an intuitive sensing out which spot in the area *feels best* and supports the greatest sense of well being. This is your "power spot" during the course of the Ritual...a place where you return to rest, regenerate and stabilize yourself. Do not attempt to locate your spot by figuring out what feels best. Instead, drop your awareness into your solar plexus and/or umbilical region and let yourself *feel* through this part of your body. Another method is in looking askance rather than directly at a potential power spot. Investigate several possible spots through these methods and any others which evolve sensorially.

Marking A Circle The next preparatory task is Marking A Circle. This is the activity of defining the boundaries of your spot...physically, emotionally, mentally and spiritually. Take complete dominion over your spot like an animal owns its territory...*own your space.* Mark the six cardinal directions: North, South, East, West, Above and Below. In fact, do anything within your spot to enhance your experience of being Safe and Alone. In Marking A Circle, you determine how much space you need to be yourself. Defining your physical and psychic boundaries will make it a little easier for you to maintain your individual integrity in the midst of the unfolding Ritual.

Stillness: Inside your spot, find its center and enter a stationary position there. In this stillness, sense the periphery or outer boundary of your spot, then, of its center where you are. The Stillness at the center has three functions: 1) Clarify your intent (Why are you here and what is this ritual for? 2) Dialogue, prayer and/or communion with God 3) Stillness. You are only as receptive as you are still.

Warming Up: Many approaches to Ritual neglect this phase. Others come to it through extended periods of repetitive movement. The intent of Warming Up is to "ground" ourselves by *feeling the body deeply.* This is so we may feel strong and flexible in the face of great forces within us. As with the previous phases, this one continues with accelerating our solitude. (Enforced solitude helps dissipate the social tendency to initiate relationship through our conditioned needs for approval, acceptance and permission.)

An effective warm-up often includes Stretching, Spinal Flexing, Breathing, Vocalizations and most important, Sweating. In Ritual, Sweat is the Holy water...the precipitation signaling heat in warm, moving bodies. The challenge in Warming Up is in remaining *within the boundaries* of your own space...your spot. This way, Warming Up is also contained and not dispersed. Sometimes, during Warming Up, our sense of personal boundaries will expand and/or contract as we energize and feel our bodies. Periodically, check your boundaries and self-dominion.

The Little Circle: Initiates the transition into Ritual. After Warming Up, stand in the center of your space and gather your forces. Then, step outside your spot and turn around so that you are facing it. This is the Little Circle. Its physical, emotional and psychic soils have been *tilled* by you for planting. You are the seed that will be planted. The process of becoming one with the seed within, our inner state of potential energy, will hereafter be referred to as *No-Form.*

No-Form: Is the *crux* of Ritual. Without it, Rituals run dry and become routines. No-Form is a state of being. It refers to that part of us which is completely OK with Being Nothing. No-Form is not supposed to be figured out but experienced. It is our direct contact with the source of our expression…the fertile void from which all forms evolve. It is our personal intimacy with Nothingness, that is also Everything. In Ritual, No-Form provides the essential bridge between pure potential and its manifestation in movement. This is facilitated through the *No-Form Stance:* Knees unlocked, Feet supportive, Stance balanced…the eyes are closed or half shut. The intent is rest…resting the head on the neck…the neck on the shoulders…the shoulders on the rib cage…and on down until the feet rest on the floor. Emphasis is on the exhale…the attitude is empty and still. In Ritual the sacred can be kept alive by starting *and* ending each ritual with the No-Form stance. It is then possible to invite the sacred into the circle because we have created space for its expression.

En-Trance: After No-Form stabilizes project into the Little Circle before you, the particular aspect of yourself you wish to evoke. Let this projection be complete and sincere. When you feel ready, enter the Little Circle and allow the force there to enter you, filling No-Form with its expression. Do not move until the force is strong enough to *move you.* Then, follow *its* direction and serve its expression. There is no need to control this or try and determine the outcome. *Relax the desire to control* by serving the expression of the energy itself. Let the energy become your source of guidance, information and direction. Discover how deeply you can surrender to its quality and then, give yourself permission to surrender more. You are simply called upon to give yourself totally to what is most true to you.

In-Tension: During the process of your surrender, you will experience variations in the intensity of the energy. Another function of Ritual is InTension, our ability to register an *energetic peak* by framing it in a gesture communicating its essence. This helps the body "record" peak moments as kinetic memory. A series of InTensions, or gestures, form the basis of a myth; a procession of tableaus. InTension keeps us aware of the energy level we are working with. Peak moments *don't always* convey themselves as intense motion. There are moments where the energy feels the most true to itself in stillness.

Completion: Sometimes, there are "trick endings" which feel done but just require a bit of stillness to release the next direction. In any event, when you *feel resolved*...step outside your Little Circle and resume the No-Form stance. Release all the expression, energy and information back to its source. Return to your own source in *being nothing.* Even if your previous experience in the Little Circle was rapturous and pleasing, let it go and *be nothing.* This practice will help assure a scrupulous approach to Ritual by restoring your individual integrity.

The previous preparation for Ritual is very flexible to suit your own needs. Ritual can be especially useful in exploring the Karmic Code (See *Karma Mechanics*) of our Excitements and Resistances. Or, it can be a simple, direct way to plunge into rapture. The crux remains in our capacity to be impressed by No-Form...the deeper our No-Form, the deeper our energetic expression. The deeper our energetic expression, the deeper the No-Form required to neutralize its "charge" so that our integrity is preserved by the act of moving on to the next thing, fresh and unencumbered by previous states of being.

Group Circle Is called whenever there is a need to talk about what is happening and/or after a particularly potent Ritual. Participants sit in a circle. *They do not hold hands.* Group Circle is dedicated to *non-judgmental feedback.* This is the place to *report* what happened. It is not a place to expound our philosophies *about what happened* but instead, to articulate the truth of the experience *as it occurred.* The Group Circle provides a time for conceptual integration, so that our minds don't get too blown away during the process of Ritual. Talking about what happened, creates a transition so that we may move on.

Polarizations: To polarize is to relate opposing forces into a unified field of directed activity. Polarizations is the Ritual process of exploring inner polarities, one at a time, towards emotional flexibility. A polarity is not actually split, but two expressions of a greater whole. To experience our totality, we pull ourselves apart and then put ourselves back together again. Examples of inner polarities are: Beauty/Ugliness, Order/Chaos, Good/Evil, Positive/Negative, Masculine/Feminine, Dry/Moist, Safety/Danger, Smart/Stupid, Growth/Decay, Hunter/Hunted, Heaven/Hell, General/Specific, and so on. Effective polarities are "charged" and provide the most direct access points to Ritual material. A polarity that feels real *exciting* is positively charged, as a polarity exciting *resistance* is negatively charged. Both positively and negatively charged polarities are essential to Ritual work. Without them, it would be very difficult to generate the kind of energy responsible for true transformation.

Writing a list of polarities is Ritual homework. Make sure and draw from as many different dimensions as possible. (The 8 Grades in *Angel Tech* provide a good multi-dimensional gridwork for this.) Fifty polarities will produce enough charged ones to start. If you've finished your list, circle the positively charged ones and underline the negative charges for reference. The proceeding Ritual depends upon the charged polarity of your choice.

After preparing thoroughly, step outside your Little Circle while facing it. Enter No-Form. Project one side of your polarity into the Little Circle. Follow instructions of EN-TRANCE phase of preparation. Discover the peak moments through InTensions. When resolved, step outside the Little Circle and re-enter No-Form, releasing previous expressions back to their source. Once No-Form stabilizes, enter the Little Circle again and repeat EN—TRANCE using the other side of your polarity. Follow through with gestures and into completion. Exit the Little Circle and return to No-Form, releasing all previous expressions.

After No-Form, enter the Little Circle again. This time expand the boundaries. Mark Your Circle all over again, stretching its periphery and take dominion over your extended territory. When you're done, find the center of your new space and gather yourself there. Then, step outside the Little Circle into No-Form, facing it, again. Mentally, divide the Little Circle in two equal halves. Designate each side to a side of your polarity. Project the entire polarity and all its emotional charge into the Little Circle. Once No-Form stabilizes, listen to the side which exerts a distinct "pull." That is the side you enter first. (Don't choose which side, you will only contrive the Ritual.) The overall objective is moving between both sides of the polarity within the Little Circle. The key is in staying on one side *until you feel the need* to enter the other. Discover the force moving you back and forth…that agent un-bound by either side but free to travel. When you're complete, exit the circle and resume the No-Form Stance. As always, return the forces to their source as you return to yours in No-Form.

Big Circle. Up to this point there has been no mention of inter-relation with others, only relationship with oneself. This is because our Ritual intent is accessing ourselves first, so that we might have some-thing of value to offer with others. (This is the primary reason for so much pre-relationship solitude). The Big Circle is dedicated to group interplay. Rituals involving the Big Circle start with each participant in their Little Circles, so group integrity can emerge and still honor every-body's uniqueness. The following Big Circle Ritual is an example of how this can work.

This Group Ritual requires eight participants who have gone through Ritual preparation and polarizations first. All eight participants locate their Little Circles on the periphery of the Big Circle, like this:

Each participant is assigned a different Grade in ANGEL TECH, or function of Intelligence, that he/she will draw upon as a soul source of energy, information and direction. For example, whoever selects First Grade, must completely surrender to their Physical Intelligence as the guiding force of their movement, and so forth. Everyone is preparing to become an ambassador of their particular function of Intelligence, complete with their individual excitements and resistances around them. It starts like this. Everybody stands facing the center of the Big Circle, with their Little Circles at their feet in front of them. It looks like this (x is participant):

Everybody enters No-Form together, individually, then the grade is projected into the Little Circle and participants step inside to be shaped by the forces inherent to their chosen function.

Once inside the Little Circle, the direction is to *resonate* a sound which matches the level or frequency of the energy itself. It does not matter *how* it sounds; what matters here is that the sound *matches the energy* and not the other way around. Let the sound change with the energy until the sound is a direct expression of the energy. The next Ritual task is to locate a rhythm which matches the energy and sound. Always create space to invite more energy. If there is a resistance, relate directly to it as energy and express it through sound, rhythm and movement. Let this gather momentum and develop into a dance accompanied by a kind of song, chant or phrase. When your dance feels strong enough to maintain relationship without falling apart, step outside your Little Circle and move towards the center of the Big Circle. This acts as a signal for others to know you are ready for interplay. During interplay with others, stay true to the source you initially began with: the function of Intelligence. If you become overly influenced by the strength of other players, stop and return to your Little Circle to regenerate yourself. When you feel ready again, step out and into the center of the Big Circle.

Begin locating the gesture which clarifies your relationship and function to the Whole. In this system of eight, it will become apparent that every player serves a highly significant role towards keeping everything alive. A final Group InTension based on this relationship to the Whole sometimes shows up as a closing gesture. In general, endings tend to find themselves and we can learn to see them if we stay aware. After the Ritual, participants return to their Little Circles and enter No-Form inside. Here, they release all energies that aren't inherently theirs and return to No-Form.

CONTACT POINTS

The following lists are comprised of workable contact points by which entire Rituals may be based.

Polarities: Contraction-Expansion, Strong-Weak, Resistance-Excitement, Hot-Cold, Fixed-Mutable, Hard-Soft, Bottom-Top, Red-Green, Nourishing-Toxic, Pleasure-Pain, Time-Space, Young-Old, Heavy-Light (mass), Guilt-Pride, Victory-Defeat, Mercy-Severity, Angels-Demons, Left-Right Brains etc.

Trinities: Red-Yellow-Blue, Creator-Destroyer-Nourisher, Mother-Father-Child, Body-Mind-Spirit, Positive-Negative-Neutral, Sun-Moon-Earth, Sleep-Dream-Awake, Savior-Persecutor-Victim, Head-Heart-Gut, No Form-Dream-Form, Heaven-Hell-Purgatory, Surrender-Control-Indifference, etc.

Quaternities: Fire-Water-Air-Earth, Summer-Winter-Fall-Spring, Physical Emotional-Conceptual-Social, Skeletal-Muscular-Respiratory-Nervous System, Seed-Sprout-Bloom-Decay, Experience-Design-Character-Story, Birth-Living-Death-Afterlife, Feeling-Thought-Understanding-Will, etc.

A BRIEF GLOSSARY OF RITUAL FUNCTIONS

ASOCIAL — non-social attitude required for maintaining a Rare Area; removing commitment to others socially; self-commitment

ATTENTION — necessary mental concentration for Ritual; capacity to by-pass and/or include interruptions to sustain continuity

AURA — self as "field"; the energy within your personal space at any given moment; developed through Rituals exercising the Body of Light

BODY OF LIGHT — those Rituals permitting the subjective experience of illumination, as if one was a "body of light"; psychic body

BOUNDARYWORK — self-generated limits necessary for scrupulous Ritual; the outer edge of your Aura at any given time and the internal adjustments required to regulate its shape and size

BREATH — connecting current between inner and outer space; self-reference during times of crisis, i.e., "Watch your Breathing" "Breathe"

CONTAINMENT — result of Boundarywork; the gratifying element of solitude; necessary crucible for tempering and mixing internal conditions resulting from intensive Ritual work

CONTACT POINT — that internal area of direct, intuitive contact with a particular quality, aspect or force; source of stimulus

CONVERSION — the point at which a particular quality or energy becomes its opposite; what usually occurs after an acceleration of self-commitment; the shift from controlling energy to serving its direction by creating space for its expression

DIRECTIONAL — movement predetermined by the will of the mover; the capacity for controlling the outcome of a movement in its style, form, tension level, tempo, rhythm and overall expression

EN-TRANCE — the moment of shifting from one dimension of reality into another, often facilitated by entering a circle wherein a particular quality or force has been Projected; entering trance

IN-TENSION — a kinetic device for framing a peak moment in a gesture to communicate its essential spirit; initiating tension

FORM — the clarity of a given shape, direction and quality

IDIOSYNCRATIC — kinetic device for claiming one's own space; the ability for instilling highly personal signature to movement

INITIATION — the result of those Rituals exciting a high degree of Uncertainty *and* creative response of the participants

INTEGRITY — necessary self-commitment for Scrupulous Ritual; a self-preservation device enabling endurance amidst intensity; the self-respect essential for respecting others' space

MAGIK — personal, living contact with the infinite; the degree of comfort exhibited amidst Uncertainty; being at home in the unknown

MARKING CIRCLES — a preliminary device for preparing a Ritual, the intent being to define a space according to a specific purpose

MYTH — a story emerging from a series of peak moments, often crystallized through InTensions, that conveys a universal theme

NO-FORM — the depth of intimacy with void, nothingness, etc., necessary for beginning and ending all rituals; crux of Ritual

NON-DIRECTIONAL — movement undetermined by the will of the mover; the organism's innate sense of direction and force, often facilitated by exhaustion, abandonment and surrender

POLARIZATIONS — the Ritual process of joining opposites toward a unified field of singular direction; method of developing inner cohesion; negatively charged polarities are resistances and positively charged ones are excitements; to balance

PRAYER — internal dialogue with your source of life; speaking with God; not necessarily verbal or conceptual, as in Silent Prayer

PREPARATION — preliminary activities essential for setting up Ritual, usually combining meditation, chanting, movement and rhythm

PROJECTION — capacity for "charging" a particular area, usually a circle, with the quality or force necessary for activating a Ritual

RARE AREA — space, as of yet, unfilled with social projections, conditions and expectations; necessary condition for inviting the sacred

RHYTHM — kinetic device for stabilizing presence and continuity; physical ability for expressing patterns of energy as sound and movement

SACRED — what one essentially lives for; point of worship; often unknown, the sacred can be evoked and invited through Ritual; holy

SACRIFICE — an offering of self to yield the sacred; to make sacred; an age-old theme for understanding the functions of Ritual; surrendering what is dear to oneself

SAFETY — necessary condition for vulnerability; the capacity for self-stabilization amidst danger or crisis

SANCTIFY — to bless or bestow an area, usually a circle but sometimes other people, with complete acceptance for the purpose of consecration; benediction; ability for granting permission

SILENT PRAYER — non-verbal resonance and/or communion with God without conditions, questions or expectations; holy sharing

SCRUPULOUS — Attention paid to Integrity; capacity for honoring the autonomy of other Ritual participants during the work itself

SWEAT — kinetic device for preparing self for the shock of Uncertainty during the more intense Ritual work; holy water; self-support

TALKING — conceptual device for integrating the social and sacred, usually implored during the non-judgmental time of Group Circle; a tool for dissipating energies

TRANCE — a primitive state of consciousness increasing one's sensitivity to light, sound, rhythm and play; shifting reality tunnels

UNCERTAINTY — condition permitting reception of new information and/or energy; capacity for confessing ignorance; Factor X

CHARISMA TRAINING
EVERYBODY IS A STAR

WARNING: Charisma May Be Hazardous To Your Privacy. The cultivation of charisma breeds magnetic, attractive and sexy personalities, proceed at your own risk. Brace yourself…you are entering the process of becoming a Positive Threat to Society. (Prepare to win friends and disarm your enemies.) Your very presence may become an object of fascination to those around you. More important, perhaps, is understanding *what you are living for* because charismatic persons tend to gain the allegiance of others…without trying.

The standard dictionary (Funk & Wagnall's) definition of the word:

> Cha-ris-ma: 1. THEOL. A gift or power bestowed by the Holy Spirit for use in the propagation of the truth or the edification of the church and its adherents. 2. The aggregate of those special gifts of mind and character which are the source of the personal power of exceptional individuals and upon which they depend for their capacity to secure the allegiance of, and exercise decisive authority over, large masses of people. [Greek…grace, favor]

CHARISMA TRAINING is possible only after understanding both the functions of Rapture and Ritual. Through Rapture, we become Bigger Than Life and give birth to our Arrogant New Self. The initiation of Ritual helps to temper our new ego and define its shape so that in CHARISMA TRAINING, we have the opportunity of learning to be holy without being obnoxious. Charisma is the natural expression of a hedonically integrated personality. The prerequisite for entering CHARISMA TRAINING is the quiet acceptance of one's own exceptional nature and the graceful surrender to the accolades of becoming a "star." *Everybody Is A Star.* To know and live this begins the process of CHARISMA TRAINING. The Training will be presented in the spirit of developing communications skills. Charisma, by itself, is not a prerequisite for communication. However, if learned, it can provide the conditions wherein communication may occur. Not just verbal but non-verbal, telepathic link ups to individuals and group minds.

Charisma communicates Sensory Intelligence and has the capacity for awakening somatic response in others. It is an animal magnetism reflecting a knowledge of deep pleasure and personal power. Charismatic individuals are instruments of this pleasure, power and light-giving influence. Feeling good and shining are charismatic attributes and most people are automatically drawn towards what feels good and looks shiny. Certain exceptional individuals just know how to turn it on and express it. What is the criteria for being an "exceptional individual"? It has to start with an innate sense of your uniqueness, like a self-aware snowflake realizing its truly eccentric nature: We're all unique and exceptional! Yes, we are unique and what else is new? Learn to wear your charisma like a necklace so it won't turn into a ball and chain.

THE "IT" IN QUESTION

Preparing for stardom isn't all hard work. In fact, you will have to give up trying altogether. Charisma doesn't try. It simply is. It's the "it" about you. And "it" just is. This is both simple and complex. That's because charisma is "simplex." It revels in its *isness*. This is partly because charisma loves to *exist*. Charismatic individuals can never go back to being Faceless People and some of them never were that way to begin with. Either way, charisma can be nurtured by learning how to act effortlessly. This is one trick to make it effortless for others to watch you. If taken far enough, you will become irresistible to watch. Not only does charisma have a great capacity for attracting attention, it has an equal passion for giving it. Charisma is an ability to give your total, undivided attention...without fear, guilt or judgment involved. There is a very pure quality to this kind of attention. It stems from our ability to Look and See, to recognize and be recognized. Charismatic attention is illuminating because in its presence, we feel as if we're being bathed in light and/or penetrated by a laser. These two extreme ends of the spectrum of radiation offer our next charismatic research area.

THE SPECTRUM OF RADIATION

A charismatic exercise tests our ability for regulating our attention between the two previously mentioned extremes in the spectrum of radiation: 1) Dispersed and enveloping light and 2) Focused laser beam of searing heat. Star Quality depends on either extreme or, with enough talent, both. With the first variety, it is possible to radiate dispersed light by being bathed in light oneself. This is the process of being effected by *one's own emanation* and it depends upon a strong sense of one's personal boundaries (see Boundarywork in RITUAL) to work. It begins with the conscious radiation of your aura, or energy, out in all directions at once, (this takes a considerable amount of practice if it's new information) while remaining firmly *in your center*. Let your energy radiate only as far as the boundaries of your personal space, or aura. Then, let it "bounce" back and effect you. Continue this practice consciously until you get the sense of your own energy "re-cycling"...radiating out, bouncing off your boundary and returning back to effect your center (where "you" are). The more you are under the influence of your own energy, the more other people will tend to be, also...unless, of course, they are as deeply under the influence of their own source. This happens when two stars get together and form a stellar dance between a mutual center of gravity.

Focusing our attention into a laser beam of searing heat is another way to stretch our charisma. This end of the spectrum can be accessed in quite the opposite manner by which the other flourished. Instead of radiating outward to be effected by your own emanation, you can create heat through *implosion*. Radiate as little as possible until you feel penetrated by yourself. This is not as abstract as it may read. The process of self-penetration doesn't work for everybody. Stars that carry "heat" are quite exceptional. They are able, somehow, to contain terrific intensity without being overly expressive about it. By and large, this type of charisma expresses itself in a much more compact and minimalist way. It smolders and burns. And where there is smoke there is fire and where there is fire, there is fuel. The fuel of this type of charisma is an intense physicality and a quality of personal density. Density is not synonymous with stupidity here (there are exceptions), but a strong instinctual sense...an earthy, gutsy style of being oneself. This kind of charisma is "hot" while the dispersed variety is "cool"...both are magnetically effective.

GOOD TIMING

Crucial to charisma is a sense of good timing, of being at the right place at the right time. The key to perfect timing is believability...the ability to believe in yourself and what you are doing. This works because timing automatically takes care of itself with a strong belief. In order to coincide with the world around you, you will need the conviction that you definitely play an important part in it. It's easier for others to believe in you when you believe in yourself. Charisma, by itself however, is not necessarily a promise of thoughtful direction. It requires a certain guidance from the wearer to become an effective communication tool. As a goal, charisma turns to "glitz"...which stands out like gaudy, fashion jewelry on a tacky, polyester pant suit. Like champagne, it must be used quickly after it's opened so the bubbles won't disappear.

You have to be something of an actor to sustain charisma. In the midst of veritable crisis, charisma not only believes as if everything is OK but makes us believe it's sparkling. The beauty of this charismatic attribute comes with its ability to pretty much flow with whatever comes up. Remember, timing is believability, no matter where you are…believe in yourself and stay "in character." The beauty of flowing with change can be cultivated through understanding the practice of *polarizing our persona.* A polarized persona is a personality balanced enough to express both sides of its nature…the Masculine and the Feminine. CHARISMA TRAINING requires flexible, spontaneous persona. If we are "hung up" or in resistance to expressing either Masculine or Feminine qualities, our charisma is suddenly put on hold. We can no longer be ourselves, completely, around others.

Whatever society we live in projects its own ideas about what is socially accepted as Masculine and as Feminine. Either we conform and adapt the socially acceptable, or begin defining these terms for ourselves based in our direct experience of Masculine and Feminine forces within us. If we choose the latter, we can expect to experiment and pass through layers of conditioned thinking about Male and Female models. This is part of the process of getting to the core of things. It is well worth the work, however, to be your beautiful self around others.

PERSONAL POLARIZATION

Along the journey towards contacting both Masculine and Feminine essences we will, most likely, encounter outdated icons and masked phantoms of what we were supposed to be when we grew up. Sometimes, for the sake of self-knowledge, we karmically live through these role models just to leave them behind. Other times, there's more freedom of choice and we select to bypass these "ghosts" in favor of holding out for the real thing.

Our self-image polarizes by including more aspects of Masculine and Feminine into the way we think about ourselves. This makes it easier to be at home with ourselves, period…an essential ingredient for charisma. With enough practice, an inner cohesion evolves and when this expresses itself openly through a personality, we have a person who appeals to both men and women. The influence of charisma is subliminal in the way the Feminine in men and the Masculine in women are simultaneously touched, instantly. A polarized ego, or self-image, effortlessly transmits its true nature and it is in this manner that charismatic individuals shine like stars. Our true nature as beings of light can only be accessed through balancing inner oppositions. When opposites are placed in equal value and experienced within oneself, they eventually unite…releasing a tremendous quantity of light. This is how a star is born.

As the persona polarizes, a type of "impersonal" quality emerges in the outward expression of the personality. A "public self" is formed… one that can be itself anywhere. It enables us to bring our radiant beings into the public to mingle socially, all the while awakening those we come in contact with to our beauty and hopefully, theirs. The electromagnetic process demonstrates charisma in still another light. If we run a current of electricity through a fibre cluster, or cable, a 360° magnetic field surrounds the cable. The thicker the insulation and fibre, the more juice we can run through it and the stronger the surrounding magnetic field. The human body is a sort of cable, or fibre cluster. The more alive, or "electrical," we are…the greater our magnetic field, or aura. We are as magnetic as we are alive. We can only take in as much Life and electricity as our "insulation" can contain. So, what is "human insulation"? How do we become energetic conductors for high power transmission? I believe it is through a greater understanding of personal polarization.

THE POLARIZED WILL

The process of polarization can be explored in a controlled setting through Ritual (See *RITUAL: Polarizations)* or more everyday situations, both of which provide excellent resources for the following experiment. There are a number of ways by which we tend to respond to an acceleration of life force. One popular way of reacting to a quickened pace of living is to resist and fight it. Another way of relating to intensity is by ignoring it and/or doing something to obscure direct contact (which is like resisting it). We are also often compelled to direct and channel the energy somewhere. Another possibility exists in our capacity for serving the force. The conversion point from directing energy to serving energy merits investigation.

When directing energy, one is in charge of creating an effect and determining its outcome through regulation of the will. One "wills" it. In the context of serving the energy, the orientation reverses. We relax our will to receive instructions from the energy itself, wherein the outcome is determined by the direction that energy takes. It "wills" us. In the first "directional" example, we are the shapers and in the second "non-directional" demonstration, we are the shaped. To be shaped, we relax our desire to control and release our compulsion to know how it will turn out. Relaxing our will is actually a sophisticated act of will, one set into motion when we are vulnerable enough to be affected. The will, as with the persona, is subject to polarization.

The human will is both active (Masculine) and receptive (Feminine); the former definition most commonly associated with "act of will." The active will acts upon the environment and knows itself through its effect on the world, whereas the receptive will sits where it is and absorbs information from its environment and is affected. When synchronized, they form a flexible kind of strength of magical proportions. In order to consciously synchronize these two halves to express your whole power, it is imperative you find out which half you're stuck on and which orientation you must restore for equilibrium.

Accessing both active and receptive modes of will tends to regenerate our personal power. The two combined endear us with the kind of emotional flexibility that is effective in relating to the unknown. This is because serving the energy (receptive will) deepens our capacity to permit uncertainty *and* directing the energy (active will) heightens our sense of self in the process. The act of absorbing information before asserting ourselves is actually plain common sense. The polarized will is effective for one last Reason...the only force which opposes it is *the ineffective.* The way this relates to charisma is the kind of personal freedom it offers in being pliable enough to be shaped by the moment and firm enough to stand your own ground in it. This kind of charisma is often worn by martial artists, shamans and other self-realizing stars.

The spectrum of human emotions introduces us to another fertile territory accessible to polarization. Emotional polarities like: Sorrow-Joy, Victory-Defeat, Love-Fear, Respect-Disgust, Indifference-Passion, etc., all require acceptance, so we don't have to spend too much time getting stuck in our emotions. Emotions come and go...to the degree we can move through each one as a fact of human living, is the degree our intuitive beauty nourishes itself along its path of least resistance...like a flowing river. We can't help but be beautiful if we surrender to the flow of life within us. This includes the resistances and negative emotions. Just going through them and responding is beautiful in its courage and faith, as long as we remain present and don't vacate. Personal vacancy is death to charisma. It's too reminiscent of the Faceless phase and besides, it just doesn't look good. It's true...if you look good, you feel good.

Through the diligent practice of personal polarization, our very bodies become instruments for sharing the illuminating, beautiful and pleasurable influence of our true nature. Our true nature, being beyond duality, can be released by uniting our inner oppositions. Like the fusions of protons and electrons (positive and negatively charged atomic particles), we release billions of photons with every unit of charisma. By training your charisma, you can become eligible for graduation into Psychic Intelligence, where being light is the status quo and our physical body *is* the insulating material encompassing the fibre clusters of the Central Nervous System.

THE CHARISMA REVIEW

Charisma is primarily a communication tool. It helps us realize that even though we have entered the Realm of the Living, we are not the only ones alive. We may have learned to become one with ourselves in rapturous bliss and entered special initiatory rituals but because we are part of a greater whole, it is that whole we learn to serve. Otherwise, cosmos might mistake us for a cog in the wheel and eliminate our once glorious selves. Charisma, in its essence, is a humbling vehicle for sharing our inner treasure with others until we have discovered still another, more uplifting way to influence those around us.

WAYS OF SHINING

Graceful surrender to stardom — Radiating our unique nature — The knowledge of deep pleasure — Act effortlessly and never try — Give your total, undivided attention — Be under the influence of your own energy by choice — Good timing, believe in yourself and what you're doing — Polarize your persona — Masculine/Feminine — Polarize your will — effect and be affected: be effective — Polarize your emotions — the beauty of a flowing river — Wear your charisma like a necklace not a ball and chain — Never compete — Learn to appreciate your influence on others to be aware of it

6

PSYCHIC INTELLIGENCE

CLAIRVOYANCE — REALITY SELECTION — DESIGNING TAROT

PSYCHIC INTELLIGENCE PREVIEW

WHERE INTELLIGENCE ORIGINATES
CENTRAL NERVOUS SYSTEM — THE BRAIN

Psychic Intelligence awakens with a greater sensitivity to the electrical and can be absorbed directly as Brain Pleasure, the essential indulgence of experiencing oneself *as light.* The Psychic process stimulates the pineal gland to secrete the psycho-active chemical hormone *serotonin,* which sensitizes the CNS to light, patterns of light (images) and trance states. Over-stimulated, an excess serotonin level produces symptoms of schizophrenia: fragmented and consciousness, hallucinations and other severe perceptual distortions. (See *MECHANICAL PROBLEMS, Second Gear: Short Circuit)* Serotonin levels can be balanced and kept in check through the release of the Brain's natural opiates, the *endorphins,* accessed through the Rapture of Sensory Intelligence.

ITS QUALITIES AND ATTRIBUTES
QUICK, ELECTRICAL AND CLEAR

The CNS receives signals at the speed of light every living moment. Psychic, or Extra-Sensory, perception explodes kaleidoscopically as clairvoyance, clairaudience, telepathy, psychometry, clairsentience, remote viewing, intuition, healing abilities and other attributes as of yet unnamed…all of which relate directly to energy itself as a means of detecting information. Psychic Intelligence "thinks" *qualitatively,* distinguishing between the various qualities expressed as the Multidimensional Self, without judging any of them and seeing all as equal in value (as colors to light). The Psychic operates from a *relativistic* attitude, regarding all information as pieces to an ever-growing puzzle which never claims one final solution or answer but a *multiplicity* of possibilities.

FUNCTIONS OF PSYCHIC INTELLIGENCE
RADAR, REALITY SELECTION AND HEALING

Radar is the capacity to pick up signals from oneself and/or the world. Reality Selection is the skill for recognizing distinctions between different types of signals, so as to determine their nature. Healing is the ability to recognize and affirm the source of a given signal. Combined, these functions are synchronized through the process of Psychic Reading.

NATURAL CLAIRVOYANCE:
NOT EVERYBODY IS PSYCHIC

Whatever is natural, unfolds of itself. Clairvoyance is a French word for "clear seeing." Natural Clairvoyance is what happens when the innate sensitivity of the CNS is allowed to unfold. There are many impediments to this process and this is why Not Everybody Is Psychic. Most children are and every animal is. The child and animal within each of us provide dues to unraveling our Natural Clairvoyance because psychic perception is both creative and instinctual. It is creative through its non-judgmental attitude and instinctual in its connection to survival and the will to live. The psychic process kicks into action whenever we are the most creative and alive. (An example is the telepathy shared amongst many lovers.)

There are many ways the "psychic switch" is turned on and off…both being equally important. We are naturally turned on in a psychic way whenever the animal gets the message that it's in danger or that it might die. Our psychic "tendrils" burst forth in an attempt to absorb as much information as possible so we don't get hurt or die. Many people have reported psychic experiences from near-death and dying conditions, some of whom retained psychic abilities afterwards. The animal is very good about living. It's also the only part of us that *knows,* without a doubt, that it will die. This is why it stays on its toes around the possibility of extinction. When our mind is together with the animal, it is possible to become *consciously* psychic and not have to wait for near-death experiences. This is the kind of "psychic" we will explore in Sixth Grade…the safe and creative kind.

You don't have to be a "psychic" to be psychic. In fact, it's better if you can just *be yourself* unless you need to identify with the Psychic Persona and get stuck in Sixth Grade as a result. That's alright, too, because in Clairvoyance School everybody travels at their own pace. Nobody gets left behind, as everyone takes as long as they need. The first lesson is understanding how clairvoyance works best when it's used as *a tool* and not made a goal. It is a device for picking up signals so we may translate them into messages of useful information…for the purpose of self-knowledge.

WHICH IS WHICH?!

As part of this education, you will have to define the word *psychic* in your own words. Until then, we shall suffice with the generic definition of: psychic equals *perceptive.* Our ordinary, or sensory, vision externalizes our psychic perception…they are a part of the same activity called seeing. (Other examples include: 1) Clairaudience and Hearing and 2) Clairsentience and Touching.) Psychic perception is *accelerated* perception and rests unconcerned with meaning. Meaning, as is commonly associated, is a psychological projection of the particular mind that is seeing. The ongoing homework for Baby Psychics is learning the game of *Which Is Which!?* Which is a genuine psychic perception *and* which is the psychological projection of its meaning? (This game will help integrate the psychic right-brain with the psychological left-brain towards their conscious synchronization: Reality Selection.)

The game of *Which Is Which!?* is, at first, best played amongst other Baby Psychics who have agreed upon being part of the Psychic Training Circle…which is any group mind based in the collective purpose of developing Psychic perception. The purpose of the Training Circle is in providing a safe place to be psychic. Members are bonded by a pact of truth. They agree to speak the truth and acknowledge the false, without the usual social and/or political considerations. The way this works is with the process of communicating perceptions verbally. If I have a perception about you which I wish to communicate, I do so. You determine, by pact of truth, whether my perception is true, false or a bit of both and tell me as clearly as possible. This works also through *resonance* because sometimes a perception will feel really true but we don't know how to prove it or figure out why it feels so true. (An example is in reading a past life) This kind of reality check is called Psychic Affirmation.

In the game of *Which Is Which!?*, it doesn't matter if what we see is true or false at first because either way, we are affirmed. The main thing is getting into the practice of *communicating perceptions* to a responsive receiver. Also, something is only true if it is shared as an agreement that it is true. If I voice a perception of you that you confess to be true, then, we are both affirmed and the truth is enhanced. If I say something that is obviously untrue according to you, the creative thing for me to do is to let it go. Don't bother trying to convince the person you are voicing your perceptions to, no matter how true it feels to you. This will only diminish your clairvoyance. Psychic Intelligence functions on a *lack* of self-investment, so whenever you get too involved emotionally, you also get in the way. This understanding will help cultivate a more relativistic attitude, one to chase the dogmas away. (See *INTRODUCTION: Dogma and Catma.*)

Due to the unspoken social law prohibiting Speaking The Truth in Public Places, it is suggested to do so only inside the Psychic Training Circle...unless you have very good friends. This is because not everybody likes to hear the truth. It's somewhat unpopular. However, this needn't put a wet blanket on your search for knowledge. If you are sincerely in need of psychic information in order to live a more intelligent and happy life, it is up to you to be open to the opportunities probably showing up as messages from the No Coincidences Dept. As we evolve and grow closer to our centers, the law of synchronicity becomes the norm, even more so in Psychic than Sensory Intelligence. In Seventh Grade Mythic Intelligence, it is the rule of thumb.

Another method of fortifying the Training Circle with enough safety to merit psychic awareness is in the elimination of any person, thing or gadget sending off "survival signals." Due to the Rare Area required for this to work, you must learn to control the setting. Survival Signals *distract* conscious psychic operation through their negativity, self-emphasis and/or overall loudness...physically and metaphysically. Psychic Intelligence expresses "post-survival" tendencies and is easily obscured in a setting fraught with interruption. The idea here is to provide a physical space where the animal feels safe enough to be open and vulnerable. The appropriate psychic atmosphere is one which permits: 1) Freedom of being (no judgments) 2) Good humor and 3) Permission to be psychic. This is a good way to develop psychic response-ability, the foundation of true clairvoyant development.

GROUNDWORK

Before moving into the actual psychic meditations, a certain common ground of knowledge is necessary. This particular orientation emphasizes *Groundwork* in a big way. Groundwork is an approach to clairvoyance which lets you bring your body with you. Groundwork is dedicated to self-embodiment and including the animal in whatever we do, physically. With Groundwork, there is no "higher" or "lower" self, there in only *oneself.* There is no need to get out of the body (sorry, astral trippers!) Nor is there any great requirement to follow a psychic guru besides your own true self.

Hierarchical tendencies recall the all but worn out tradition of this "higher" and "lower" self business. Hierarchy jams communication and Groundwork means literally...*working on the ground*...our body. (See *KARMA MECHANICS: Everything about First Gear.*)

Another form of Groundwork is *psychological grounding.* As pointed out earlier, our psychology is how we interpret the impressions and perceptions received psychically. Psychological grounding grows from several sources: 1) Knowing what we want 2) Thinking for ourself 3) Making sense of things in our own way...basically, it is the strength *and* flexibility of our conceptual framework. Psychological grounding is highly recommended for developing in a safe and creative way. You may initiate yours by answering the following questions:

1) Why do you want to be psychic?
2) What is your basic philosophy in life?
3) How do you go about solving problems?
4) Would you consider yourself "mentally balanced" at this time?
5) How many hours of TV do you watch every day?

WARNING

It is imperative you answer the previous questions before reading any further. Clairvoyant Training will, with practice, render you more Perceptive. Are you willing to see and know more of yourself and the world you are part of? If not, think about it and come back. If so, we resume our approach to safe and creative psychic development.

Once you have procured the appropriate setting for psychic work, it is possible to proceed. The first meditation is called "grounding" and its function is to *stabilize your energy.* There are many different forms of grounding. The one presented here integrates three facets of self-stabilization... 1) Centering 2) Owning Your Space and 3) Earth Relationship. To practice the preliminary orientation, you need to sit down somewhere in your controlled setting. Once you learn the meditation in the sitting format, feel free to apply it in as many different forms as is necessary to assure your energetic stabilization, i.e., while walking, jogging, standing...experiment.

FACET ONE: CENTERING

Center yourself in whatever way you already know how. (If you don't know how to center, return to Fifth Grade Ritual and/or sit still for awhile without doing anything except letting yourself settle) From your center, get a sense or image of the periphery boundary of your personal space...your aura. Be in the center of your aura. Close your eyes.

FACET TWO: OWN YOUR SPACE

From the center of your aura, *own your space.* Take complete control of the space within your boundaries. Now, while remaining in the center, own the room you are in. Control the space in the room, not the people or things in the space. As long as everybody remains centered, nobody will bump into anybody else. Mutual ownership is possible if everyone remains in their centers.

FACET THREE: EARTH RELATIONSHIP

From your center, feel the base of your spine and let it sink and be heavy. The base of your spine is your body's anchor and is a source of Physical Intelligence. (See *The Energy Centers)* Let your entire spine relax and settle with gravity into its base until it starts feeling more dense and thick down there. Now, open the base of the spine…open your first energy center and let it become "porous."

Send a column or cord of this "density" down from the base of your spine into the planet. Let it pass through the layers of rock and sediment until, finally, it reaches the core. *Hook it in.* (If it doesn't go that far down, stop trying. The trick is to let it find its way down after your initial command of sending it down. This takes practice.) Be with the feeling of being hooked into the planet's core. (If you cannot "feel" this, practice visualizing it. If you can't visualize, imagine. If you can't imagine, pretend. Where there's a gap, there's a bridge.)

Now adjust your feet so they are flat against the ground. Watch your breath. Don't change it, just watch it. After a few moments of watching, open your arches in the same way you opened the base of your spine. (If you can't, visualize camera shutters in each arch opening up to the max.) On your inhale, breathe in "Earth Energy" up through your opened arches. On your exhale, circulate this Earth Energy around the base of your spine, so it spirals around it. After several cycles, start exhaling the Earth Energy down your "grounding column" so it's sent down to the Earth's core. Start inhaling in more Earth Energy by taking deeper breaths. On the inhale, the Earth Energy comes up the legs and spirals around the base of the spine. On the exhale, it flows down to the Earth's core. Repeat this process until you are cycling and recycling Earth Energy. Continue cycling until you feel you've gotten what you've needed…until you feel stabilized

FROM THE GROUND UP

The process of grounding, articulates a specific source of energy...*the Earth.* Earth Energy is the epitome of energy in its most tangible, manifest state without being as "physical" as the chair you're sitting on or the book you're reading. The function of Earth Energy is to stabilize and/or render more ethereal or volatile energies manageable. The best times to ground yourself are those moments wherein the need is the most apparent...like before you go for that job interview...or...when you need to pull the emergency brake to a non-stop day...or just when you want to settle yourself and be calm. The Earth is a vastly intelligent and compassionate entity who selected to incarnate as this planet. Any way you personally resonate, commune and/or dialogue with this entity is about as grounded as you'll ever get.

Grounding prepares us for opening up to an altogether different source of energy...the Cosmos. In the following psychic meditation, we will refer to this energy as Neutral Cosmic Energy...which is energy that has not become manifest yet. It exists, however, in a potential state. In Fifth Grade Ritual, it was introduced as No-Form. Here, it becomes Neutral Cosmic Energy, or *NCE.*

TRANCE MEDITATION

1) Ground yourself as was previously described by centering, owning your space and establishing a relationship with the Earth. Close the eyes.
2) Upon Grounding, place your attention in the center of your brain. Do not try...simply be at home in the center of your head.
3) Like you opened the base of your spine and arches, now open your crown (top of head) to about 80%. Let *NCE* drift down from above in the manner *it* so chooses. Do not bother to direct or control the *NCE* but simply create space for it to fill. Let the *NCE* settle and mingle at the base of your spine with the Earth Energy.
4) Watch your breathing. On your inhale, draw the *NCE* and the Earth Energy into your body from their respective openings *simultaneously* and let them meet at the base of your spine. On your exhale, wiggle this mixture up your spine and out your crown like you were a fountain.

CONSCIOUS TRANCE

5) Repeat this cycle of simultaneously inhaling both energies in and wiggling their mixture up the spine and out the crown. Repeat it enough to be comfortable with it. If it makes you uncomfortable, *stop*. (Get up and walk around. Try it again when you feel safe.)

6) Repeat the cycle outlined in #4 & #5 for about 10 minutes, then open your eyes and register any change in your state of being and/or perception. If you are with others, talk about it. If not, write it down. If you feel light-headed, re-ground. If you still feel spacey, make animal sounds like growling, purring, barking, etc. This will remind the animal that you are back again. This is always good news to the animal.

With the preceding exercise and every other psychic meditation, it is mandatory that you ground first. This gets you in the habit of bringing your body with you. As the animal is included, it'll help the *NCE* become more tangible to you. As your overall energy, or aura, becomes more obvious to you it will be easier to read, heal and work with. The suggested time requirement for this psychic meditation to start working for you is 15 minutes a day for at least two weeks. If you are opening up psychically anyway, it may take less time. If you are a hardcore skeptic, or closet psychic, it may take more. The long-term effect of this meditation, properly practiced, is called Conscious Trance, and it will tend to accelerate perception.

Conscious Trance enables us to work with our own energy more directly, through picking up signals from the body's energy centers and translating these into useful messages. Eventually, with enough diligent practice, it is possible to sense, see and read the auras of others while engaged in this Conscious Trance state. It is called Conscious because the participant does not lose consciousness. This is in no way related to the kind of trance certain "mediums" enter, so they can leave their body (yikes!) and let another entity come inside to speak through their vocal circuitry. That kind of "psychism" is not recommended because it negates our Groundwork. It is, perhaps, fascinating to many but still projects the source of power, knowledge and clairvoyance onto somebody else...even though they don't have a body on. Our intent remains with *individual integrity;* claiming these attributes ourselves and *at our own pace.*

THE HUMAN AURA

The word *aura* is derived from the Greek "avra" meaning *breeze.* Just as breezes come in many forms, so do auras: warm, gulf winds...cold gusts...autumn breezes...hurricanes...perhaps there is something to the expression of "being blown away." Like a breeze, the aura is a moving field able to be registered by the things it affects...like a rippling meadow. The aura is an electromagnetic field of energy surrounding and permeating all living forms. Everything living has one and, like snow-flakes, each one is unique. Clairvoyance is the ability to *see* auras. The clairvoyant experience is also unique in that two "psychics" looking at the same aura are likely to see differing manifestations of the same field. This is because each person's psychological filtering mechanism is unique, as well. There are no "clear channels" just different interpreta-tions. (See *MECHANICAL PROBLEMS, Second Gear: Short Circuit.*)

Nobody actually knows what an aura is or what one really looks like. The previous statement was meant to clear the air about what to expect. Life is a mystery at best. Due to our individual bias' and psychologies, auras can appear in a variety of shapes and forms: colors, images, textures, illuminated eggs, clouds and other assorted curiosities. There are no "ideal" auras, as some books would have you believe by even including "pictures" and drawings of them. Maybe through bypassing our preconceptions of "auras", there is a living chance of detecting its qualities. When what we are trying to describe is obscured by our defini-tion of it, we shall only witness our own illuminated limitations. We turn ourselves on clairvoyantly by supporting our initial impression while side-stepping its translation. Interpretation will come naturally enough with our need to communicate what we see in the manner most condu-cive to the person listening.

We are our auras. The aura (us) is generated and sustained by Con-sciousness as expressed through specific energy centers in our body. These centers are vortices of swirling energy referred to originally as *Chakras,* a Hindu Sanskrit word for "wheel." These centers spin at different rates, from the slowest spinning first center (base of spine) to the fastest spinning eighth center (above the head) and express eight functions of Intelligence. Subjectively, this can be felt as the densest quality of consciousness available to us (first center) to the dearest con-sciousness we can access (eighth center). From a psychic perspective, there are no right or wrong qualities of consciousness. Clarity is no better

than density and vice versa. From a relativistic outlook, each quality has
its value, function and ace in sustaining the whole being. This is not to
say we don't get stuck in one of the centers...we do. Psychic work is
learning to read the center we're having problems in and the ones where
there's no problem whatsoever. (More on The Energy Centers themselves, later.)

The overall size, shape, density, depth and quality of an aura varies
widely with each individual. There are basically two major auric levels:
1) The central axis of the energy centers (spine & brain) and 2) The
periphery into the area of the central axis. The second level goes through
the most noticeable and dramatic changes, while the central axis takes
much longer to actually transform...it's more fixed. It's like the ocean in
that the surface wave action goes through a lot more noticeable change
than the deep ocean floor. The energy centers at the axis can reconstruct
but only with prolonged self-work. These centers express long-term
fixations and excitements...in a word, the karmic code of each individual. This is because all experiences impress us at the auric level. Each of
us are open books to those that can read. If you could see auras, would
you want to see them all the time?

The auric periphery changes with shifts of mood, thinking and physical activity. Some of us possess the uncanny capacity for appearing
different hour by hour, day by day, depending on how vulnerable we are
to being under the influence of our own energy and others'. Good actors
in the Theatre are able to "charge" their aura, or atmosphere, with a vast
spectrum of colors, moods and textures. These actors permit themselves
to be shaped and affected by their creations into characterizations com-
pelling to witness. Certain individuals, as you've no doubt noticed, carry
an "edge" about them, as if the boundaries of their aura were more well
defined. Others, almost mist-like, blend so well with their immediate
environment that they become chameleons and unnoticeable except in
relationship. Then there are those exceptional individuals who, after
defying all attempts at categorization, continue standing put in crowds
like a spotlight amidst candles. Sometimes, these spotlight people appear
normal in every other way except for the psychic fact of shining brighter.

Every aura has its bright and dark side...or put more succinctly,
bright and dark "spots." Dark areas in an aura refer to resistance...a
condensation of energy resulting in an endarkenment. The bright spots
convey a free flow of enlightened energy. Depending upon which energy
center the spots are in or near, pinpoints that particular area where the

action is taking place, i.e., dark spot around the first center (base of the spine) indicates resistance around physical survival and security issues. From Conscious Trance, it is possible to look into the "heart of the dark spot" and see the image we are stuck on. It becomes useful information when the resistance is articulated in a manner which makes sense to the person in resistance.

A psychic indicator of a lot of resistance in an aura is that its periphery is "brittle." Our periphery is where we are most subject to emotional, psychological and psychic attack. If we don't know how to be *in our center,* we are probably hanging out along the periphery. When the aura is brittle, it is easier to shatter. It is a moving target for whatever is inclined to be thrown at it. You will tend to draw towards you the very thing you resist.

The most effective counterpoint to psychic attack is *non-resistance.* We begin by adapting a less judgmental attitude. Non-resistance, from a psychological standpoint, means letting yourself and others be whatever everybody wants to be. (Stop picking on yourselves and/or others.) Every judgment rigidifies the aura. How many times have we seen someone shattered over an event because they couldn't stop judging it as being "wrong" the way it happened?

Bright spots in the aura can indicate healing abilities. Whenever there is an acceleration of energy and a great opening in the area of the heart, hands, knees, and sometimes solar plexus…there exists the tendencies for catalyzing openings in other auras. Many people are natural healers and don't even know it or wouldn't even think to call themselves "healers." They just have a penchant for making people feel better and more of themselves. This is what healing is all about…touching the innate self in others, so they help themselves by coming out more. All healing might just be self-healing. If you don't want to be healed, you probably won't. If you believe you will, then you just might. Such is the power of belief when focused with positive intent.

The following psychic meditation has the intent of acquainting us with our dark and bright spots. It can be facilitated alone or in a group, just so long as the setting is controlled.

THE CRYSTAL BODY MEDITATION

1) Ground yourself thoroughly as previously instructed and/or with any other stabilization methods. Sit with your eyes closed.

2) Place your attention into the middle of your brain. This is your Psychic Command Post…where your mind controls your reality.
3) From the middle of your brain, visualize or imagine a replica of your own body, in its present shape and posture, cast from clear crystal in front of you about five feet.
4) Inspect your crystal body for any cracks or flaws; mend them.
5) Project your consciousness out into the crystal body. Then pull it back to fit in your physical body.
6) Repeat #5 several times; each time go a little deeper into each body.
7) Inhabit your physical body and pull the crystal body into it, so it fits like a glove. Be there with the crystal body synchronized with the physical one.
8) Scan your body for dark spots. When finding one, see if it is OK to give yourself permission to let it go. If you can, let it drop into the planet. If you can't, no worry, move on to another dark spot.
9) Spend as much time as you like dropping dark spots but don't be too hard on yourself…besides, the important ones will reappear.
10) Visualize and/or sense a horizon out to the distance stretching 360° around you on all sides.
11) Let a sun rise over a horizon. Don't predetermine this. Simply permit the sun to rise at its own pace over its own horizon.
12) Absorb whatever light you can with your crystal body. Let *it* work.
13) From the center of your brain, invite the sun to come twice as close, so it moves to a point half way between you and its horizon.
14) Let your crystal body absorb its light and refract it within itself.
15) From here, gradually draw the sun closer…all the while absorbing its light. Find out how much light you can take…how much your crystal body feels safe enough to absorb.
16) If you're able, bring the sun inside your body and let it find its own place there. Let it radiate from its self-appointed position and fill your entire body with light.
17) Check your grounding. Re-ground. See how this affects the light.
18) When you feel resolved and have met your needs, open your eyes and register any change in your state of being and/or perception. If there are others around, talk about it. If not, write it down.

The preliminary phase of Psychic Intelligence is Brain Pleasure. The preceding meditation is set up for the essential indulgence of experiencing oneself as light. It also will indicate the degree of illumination you are presently capable of. The "sun" in this meditation is an ambassador

from your True Source in that you can determine your present-time
Source relation by which horizon it came over. Were you facing your
True Source? Did it surprise you from behind? Did you catch it indirectly
from the side? Further investigation on your own, in perhaps, Ritual, will
provide more information still. You are your aura. We are all beings of
light.

REALITY SELECTION:
WHAT CHANNEL ARE WE ON?

Psychic Intelligence views reality as a Multiple Choice Question; not a
True/False Test. To see relativity in action, permit *multiplicity,* the
simultaneous and inter-dimensional existence of multiple realities equal
in value. Read that last sentence over again. Simultaneity refers to things
happening at the same time, while remaining distinctly themselves...like
the convergence of several directions in time and space to produce the
meaningful coincidence of *synchronicity.* To witness relativity, we have
to stop getting our minds blown so much by the cosmic nature of things
and just start allowing their expression as the norm. According to
relativity, there's really no such thing as true or false, unreal or real...
something is true or unreal according to the perceiver who calls it so.
Shift the perspective and what was once profoundly true turns hysteri-
cally absurd and vice versa...

In Fifth Grade Sensory Intelligence, we learned about unity and being
at one with ourselves. In Sixth Grade Psychic Intelligence, the mantra is
not ALL IS ONE but I *AM MANY.* Not to be confused with schizophrenia, the Multidimensional Self introduces us to Soul Consciousness, of
which the CNS is the instrument of expression. Schizophrenia, by the
way, is two words...schiz (broken) and phrenia (soul or heart). We shall
refer to this process of relating to the pieces of oneself as Reality Selection. This process begins with our capacity for distinguishing the qualities of each piece and an understanding of their relation to the whole self.
The analogy of colors to Light demonstrates it very simply. Color is the
suffering of Light. Reality Selection is the skill of distinguishing levels
of reality for the purpose of increasing *inner freedom and dominion.*
(Second Grade Emotional Intelligence is the need for *external* freedom
and dominion.) Reality Selection starts with tuning into a reality to
determine if you'd care to be included or not. What channel are we on,
anyways?

Sensory Intelligence and to some degree, Brain Pleasure, lets us be the energy. To develop the skill of Reality Selection, we learn how to *read* energy, or auras, instead of merging. Reading auras and other energy forms requires a certain ability enabling us to extract information from energy. Pulling information out of energy is something like pulling a rabbit out of a hat. The trick, or technique, of reading energy is in having very strong guidelines to get started. Once you no longer need the training wheels, you simply *read*. The training wheels are the Eight Energy Centers, as already presented as Eight Grades in this book. However, the localization of these Eight Centers *in the human body* provide a major key to unlocking psychic information right where you are sitting now.

THE ENERGY CENTERS

There are eight major energy centers and eight minor ones, all localized inside the body except one which positions itself above the head. The centers are an interdependent network and all carry innate psychic abilities to some degree. When functioning naturally, each are able to receive, store and transmit signals and/or messages. From a psychic perspective, all energy originates in Consciousness and eventually materializes into what we know to be real. What we know to be real also spiritualizes, transmuting back to Consciousness. Both of these directions occur simultaneously and inter-dimensionally in that they also happen within each other. The first seven major centers are expressed physiologically as the human glandular system, secreting certain hormones when that energy center is open. The bridge between the psychic and the physiological is our *psychology*. To the degree we find *our own way* of defining and describing these Energy Centers, is the degree they can be *accessed* by us.

THE FIRST CENTER

Located in the base of the spine, the First Center is our source of *survival information*. It tells us what we need to know to survive on this planet and contains not only our personal experiences but the survival code of the race as *instinct*. This no-nonsense center activates when our security and/or physical well-being is threatened. It carries within its core what the Hindus call Kundalini Fire…a powerful source of volatile energy activated in very small dosages during: 1) Second-wind Experiences 2) Psychic Trance and 3) Near-death states. It is released in larger currents through the practice of Kundalini Yoga. When active, it travels up the spinal column seeking expression. If one of the Energy Centers along the spine is blocked, then the Kundalini Fire will release itself through the center directly *below* the resistant one and greatly amplify its orientation. If the Second Center is blocked, for example, then Kundalini will express itself through First Center activities, exaggerating survival and security issues.

The First Center registers *self-commitment;* the soul's willingness to embody itself. This, in turn, expresses an individual's overall sense of personal integrity. On a psychic level, the First Center shows how grounded somebody is and how they tend to relate to Earth Energy in general. The psychic ability of this center is "clairsmellen"…a rather rare ability to detect scents and extract information by how people and places *smell.* Animals are usually very clairsmellent, especially dogs. The First Center is our source of Body Wisdom. This center also expresses itself glandularly as the gonads. The First Energy Center is the support for every other Center, providing their basic foundation for how safety is defined and to what degree it actually is.

THE SECOND CENTER

The Second Center is felt a few inches below the navel and governs *emotional style.* This Center is actually closest to being the center of the physical body itself, so it is intimately connected with *motivation* and has been referred to by G. Gurdjieff as the Movement Center. We can read someone's "thrill criteria" here, as well as their sexual preference. This center works off sensation and excitement for the most part, so any issues related to these areas can be read by looking here. This includes a person's ability for giving and receiving "strokes" or emotional support. Territorial concerns are most likely to show up in the Second Center, as are negative emotions around violation, aggression, and rage…especially if they are repressed. Repressed emotions are one of the more effective ways to keep this Center blocked up. The primary signal absorbed and communicated by the Second Center is the need to be felt and the need to feel others. In its extreme, the psychic ability of "clairsentience" develops. This enables us to feel what others are feeling without having to converse with them about it. When clairsentience is out of control, we cannot tell the difference between our own emotions, pains and pleasures and those of other people. Creatively, the Second Center lets us become self-motivated, once we figure out how to turn ourselves on and off, emotionally. The spleen is its glandular expression.

THE THIRD CENTER

The Third Center radiates from the area of the solar plexus and expresses *orientation to power*. This Center absorbs the sun's rays and distributes the energy throughout our body. The Third Center loves to be outdoors and in the sunshine. Our capacity for self-regulation can be read here, as well as the power of our will. The *force* of your personality comes through here and your ability to focus and direct this force. Externally, it is our ability to *act in the world*...to project our presence and get things done. The Third Center revolves around a "doer" who is defined by doing and making decisions in order to create effects around him/her. More than any other Center, this one is responsible for manufacturing "psychic shields." An over-developed Third Center is one which has *outdone itself* and has become externally invulnerable, unable to be touched and affected by external influences. However, consciously approached, psychic shields are often useful if you don't make a house of them.

Psychologically, the Third Center expresses the survival-oriented and often scheming-manipulative mind...the one dedicated to its own individual survival. On the bright side, this center offers information about our ongoing orientation to *success*, both financially and personally, as well as our ability to *portray roles*. In an overall sense, this Center is The Actor. Psychically, the ability to project ourselves outside of our physical bodies, whether through dreaming or out-of-body experiences...are Third Center attributes. Similar but not quite as dramatic is this Center's capacity for "ego-state cathexis"...the psychic ability to invest or charge an object, person or space with our energy. This is related to telekinesis, another psychic ability enabling us to move objects without physically touching them. A psychological ability of the Third Center is dream memory, as well as our capacity for "lucid dreaming"...waking up in a dream and making choices which instantly turn to dream realities. Finally, and perhaps most significant from our spiritual perspective, is the degree by which a person requires outside approval for their actions and to what degree self-approval, or empowerment, determines initiative. The Adrenals are the Third Centers glandular counterpart.

THE FOURTH CENTER

Breathing from the upper chest area, the Fourth Center evolves through the many colors of *love;* from romantic fantasies to compassionate detachment. From the perils of Fatal Romance to the solitude of Religious Devotion, the Fourth Heart Center governs our capacity for affinity; being one with ourselves, others, an idea or belief...anything it desires. The Heart Center operates off of *empathy,* which is different from sympathy. (Sympathy is a Second Center emotion letting us feel others at the cost of losing ourselves.) It resonates with another because it knows that what it resonates with is first within itself...there is no longer any need to go out and try to find it. Empathy develops in many ways, most directly with our capacity for love...to give and receive.

The Fourth Center expands with self-acceptance. When we let ourselves *be,* it's easy and natural to let others be themselves around us. As the Third Center expressed itself spiritually as self-empowerment, the Heart Center spiritualizes as *self-embodiment.* As our inner oppositions unite, the soul wears the body like a hand in a glove. When the animal and the mind agree on more issues, the Heart gets happy and opens. An open Heart is healing to itself and those in close contact. Healing is love made contagious. There are no "healers" in this sense, only open Hearts and the love circulating throughout them. A psychic ability associated with the Fourth Center is "sensing" which is different from the Second Center mode of feeling. Sensing can determine something's nature without becoming it. There is a certain detachment about sensing because it requires space to work. The Fourth Center, in general, requires great space to open...as it is related to the connecting current of air we breathe in and out of our lungs. Without air, it's obvious that we can't open our Hearts...the physiological organ is the Heart and the Thymus gland.

THE FIFTH CENTER

Voiced from the base of the throat, the Fifth Center concerns itself with the multi-faceted forms of *communication.* Communication naturally follows empathy, affinity and a strong sense of the mutual. The Fifth Center works with our ability to *listen.* When activated, it offers the psychic gifts of *inner voice* (speaking with your core self), *clairaudience* (hearing sounds, voices and/or music not in time/space) and *telepathy* (non-verbal communication with another and/or groups). Various creative talents like music, poetry and other audio-arts are inherent to the open Fifth Center. This Center tends to open with our willingness to speak the truth and in letting others' truths exist alongside our own.

The bottom Four Centers are dedicated to individual survival and the upper Four, to creativity. The Fifth Center in particular is highly creative in that it is, along with the Fourth Center, a bridge between individual survival issues and creativity. If the Third Center were The Actor and the Fourth Center, The Lover...the Fifth Center might be The Artist.

Another set of attributes innate to the Throat Center is the ability to be a parent. This requires a certain sacrifice of one's own needs in favor of meeting the needs of the children. This is possible after one is able to meet one's own needs effectively, first. This is the gift of nurturing...to quickly see into the needs of others and help them help themselves. Good psychotherapists will have radiant Fifth Centers...as will mothers, teachers, rock stars, saints, etc. The Thyroids and Para-thyroids glandularize the Fifth Center, as well as regulate our growth and fine-tune the Central Nervous System (CNS).

THE SIXTH CENTER

The Sixth Center envisions itself from the center of our brains, governing all modes of *possible perception*...from imagination to seeing auras. Referred to also as the "third eye" and "seat of the soul," its home is nestled deep within our central, "reptilian" brain...stewing in the juices of our exotic brain chemistry. The Sixth Center determines our Reality Perception of how we see the world. Its functions are primarily psychic: *clairvoyance* (ability to see auras), *remote viewing* (seeing events over great space and time spans), intuition (coming to conclusions, non-linearly) and other abilities as of yet, unnamed, hence uncharted.

The Sixth Center claims the distinct privilege of being the Psychic Command Post where instructions can be issued to the body/subconscious. The type of perception typical of the Sixth Center bypasses thoughts, meanings and/or symbols. This is not to say that it doesn't see these things. Sixth Center perception just has more *structural insight* and sees into how things operate and where they come from. It is in this manner that precognition, prediction and prophecy develop...from a profound sense of where a direction is going from knowing whence it came.

Psychic vision tends to see more similarities between the so-called "cosmic" and "mundane" than their apparent differences. This ability to detect the associations between illusory opposites, gives this Center a certain *continuity of consciousness*. Psychologically, the Sixth Center functions as an organizer of psychic perception…sorting out images for easy recall and quick reference. Where the Fifth Center oriented around the vibration of sound, the Sixth is "light sensitive" and knows itself through illumination. It receives signals at the speed of light and, when trained, extracts information from energy received *instantly*. This initiates the discipline of psychic reading. The pineal gland houses this Center.

THE SEVENTH CENTER

The Seventh Center crowns the top of the head and, when contacted, introduces our *totality and beingness*. When operative, psychological and psychic attributes unite in an unbreakable bond of inner perception and outer response…seeing and acting at the same time. The Seventh Center is as close as we're going to get to God and The Infinite while inhabiting our animal bodies. This is personal contact and fusion with the God Within. Its ability is *knowingness* (being still enough to draw upon the Universal Source of Knowledge…knowing without having to know how or why…knowing and being *dead correct).* This Center signifies your capacity for relating to DNA and genetic memory matrixes.

The Crown Center expresses Identity and carries inside it all those experiences which mark us as *unique* and how these affect our lives. This Center communicates the degree of unity between cosmic and mundane factions of our life, thus, stabilizing a true continuity of consciousness. Besides being the direct, uninhibited contact with infinity, the Seventh Center is catalytic in sharing this with others. Seventh Center catalysts are referred to here as "can-openers" in that they, inadvertently, open the Crown Centers of others as a result of just being their Infinite Selves. The Crown Center expresses itself as the pituitary gland, which serves to govern the other glands, as well as secrete endorphins when stimulated.

THE EIGHTH CENTER

The Eighth Center is suspended anywhere from 6 inches to a few feet over the head, in space, as it were. It governs all assortments of *out-of-body* experiences and because it's not in the body directly, there is no corresponding gland (however, speculation places the hypothalamus to the closest proximity). Here, we find contact and fusion with our deepest unknowns. The invisible realm of sub-atomic activities play out their strange and charming dance where matter transforms incessantly and nothing stays the same. At this level, there is no such thing as prediction, only the random permutations of atoms falling apart and coming together; unless, of course, Consciousness awakens here and randomness *lived* reveals itself as a message from a still higher state of intrinsic order, as of yet, undeciphered.

THE EIGHT MAJOR ENERGY CENTERS

1) *BASE OF SPINE:* survival information; Kundalini storehouse; security issues, physical grounding; body wisdom; self-commitment; integrity
2) *JUST BELOW THE NAVEL* emotional style; thrill criteria; sexual preference; feeling others and self; clairsentience; motivation; sensation
3) *SOLAR PLEXUS:* energy orientation; will power; personal force; acting; success style; psychic shields; dream memory; self-empowerment; "mind"
4) *UPPER CHEST (HEART):* love, empathy, and compassion; romance; affinity and resonance; healing ability; self-embodiment; sensing; the breath
5) *BASE OF THROAT:* communication; listening; creative skills; telepathy, clairaudience and inner voice; parenting; ability to speak the truth
6) *CENTER OF BRAIN:* reality perception; structural insight; clairvoyance, intuition and remote viewing; precognition, prediction and prophecy
7) *TOP OF HEAD (CROWN):* spiritual orientation; knowingness; total being; personal contact with infinity; identity; continuity or consciousness
8) *ABOVE THE HEAD:* out-of-body experiences; unknown & paradoxical; fusion with subatomic activity; apparent randomness; incessant transformation

THE EIGHT MINOR ENERGY CENTERS

a) *THE FEET (arches):* capacity for absorbing Earth Energy; state of commitment soul has to being embodied; connected to First Center

b) *THE HANDS (palms & fingertips):* creative abilities that are ready to manifest; psychometry (reading energy by physical touch); healing abilities...connected to Fourth Center; scanners of energy fields

c) *THE KNEES (fronts):* healing capacities; tuning into needs of others; sense of personal command; ability to stand one's ground; leadership

d) *THE ELBOWS:* amount of personal space required (elbow room); overall flexibility; degree of self-support

HUMAN RADAR

Psychic Intelligence works as our Human Radar...picking up signals, translating them into readable messages. Our hands are natural radar disks, or "scanners," capable of picking up bits of information from the energy field, or aura, they are scanning. Since the hands are connected to the Fourth Center (via the arms) and the Sixth Center is the seat of clairvoyance, the relationship between the Fourth and Sixth Centers is instrumental to a fine-tuned radar. Clairvoyance thrives on empathy. Love is clarified with vision. The Heart learns to see and the Head learns to sense. These are prerequisites of developing Human Radar.

When the Fourth and Sixth Centers harmonize, the new energetic synthesis naturally voices itself in the opening Fifth Center. The Centers work like this. Unify the Fifth and Third Centers, and the Fourth Center blossoms...and so forth. This way, we can "work on our centers" by recognizing their inter-relationships. Like anything truly alive, a Center may become inaccessible if approached too directly and without regard for its innate Intelligence. (Even wild animals will come to your call if given the right kind of invitation.) The following meditation carries within it the intent of scanning...of testing your Human Radar.

SCANNING

1) Ground yourself thoroughly. Close your eyes and rest in your Sixth Center.

2) Enter the Trance Meditation as is previously presented while remaining in the Sixth Center. Periodically, check your grounding.

3) After you have moved the mixture of Earth and Cosmic Energies up your spine for about ten minutes, let a portion of this mix run through your arms and out your hands. Place your hands apart, resting on your lap with palms facing up.

4) Designate one hand to be a "receiving" scanner. Place this hand over your head with its palm faced down. Let your palm center open up.

5) Scan your Seventh Center. Be receptive to *any* sensation, impression and/or image…no matter how small and *without* naming it.

6) Then, move your scanning hand in front of the Sixth Center out about a foot. Is there any difference in what you're picking up? Feel free to bring your hand closer to you or pull it father away to get more information.

7) At your own pace, start scanning the rest of the Five Centers (skip the Eighth Center for now) in order with the intent of distinguishing between them as energies. Periodically, check your grounding.

8) After completing #7, scan for "bright and dark" spots, also where there doesn't seem to be any flow of energy at all.

9) Remember the Centers which had dark spots and/or energy blockage.

10) Open your eyes and come out of Trance Meditation by stretching and making animal sounds…growl, purr, bark, etc….this is not a joke.

Healing is what happens whenever we are left with our own energy. Whatever the Cosmic Energy blows out was never ours to begin with. An excessive level of other people's energy in our aura can prove draining and parasitic. Those strange emotions you're feeling…voices you're hearing…thoughts you're thinking…may *not* be your own. Claiming Psychic Intelligence within ourselves is one way of confessing a preference for certain emotions, voices and thoughts…the ones *you* want inside you and not the ones which run amok and are mysteriously activated around certain people. This is the kind of inner freedom and dominion assured through understanding our own place in Sixth Grade. Psychically, we are fighting for territory until we take a stand and mark our positions. This is not a paranoid or fearful attitude but one borne out of a realistic preference for more freedom. We are only as free as our integrity permits.

INTRODUCTION TO DESIGNING TAROT

A tool for stabilizing your psychic freedom and internal dominion can be found in designing your own Tarot. There are basically three paths to follow: Traditional, Non-Traditional and The Combination. We will travel along a three-lane highway, giving everybody a chance to shift lanes when they are ready to do so. Until that time, feel free to relax. Designing a Tarot is a lot of fun and a profoundly instructive experience. Contrary to popular belief, you do not have to be an expert in Traditional Tarot to design a Non-Traditional deck of cards. You do, however, require the nerve and audacity to make strong statements about your ultimate values. For those of us already adept in Traditional Tarot, perhaps it is time to design a new version for yourself. For the rest of the eclectics, perhaps combining the best of old and new will shed light where none has ventured before.

There are also basically three ways to technically design a deck of Tarot cards: Illustration, Collage and The Combination. Once again, there are no hard, fast rules…only the honest evaluation of what you feel capable of executing. Guidelines will be presented, both psychically and technically, along the way to initiate and sustain the process. What remains pivotal to designing a Tarot is the importance of communicating our true values.

THE ORIENTATION

The Tarot conveys a psychic language which combines a picture with a word to form a symbol…representing an archetype…a force of nature. Seeing as we are part of nature, these forces are at constant play within us. The Tarot is one way of framing, articulating and thus, evoking these forces into conscious recognition. Designing your own Tarot will probably change your life. It will certainly release a great deal of latent psychic energy. The process itself is highly integrative, in that the energy released will have somewhere creative to go. It will go wherever you are required to *live out your values.* Designing a Tarot is not a mind game. It is a self-drawn map to help you get to the territory itself.

Tarot is a working model for the Multidimensional Self. Each card reflects a facet of who we are. A deck is a neurological autobiography. The deck you design, for it to ring true, will have to communicate what is true to your own Central Nervous System and not just socially conditioned assumptions. The more true something is to you, the more likely it will be true for others as well. Read that last sentence again…it holds the paradoxical key for an effective Tarot. It may be difficult to grasp immediately, but The Fool that persists in his folly becomes wise.

Our task is to design the pieces to a large puzzle, that, when put together tells the story of our personal (and maybe, collective) evolution. If you are working on a particular card and get stumped, relax…move on to the next because all the answers may not come in linear order. You may have to design many cards before you get just the right piece of information you need. Another clue is in being specific and personal.

Look to your own experience for the source of your information. *You are the territory.*

TRADITIONAL TAROT: Research the meanings of color...specifically, the primary, secondary, black, white, brown, silver, grey and gold colors. Discover the Kabbalistic meanings of the numbers 0–21 and how they relate to the Hebrew alphabet. Designate the correct Astrological symbols for each of the Major Arcana cards. Color code the cards so as to reveal their inter-relationships qualitatively. Read *The Tarot* by Paul Foster Case and then, re-read it as if you are designing it another way.

NON-TRADITIONAL TAROT: Designate *your own meaning* to each of the colors mentioned above. Make a list of at least *25* opposites and circle the pairs that are the most *charged.* Think in terms of contrasts while you are designing, i.e., humor/serious, safe/dangerous, etc., so as to instill your cards with both sides of the story. *Naming:* Get used to renaming big issues like Death, Rebirth, Sex, etc. in words that are more personal and exciting to yourself.

THE COMBINATION: Look through the Traditional Tarot deck itself and *rename* the cards according to what you see is a closer articulation of that archetype. Do the same with the images. Envision a more direct and true picture of what that card's all about to you. Don't hesitate to update the imagery a few centuries or...put it back a few. Play with Time. Do the research suggested for both Traditional and Non-Traditional Decks.

TECHNICAL MATERIALS

If you plan to illustrate, you probably already know your medium and its tools. If you are comfortable with pencil or ink pen, it's suggested you go with a more graphically explicit approach until you have enough information to do it with colors, oils, etc. Black-and-white is more inexpensively reduced with the advance in xerox technology, as well. Draw on whatever size is best suited to your creative style.

If you plan to collage, there are materials to purchase. They are: 1) 100 3×5 *or* 5×7 (depending on how large you want your cards) *white* index cards (lined or unlined). 2) 100 of the same size colored index cards (choose the one color you wish to grace the back side of your finished deck) 3) Scissors 4) Glue Stick 5) Scratch Paper 6) Black Felt-tip Pen 7) 12 Multi-Colored felt-tip pens or colored pencils or crayons.

PHASE WON

Next thing you'll need is a lot of magazines. Cut out pictures and words which interest you and spread them in piles on the floor before you…words to the right and pictures to the left, so there's space in between for designing cards. Combine pictures and words in *evocative* rather than explanatory ways which have a strong personal resonance.

Above you can see the three primary parts to a Tarot Card made by a collage Method: 1) Foreground image 2) Background image 3) The word. Sometimes, with the right image, you won't need a background...other times, you'll want to experiment with multiple backgrounds and foregrounds within a single card. Perhaps some of your cards will remain nameless because the image will speak strong enough for itself. When you're ready, move on to Phase Number Next!

THE PHASE NUMBER NEXT

Combine the three parts into a single card by gluing them together on to an index card. Then, draw a border around the edge with your black felt-tip pen and add any other embellishments you feel are appropriate to this card. Then, glue another colored index card behind it (glue it along the side borders for durability) to make your card more stiff. Then, with a rubber stamp, seal or sticker...mark the colored but blank back. Mark the backs of all cards with the same signature, that way you won't be working with a marked deck. As a finishing touch, bring your cards to a printer or laminator to have them *laminated* and sealed in clear plastic, like certain identification cards and menus.

Once you've gotten the gist of it, it'll catch on real fast. Do the best you can, have patience and don't hesitate to expose yourself. Your Tarot cards can only give as honest a reading as you give yourself. When you are ready to incorporate a more structured approach, move on...

TRAINING MODELS

We will incorporate elements of the Traditional to honor the age-old maps drawn before us but also provide the option of opening up wild and unorthodox directions to follow which may start establishing their own traditions some day. To start the process, it's sometimes helps to work from a particular system or model we are familiar with until we feel safe and strong enough to break away to forge our own. The most obvious grid to start with is the one outlined as the 8 grades in this book. Each grade operates by absorbing, organizing and communicating its Intelligence. An entire deck of thirty-two cards (24 plus 8 equals 32) can form the basis of a Tarot. (When working non-traditionally, there is no need to confine yourself to any particular number or numerology unless your idea of a Tarot depends on it).

For those versed in Astrology, a deck may be based on the 12 signs, 10 planets, 12 houses and the 5 major aspects for a grand total of 39 cards. The Kabbalistic Tree of Life lends itself easily to a Tarot Deck with 10 Lights (plus the invisible 11th) and 22 paths between them all, making 33 cards in all. In fact, every conceivable body of knowledge can be taken apart and its pieces designed into a deck of cards. However, that doesn't necessarily mean it will work like a Tarot deck. A real Tarot is as mysterious as the mystery instilled into its design by the designer...you. One way to bring the unknown into your deck is by including it as a card. We'll refer to this as:

ZERO: The zero card *isn't* anything at all. It represents the void. Personally, it's that part of you which exists as nothing, nobody, no-form. It is your relationship with the realm of possibilities and, as of yet, unmanifest potential. Name the zero.

ONE: The one card *is* when everything comes together into a single, unified direction. After the realm of possibilities (zero), a path is chosen or is presented towards the manifestation of a singular possibility. Here, we have a sense of being in control and in the driver's seat. On Target!

TWO: The two card *reflects* on what just went down in the number one card. It's our capacity for seeing ourselves in action yet remaining detached about what we're doing. There's a mirroring ability here, one which is able to create a picture of our reality. Get the picture? Think.

THREE: The three card *feels* a response to itself and is affected. There is a certain vulnerable fertility to this principle because it is soft enough to respond and be moved by its own responses. Its energy recycles and renews itself constantly. Feel it out. Let you heart in on this one.

FOUR: The four card *establishes* itself and whatever it comes into contact with by defining things for itself. This is the authority figure card…where you stand with power, initiative and the masculine principle. How you design this card will express your willingness to be powerful and do things your way. This is the "boss" card. WHO OWNS YOU?

FIVE: The five card *sanctifies* and approves of whatever card four put down as law. This card recognizes the sacred and how we relate its knowledge. It conveys our relationship to the Teacher archetype in general. This is how we personally bridge our inner experience to the outer world. Express yourself.

SIX: Card six *separates* in order to understand how things can come together in deeper ways than before. This capacity for distinction makes relationship possible. Without it, we'd be lost in the sauce of our own expectations and delusions. Design this card with the Significant Other in mind and how you'd like to co-create with your partner. Polarize!

SEVEN: The seven card *protects* and harnesses the sacred powers released in relationship. If 7 is your lucky number, make this your lucky card. If it's not, let it express your relationship to discipline so that whatever you can't get by luck, you can with hard work. This principle is related to the warrior archetype and his/her weapon, the shield. Shield yourself.

EIGHT: Card eight *tames* the animal. Communicate the importance of the ongoing relationship between the soul and animal elements within yourself. This card could also convey the wild, strong force of the animal itself tempered by a benevolent owner. Grounded.

NINE: The nine card *illuminates* through the heights of spiritual solitude, peace and singularity. This quality speaks of a mystical clarity from the blissful merging with God. It is a sense of being complete within oneself…wholeness. *9* marks the end of a major cycle. Tie up loose ends.

TEN: Card ten *merges* us with destiny. This symbol represents great forces moving lives, times and places together for definite purposes. Random, chance meetings are no longer accidental. Synchronicity.

ELEVEN: The eleven card *restricts,* orders and clarifies the previous acceleration for the purpose of restoring grace to chaos. When you need reminding to get your act together, this card works well. Sometimes life's ups and downs require tempering influences, something to help us take the reigns, again. How do you get back in control?

TWELVE: Card twelve *surrenders* to the forces of nature. The personal life gives in to Life Itself…our ability to flow and roll with the punches. This card symbolizes the socially disconnected state of Rapture and Floating aimlessly like a leaf in the wind. A state of total grace. Let go…

THIRTEEN: The thirteen card *transfigures* whatever it touches. Transmit intense transformation in this card. This card should remind you of your need to go through changes. Growth and decay are part of the same motion. Let this card destroy anything which inhibits freedom. Grow!

FOURTEEN: Card fourteen *purges* whatever is left over from card thirteen as a test to its true strength and resiliency. This is trial-by-fire time. This card dedicates itself to right action and experiment to determine which direction is appropriate. What is Ritual? Test Yourself.

FIFTEEN: The fifteen card *disillusions* us so that we might see clearly again. It reminds us of our human weaknesses, foibles and flaws. The card symbolizes the pain and difficulties we endure when we either see the part as the whole, or reject a part from the whole. Silly, silly you…

SIXTEEN: Card sixteen *activates* adjustments and change in those areas requiring a reality check. Whenever you'd like to know when to stop fooling yourself, design this card to reflect the reality of sudden change…as unpredictable as lightening itself. Frame the unexpected and give it a name.

SEVENTEEN: The seventeen card *settles* the energy disrupted in the previous phase. This card expresses the principle and practice of meditation. Design this card to remind you of your serenity, so that in times of upheaval you may access your calm. These are the still, deep waters of your innermost being…unaffected by the turbulence of surface realities. Center.

EIGHTEEN: This card *humanizes* us, helping to recall our emotional fragilities in the midst of our strengths. Let this card reflect our capacity for external dependency…the "needy" side of our nature. It should recall our unconscious and as of yet, unintegrated "shadows" of ourselves…our fears, addictions and insecurities. Sleep.

NINETEEN: This card *integrates* previously unconscious parts of ourselves into the daylight of Consciousness. It also relates externally to our choice to become a member of a collective. Make this as bright and cheerful as the previous one was dark and perhaps, dreary. This is the light at the end of the tunnel.

TWENTY: This card *perpetuates* the lives of those who have come in contact with their eternal, infinite selves. Transmit the possibility of living forever or at least, the inspiration of eternal moments. A highly spiritual card, its quality is timeless and ever-expanding spaciousness. It signifies the conscious union with Spirit. Rebirth.

TWENTY-ONE: This card *centralizes* the self. This is the end of the cycle...expressing the epitome of material manifestation, where the whole is self-organized. This card is you as the executive and chief administrator of yourself...the central core of your true self. Govern Yourself.

THE MINOR ARCANA

The previous twenty-two cards make up the Major Arcana. The Minor Arcana consists of Four Suits with fourteen cards each. The first ten are numbered, the last four depict "royalty": page, knight, queen and king. You are not required to build a "minor arcana" as the "major" may suit your needs. However, the following provides guidelines for the Minor Arcana. The Four Suits represent the Elements of Fire, Water, Air and Earth. Discover your own personal metaphors for these: Earth, Instinct, Water, Feeling, Fire, Intuition and Air, Thought. Other examples should be explored to make these suits *personal to yourself.*

7
MYTHIC INTELLIGENCE

A Synchronicity B Alchemy C Astrology

7   CHARIOT   ♇

SEVENTH GRADE MYTHIC INTELLIGENCE
A PREVIEW

WHERE INTELLIGENCE ORIGINATES
DNA AND THE PLANETARY ENTITY

DNA is how the Mythic Intelligence of Planetary Consciousness knows itself. DNA creates Central Nervous Systems (CNS) which, in turn, control The Body via neuromuscular feedback. The internal DNA-CNS dialogue forms the basis for revelatory activities such as prayer, inspiration and transfiguration, or mutation. The DNA-CNS dialogue of the planet itself provides the prototype for our own experience. As we awaken to the coordinates intersecting human and planetary life, Mythic Intelligence is absorbed. Subjectively, this may excite Synchronicity, Future Memory, Past Lives and other mythic functions. Mythic Intelligence originates from our personal dialogue with the planet and/or the Collective Unconscious, wherein racial and planetary memory is stored. Occasionally, this vast storehouse is accessed through our dreams and larger-than-life numinous imagery...charged and animated by the living forces governing existence: archetypes!

ITS QUALITIES AND ATTRIBUTES:
MANDALIC, CENTRALIZED AND RADIAL

Mythic Intelligence thinks "radially"...incorporating Past, Present and Future into its scope. From this perspective, Time moves simultaneously from the Future into the Past, as it does from the Past into the Future. Its qualities are Mandalic. All outgoing forms of life are connected at their singular source in DNA. This enables Consciousness the extended mobility of traversing amidst simultaneously juxtaposed destinies for the purpose of gathering information on itself. Mythic languages such as Alchemy and Astrology aid to organize and communicate in metaphor planetary consciousness, thus articulating its intersection with humanity. DNA receives its instructions from the central nucleus of the atom, whereby it encodes this information for the CNS to delegate the necessary processes for its survival. *Synchronicity initiates us into the Realm of the Archetypes, its signals indicative of our close proximity to being "in sync" with our destinies. Alchemy* is a mythic tool for naming the phases of natural transformation which tend to accelerate when we get closer to our centers. *Astrology* maps out the energetic styles by which we most effectively access the territory of our alchemical realizations.

SYNCHRONICITY

When does "mere coincidence" cease being merely coincidental? When it happens more often than not. Carl Jung spoke of the "relativization of time and space in the unconscious mind" and how this influences our outer environment. This relativization process expresses itself as one of many functions given to the deep, centralizing Intelligence at work within the psyche. Terence McKenna's *The Invisible Landscape* chronicles the inner sojourn he and his brother took while eating psychedelic mushrooms along the Amazon River Basin. Their mystical visions related the universe as a *hologram* of 64 time scales, each corresponding to a hexagram in the *I Ching* and the 64 codons of DNA. Another author, that ingenious iconoclast Robert Anton Wilson, has written *Cosmic Trigger,* a veritable source book of synchronistic experiences. Since then, every book he has written reeks of synchronicity until the reader finally becomes accustomed to accepting it as the norm.

Jose Arguelles, an artist and scholar, channeled his book *Earth Ascending,* a bird's-eye view of human evolution as "determined by the living entity of Planet Earth." In his book he has managed to find cross-references between systems and languages connecting the Mayan calendar, *I Ching,* DNA, Geomancy, Geology, Cultural History, Astronomy, just to name a few. Populist author, Marilyn Ferguson's *The Visionary Factor: A Guide for Remembering the Future* is also suggestive of synchronicity. On the psychic frontier, West Coast psychic Alan Vaughn's *Synchronicity* presents a book on the clairvoyantly-related facets like premonition, prophecy and other abilities inherent to the synchronistic.

> *"Vuja Day: 1 feel like I've never been here before..."*
> — Robin Williams, Coincidentalist

The biological expression of Mythic Intelligence is the DNA code, which was "accidentally" discovered to be a double-helix spiral by Dr. James Watson after his "flash" while descending a spiral staircase at Oxford. The number "23" connects the DNA code with the I *Ching;* there are bonding irregularities every 23rd angstrom units and the 23rd hexagram is called Breaking Apart...there are 23 chromosomes from each male and female cell. There are numerous other examples using the number 23 to demonstrate synchronicity, all of which can be read about m Wilson's *Cosmic Trigger.* Synchronicity seems to unveil the underlying network of All Life Being Connected To Itself.

PARADISE CENTRAL

Synchronicity is an attribute of that aspect of ourselves capable of thinking like a *mandala.* To think like a mandala is to recall the African Fan-shaped model of destiny…that from the center, there are numerous paths to follow outward and we can, at any time, jump from one reality tunnel into another thanks to our union with the center. Like the mandala, all paths of destiny come from and return to the same one source. To the degree we recall this center, is the degree we may shift from one time-scape into another, as all times and places are expressions from This Source, here-after called Paradise Central.

Paradise Central is the Consciousness enabling us to bypass the illusions of: 1) Time and 2) Coming and Going. If there is no Time, there can be no Coming or Going but only a continual Arrival in our Being. We become more present under the influence of Mythic Intelligence because from here, we are literally living out our distinct expressions of the Archetypes: those autonomous, numinous forces visiting our dreams and occasionally frequenting the daydream we call "reality." Oftentimes, we fall completely at the mercy of these Larger Than Life forces… watching helplessly as we are strung about like puppets on strings. If we do not resist and fight too much, we learn to surrender and live life as a servant to these forces for awhile. As a servant, we understand (bit by bit) how to operate in the Realm of the Archetypes until eventually, we know enough to claim a sense of identity there. It is usually a Trial-By-Error/Success process requiring one humbling experience after another until we learn how to "play" the Archetype without taking ourselves too seriously. (This kind of knowledge usually emerges with Eighth Grade Graduation, where Spiritual Intelligence reminds us that we're not necessarily the stuff we're made of. Also see *Mechanical Problems, Gear 3*).

Mythic Intelligence conceives in a radial manner, including Past, Present and Future awareness of ourselves. As we have had "past lives" we also have "future lives." Future Memory is a function of Mythic Intelligence that lets us recall the Us In The Future…that part of ourselves which has already reached its destiny. What we are experiencing in the present are the ripples of who we are in the future. That's right, *we have already happened* and as you enter the future, you will ride the outward expanding waves *inward* to your inevitable center…of who you have become…who you have always been. Future Memory recognizes, what Arguelles calls "the aboriginal current of time" which moves from the future to the past simultaneously as the "civilized current of time" runs from the past to the future. This is one way of talking about "radial time" and what Arguelles calls the "synergistic function of the Earth's energy fields…the PSI-Bank Memory Matrix of the planet…"

Myth conveys the language of Spiritual realities. A true myth is not bound by any culture, as it bypasses the conditioned intellect to relay a story obvious to all. Its story follows an evolution and its players are personifications of Archetypical Forces at work. The action relays universal experience unhampered, for the most part, by time zone or space. Its intent is to transmit living, spiritual signals. Permit, if you will, the following heuristic possibilities. Myth is God-Food in that when one is lived out, it is an offering of oneself to the Creator. Gods eat myths like DNA consumes protein. Living through our story, we are consumed and must recombine our elements in different ways to recreate another story…*another myth to live by.*

SIMULTANEOUS DEFINITIONS OF SYNCHRONICITY

1) The simultaneous occurrence of two or more events coinciding together which bypass the linear laws of cause and effect to create a sense of meaning.
2) The convergence, in time and space, of seemingly unrelated coordinate points serving to evoke depth and psychological significance.
3) When an internally perceived event (as a dream) is seen to correspond to an external reality by means of premonition.
4) Psychic parallels between individuals and groups of like mind, as in the simultaneous occurrence of thoughts, feelings and activities.
5) The relativization of time and space in the unconscious mind.
6) Two or more directions originating in different dimensions coming together at the same time and space coordinates, suggesting a previously meaningful and conscious intent.
7) Incongruous juxtapositions combined for the purpose of new information.

GENETIC ALCHEMY

Another synchronicity for heuristic speculation is the relationship between the mystified codes of Alchemy and the modern, clinical experiments of Genetics. Both disciplines honor the same deity of a different name. Geneticists call her DNA and Alchemists call her Prima Materia, or Nature. The symbol used by both teams as an emblem for their Goddess is a *double spiral*...the double helix of DNA and the sideways #8. The molecular structure of DNA consists of Mostly Carbon, Oxygen, Nitrogen and Hydrogen atoms. It was thought that the Four Elements held Prima Materia together: Earth (C), Water (O), Air (N) and Fire (H).

Genetics understands that DNA replicates itself into "RNA Messenger" molecules for the purpose of templating RNA with the instructions for manufacturing Sulphur and Nitrogen-rich protein to feed Itself, thus, perpetuating life as we know it. Prima Materia replicates herself as the Mercury of Human Consciousness (Hermes the Messenger) for the purpose of instructing Consciousness to manufacture protean-rich mythologies for the evolution of soul-consciousness towards global enlightenment. Phosphorus-rich DNA lacks the minerals of Sulphur and Nitrogen, so it burns and consumes these incessantly to sustain life. According to alchemical code, Phosphorus is the Feminine side of Nature, as Sulphur is the Masculine. Chromo equals color *and* some equals body, container, house...the alchemist's "vas hermeticum" (body within the body) which contained and mixed the various phases referred to by *color,* "blackening" "whitening" and "reddening." These stages marked a specific evolution of cycles pertaining to natural transformation. (See *Seventh Grade, Alchemy.*)

THE MESSENGER: A RELATIVE MYTH

Once upon a space, a very hungry man roamed around the outskirts of The World searching the Wide Periphery day after day for food, be it fruit, fowl or cheese. The Periphery was already gaining critical acclaim for procuring the longest and coldest nights in The World, which left its Stalkers (for that is what they called each other) the hard knowledge of starvation if food was not found. On one such night, this particular Stalker whose name was Ronald and he knew it not, ay, on one such night our Ronald the Stalker had not found enough food. SO...in stark blindness and bitter cold, he ventured out beyond The Periphery and out to The Edge. And fell over. Down Ronald fell, head over heels, with the swift certainty of a hawk to a bunny.

Meanwhile, at the other end of The World, a Magician had been promoted and was beginning his long ascent to Paradise Central where he would meet with a host of Silly Angels who, as rumor has it, will attempt to engage the Magician in the seemingly harmless game of Make Me Laugh. The Magician, of course, knew of this test and was taking all the necessary measures to remain quite serious in spite of himself. On his way up to the Silly Angels, the Magician espyed poor Ronald falling. It was here that the graduating Magician made his Mandatory Last Gesture by catching Ronald, by the ears yet, with the intention of putting him to work as the new Messenger (which is what Magicians were before they graduated).

As they rose over the outer ring of the Center of the World, Ronald was dropped and down he went. Looking up, all Ronald could see against the cobalt blue sky was a small puffy white cloud with two outstretched hands waving good-bye to him before it disappeared, completely. Ronald crashed, rolling around on the ground, gangling like a spider without a web.

The sky spun circles inside his head. As Ronald got up on his feet, trees uprooted…rocks and earth flew about him in a kaleidoscope of magnificent confusion. It was the most confused Ronald had ever felt. In fact, he'd never known confusion like this before, as it more or less became his only reference point to reality. Confusion was solid as a rock now, weighing his head down like a great swaying pendulum of maximum density.

"This is Earth," a woman's voice rang out. "Mark it well, as there is no beginning without it."

The voice overwhelmed Ronald. It was tremendously reassuring as it spoke so precisely of the very thing he was experiencing. Involuntarily, Ronald wept, as if a dam had broken flooding his mind with water so he could not see anymore.

"This is Water," the voice chimed. "Mark it well, as there is no Life without it."

Instantly, the tears dried and Ronald was left feeling empty, relieved and then, full with pleasure. As his vision cleared a house appeared before him…a multi-colored house with a door swinging open and shut with the wind.

"This is Air," whispered the voice. "Mark it well, for there is no motion without it."

Ronald approached the door and when he got close enough to read the inscription across its oaken veneer, his mouth opened and spoke the letters, "D-N-A". He walked through the door. Inside, Ronald noticed a fire burning in a deep stone pit in the center of the large room.

"Enter the center," the voice spoke as it cracked the air.

Without thinking, Ronald entered the center and stepped into the fire. All around and inside him, he heard fantastic popping sounds, as with every pop…Ronald could see more clearly. Ronald liked the fire.

"This is Fire," she said. "Mark it well, as there is no light or heat without it. You are standing in The Center of the World now. Know its presence and solitude. Here, you will prepare for service as a Messenger. Once you understand the structure, function and quality of each of the Four Elements, you will learn how to combine them in the way I shall show you. You will do this to keep me alive."

Ronald thought of asking the voice who it was, when just as the words were leaving his lips, they changed and instead asked, "Who am I?" He tried again to ask the voice who *it* was and once again…his words reversed against his will, on their own and spoke,

"Who am I?"

"You were Ronald at The Periphery but you are RNA Messenger, here, in the Center of the World. You were created by me to keep the world from collapsing. You are now, as I have said, in the Center of the World. It is the safest place you will ever know. Your purpose here is to bring me food."

Ronald, involuntarily, closed his eyes. When he decided to open them, the house was gone! Listening closely, he realized the voice was also gone and when he looked at his hands, they were gone as well. In the time it takes a single moment to unfold, Ronald realized that he did not exist. And yet, he did…he had to. How else would he know he didn't exist if there wasn't someone there to notice it? It then dawned upon him what the voice had last said to him about bringing it food to keep alive and understanding the elements and how to combine them. It occurred to him that he had sacrificed himself to the voice and now it was time to recreate himself through the elements to restore an offering to the voice. He was beginning to get the picture.

ALCHEMY

Alchemy is the study of the evolutionary phases of transformative process. Every culture which has reached some degree of maturity has developed its own approach to Alchemy…the Egyptians, Chinese, Indian, Native American, European, etc. The cultural basis for Alchemical Studies in *Angel Tech* stems from the 16th Century European Tradition.

The form of Alchemy introduced here is spiritual in that it rests unconcerned with the material attempts of transmuting base metals into gold. Instead, we will explore a more agricultural model for cultivating internal conditions conducive for the unification of the Multidimensional Self. In Sixth Grade Psychic Intelligence, we learned about the multiple facets of ourselves, as well as their functions and attributes. (See *Sixth Grade Reality Selection and Designing Tarot.*) In Seventh Grade Mythic Intelligence we relate to the inter-connectedness of all our various "selves." In Fifth Grade, we chanted *ALL IS ONE.* In Sixth Grade, we reveled in *I AM MANY.* Seventh Grade Mythic Intelligence confesses, *WE ARE A NETWORK.*

The word "alchemy" means *black earth* in its root origins, referring to a key Point in alchemical process and demonstrating the agricultural model mentioned earlier. A seed, when placed in fertile soil, sprouts and continues to grow *with the proper conditions.* Alchemy provides the guidelines for cultivating the proper conditions for real growth to occur, so we may finish the work Nature has started within us. The black earth signifies many things but primarily it is a metaphor for fecundity, fertility and fertilizer. Humanistically speaking, the cultivation of the alchemical black earth is a life-long process…an "opus." Emotionally, it is a psychic death/rebirth; what has been called The Dark Night of the Soul.

In the spirit of *following through,* we return to the agricultural model of the seed planted in fertile soil. The seed sprouts and in time, let's say, grows into a tree. The tree blossoms and bears fruit, which ripens and drops to the ground. Here, it rots and goes to seed, the combination of which provide fertile soil for the next generation of seeds to sprout and grow…perpetually regenerating its life cycle. Close study of this cycle will reveal the fruit of alchemical knowledge wherein decay precedes growth. The turning point in alchemical process is always this black earth phase. Everything up to there is Preparation; everything following initiates the Greater Work.

Alchemical understanding rests upon the depth of our own personal insight into the black earth phase…the catalytic nature of death and decay. Without an individual sense and experience of this, Alchemy becomes an empty philosophy. (Indeed, this is why alchemy has fascinated so many intellectuals who sense promise of redemption from their ivory tower ways. Jung spent ten years researching and writing alchemical treatises alone.) The goal of Alchemy is identical to the long-term objectives of Nature *and* DNA…the realization of immortality. Nature knows that death is no end but the essential ingredient for transmutation and rebirth. The study of Nature provides dues to its perpetuation and reproduction. The alchemist's goal is *self-reproduction…*finding another way to perpetuate him/herself besides the genetic imperative of yielding offspring (Hyatt's Reproduction Bias).

Alchemy is a natural myth. It is a special language and code for deciphering spiritual signals into applicable messages. These messages, according to the 16th Century European alchemists, relayed themselves as eleven phases of natural transformation, all of which have been preserved in eleven wood-block prints. Before actually going on the study of these, it is mandatory research to investigate the nature of the Four Elements: Earth, Water, Fire, and Air…and their originating AETHER.

ELEMENTAL RITUAL MEDITATION

The following Elemental Ritual Meditation provides internal guide-lines by which one can access the living forces of Earth, Water, Fire and Air as *Allies* towards restoring balance and equilibrium during times of crisis, imbalance and/or upset. The meditation depends entirely upon your capacity to permit uncertainty by letting the elements have a life of their own.

1) Sitting down, center, own your space and ground. (See *Sixth Grade, Grounding.*)
2) Project the living force of Earth in you down below your body about three feet. Enter No-Form. (See *Fifth Grade, Ritual: No Form.*)
3) Invite the spirit of the Earth to enter your soles and move throughout your body. Connect your breathing so you inhale Earth and circulate the energy throughout your body on the exhale. *Stabilize.*
4) Project the living force of Air within you up above your head about three feet. Enter No-Form. Invite the spirit of Air inside through your crown and let it circulate *as it will,* without your guidance, throughout your body until you feel *circulated from within.*
5) Project the living force of Fire within you out along the right side of your body about three feet out. Let it flicker there in all its light and heat giving properties. Enter No—Form. Feel the entire right side of your body, then invite the spirit of Fire into that area of your body which it feels most attracted to at first. Let the spirit of Fire move throughout your body, consuming everything it doesn't illuminate until you feel *activated from within.*
6) Sense the entire left side of your body. Then, project the living force of Water within you out along your left side about three feet out and let it flow and move in its own ways. Enter No-Form. Invite the spirit of Water to enter that part of your body which is in *least* resistance to it. Let the spirit of Water flow throughout your body, dissolving any resistances you no longer need until you feel *fluid within.*
7) Command all four elements to their places outside of your body and invite whatever element in that meets your need for internal balance. Repeat whenever needed. Practice this while standing and walking.

EARTH

The primary intent behind understanding the Four Elements is to develop an internal reference for balancing one's energies. Each element has a distinct function and acts in very specific ways. It is possible to start determining where we are over-emphasized and with what element we lack. The elements are forces within us. They are *autonomous* in that they have lives of their own and can be invoked as allies as soon as we are intimate enough with their ways. The element to understand first, before any manifestation of forces is possible, is...EARTH.

Earth is our magical physiology. The realm of matter, thanks to Modern Alchemy (Quantum Physics), has become infinitely mysterious and so, what was once thought to be fixed is, in fact quite malleable. The element earth manifests most directly in our immediate experience of *gravity*. Gravity, in spite of contrary belief, is a source of energy and not something to fight against. Giving in to gravity is a direct link to releasing its Intelligence, as is expressed by all cats, some dancers and a few publishers. Earth requires that we become like animals and live by instinct. We are all creatures of the Earth and to the degree we can live openly with this fact, is the degree our alchemical orientation has begun.

The two primary gifts of Earth are: 1) Fuel and 2) Definition. Earth gives Fire fuel to burn. Another analogy is that the Fire of "spirit" consumes the Earth of the body. Earth stabilizes. When we are not grounded during periods of high-velocity acceleration (Fire), we get "burned out."

Earth is our sustenance and the depth of our resiliency. Earth provides Water with the vehicle necessary for its flow and its sense of direction. Earth renders the ethereal (Air) *tangible* and the fluid (Water), a sense of purpose in *containment*. The molecule closest to corresponding with Earth is *Carbon* and its atomic structure is 666: Six protons, six neutrons and six electrons (Hello, Mr. Crowley...)

To integrate Earth is to consecrate the body, *nothing less will do.* (Physical hang-ups are among the greatest impediments to our creativity... See *Mechanical Problems, Gear One.*) The body is the temple and crucible responsible for containing, mixing, separating and reuniting the natural forces at work therein. Earth is, by far, the most significant alchemical element for the most obvious reason of all...*the black earth phase.* The quality of black is distinct in its capacity for absorbing Light into itself, the most extreme example being The Black Hole phenomena. Without going into the evolution of Black Holes, suffice it to say their dominant characteristics are ultra-gravitational and extraordinary density.

The alchemical relationship to the *density* of the black earth phase is one of *conscious surrender*. This means there is no need for panic…on the contrary, it's time to *be confused*. This exaltation of confusion as an alchemical value *during the black earth phase* is only confusing if clarity has been made an ultimate goal.

Alchemists are also *Confusionists* due to their veneration for the black earth phase and especially what it produces: rebirth. The real earth lesson is in *yielding to density*. The denser Consciousness gets, the blacker the Earth turns and the greater the rebirth. Earth, in its densest and blackest manifestations, wields a mighty pressure capable of shaping our destiny from the darkest coal to the brightest diamond. It is the diamond self that the alchemist strives to forge and this hardest of all stones is called *lapis*.

WATER

Water knows itself through adaptation. It does not resist until captured in its frozen state of ice. It usually follows the path of least resistance unless moved otherwise by Earth, Fire or Air. Water changes form to suit whatever purpose it is called to perform. Its overall effect soothes, moistens, and renders flexible whatever is prone to be rigid without it. Humanistically, it is our emotions and capacity for feeling which most directly incorporates the spirit of Water. Due to Water's prediction for fluidity, it is our Feeling Self which lets us *be* whatever comes up. When the *Water* element is over-emphasized, we're flooded with contents from the subconscious. This is because we are unable to stop *being* everything that comes up. Water does not know distinction without Earth to give it boundaries and without a container, we "spill our death"…and feel shipwrecked or worse, drowned.

A lack of Water shows up as emotional dryness and/or psychological rigidity…uptight and tense. Emotions move a lot and tend to be primitive and unpredictable. They need lots of psychological space to even be alive in the body. And alive they are unless they're dead, and when they're dead, *so are we*. The Feeling Self is vulnerable and impressionable to outside energies which keep it stimulated, nourished and healthy. Water people tend to possess a "ripened and full" look about them, as Water depraved persons appear more stark and barren. Water is the element which nurtures Psychic Intelligence in two ways: 1) By balancing the Fire, and 2) Letting us in on other peoples' feelings. Water aids in our overall sense of relatedness to others, without which we would become isolated.

The psychic advantage of having access to the Water spirit is that it's a lubricant during times of high-velocity acceleration. Water minimizes the inertia that would otherwise cause friction at high speeds of living and create insensitivity to oneself and the world. However, Water is by nature slippery and, too much would create even more inertia. It takes a careful balancing act to regulate the spirit of Water.

FIRE

As we become more comfortable with (Earth) and (Water), we can acquaint ourselves with the correct use of Fire. The two primary properties of Fire are *illumination and heat.* Fire requires fuel to burn (Earth) and *the need to be regulated* (Water). The spirit of Fire is excited every time we *pay attention.* Our attention *is* the medium by which we can regulate the intensity of Fire. This spirit is particularly well sustained during the *acute and prolonged attention span.* Fire is our power of concentration. It expresses itself joyously as the Will in its capacity for focusing and directing energy.

The neuro-electronic impulses of our Central Nervous System provide the biological basis for the spirit of Fire within us. *Following your impulses* will tend to fire up your energy…especially if there's not too many emotions (Water) or thoughts (Air) in the way. There are basically two types of *heat* Fire produces: 1) Pleasant and 2) Unpleasant. Anything *that feels good* to the consecrated body immediately gains favor. The second type of heat, however, is the effect of friction; of forces rubbing the "wrong way" inside the body. They are rubbing the "wrong" way because *it hurts.* The body instantly resists pain because it recalls threat, danger, and death. The two types of heat can be concurrent as well. This happens when we fall in love with pleasure to the point of ignoring its limitations and then, the previously stimulating Fire over-stimulates our sensations into irritation pain and on into numbness. The correct use of Fire is knowing when to stop.

The Will defines itself in terms of its effects on the world by its actions. Fire tempers the Will, forging its shape and sharpening its edge like a fine, crafted sword. Fire can be invoked through conscious intentions meeting their manifestation in directed activity. Wherever there is skill, manipulation and technique acquired, you can be sure the element of Fire is burning something. This is why Water is important to its regulation…Water doesn't really have a will of its own and couldn't manipulate if it tried. Mixing Fire and Water in the crucible of Earth will quickly invite the spirit of Air to join in the elemental drama.

AIR

Of the Four Elements, Air is the most spacious and expansive. Air is also closest in nature to Aether...the originating fabric of the Four Elements. Clarity and buoyancy are to Air what darkness and density are to its opposite, Earth. Air relates with its pervasiveness and can travel practically anywhere; it doesn't require the gravity or fuel necessary to the survival of the other three forces. The overall effect the spirit of Air has on consciousness is to *mobilize and circulate* it. It doesn't need boundaries and moves freely within and outside ourselves as the air we breathe.

An excessive degree of Air can leave us breathless and spacey because we get to moving too fast. Too much air can also breed delusions of Not Being Enough (the way we are) as well as an overall fear of existence and sitting still. Maximum Air tends to be so highly interactive that it utterly loses itself in relationships. It needs the definition of Earth so it won't immobilize itself in mobility. The spirit of Air is effective for creating space and a cooling effect. Due to Air's highly reactive nature, it is quickly affected by the other three elements, most notably Fire, which requires Air for fuel, as well.

AETHER

Aether is, perhaps, the most difficult element to describe in that like black, it's not a color or element at all but a quality unto itself. Aether is the refined substance of all Four Elements combined into a fifth expression or dimension. Earth being the first dimension of existence itself...Water being the dimension of depth...Fire of height...and Air of movement or time. The fifth dimension is beyond time-and-space...a doorway to that place where we may begin the next phase of our alchemical research...

> **The life of Fire comes from the death of Earth**
> **The life of Air comes from the death of Fire**
> **The life of Water comes from the death of Air**
> **The life of Earth comes from the death of Water**
> **Form lives In the light and dies In the Dark**
> **Life lives in the Dark and dies In the Light...**
> **Alchemist Anonymous**

THE MERCURIAL FOUNTAIN

THE KING AND QUEEN

THE NAKED TRUTH

IMMERSION IN THE BATH

THE CONJUNCTION

THE FERMENTATION

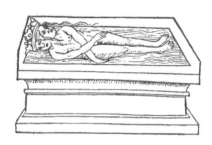

DEATH

THE ASCENT OF THE SOUL

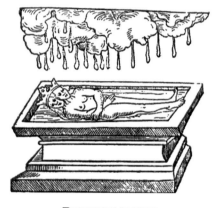

PURIFICATION

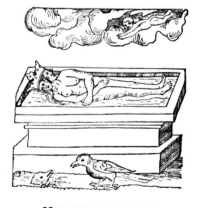

MULTIPLICATION

REBIRTH

The Mercurial Fountain — The mysterious Vas Hermeticum, or Human Body, is the container where all transformations occur. The Fountain is made up of The Four Elements (6-pointed stars), Masculine and Feminine Natures (sun and moon) plus the transcendent principle of Consciousness itself (2-headed serpent) all interwoven into their undivided state as the "aqua permanens" (infinite sea) of the fifth dimensional Aether. This is the unknowable source of all forms, colors and expression. The significance of the number six in this picture refers to the six cardinal directions: North, South, East, West, Above and Below. These alchemists called Aether, *materia prima* for the "source of matter." They claimed it could not be seen, described or explained but could, however, be *touched*. It was, perhaps their way of speaking about Factor X.

The King And Queen — Here, is the first recognition of inner opposition during its superficial ideation phase. The self-images of Masculine and Feminine (& other polarities) are confronted, alongside those imposed by society, parents, friends, etc. in order to become more aware of their existence as *images*. This phase marks the beginning of Image-awareness and a gradual disidentification with images in general. There is a conscious choice to "regress" and "descend into matter" for the purpose of living the truth. The 6-pointed star of The Source is still visible, signaling the message that it's still not too late to turn back to the undifferentiated state.

The Naked Truth — This phase marks the sacrifice of the Image altogether, revealing King and Queen in their natural, naked state. The social persona and "act" have been dropped for a still deeper descent into the truth of Masculine/Feminine instead of their conditioned images. The dove of transcendence is still present to refer the polarity back to its Source in The Fountain, so they do not forget they are still part of a Whole. Both hands of each polarity grasps the central "twig," initiating a deeper engagement towards merging or fusion of opposites.

Immersion In The Bath — This phase is the "solutio" and is dedicated to dissolving the differences between polarities before the final merging. Here, a further descent into the Sea of Experience that "devours, dissolves and cleanses" all that still clings to distinction. The dove signifies the love from complete acceptance of both polarities within oneself. Due to the encompassing nature of The Bath, it may excite fears of drowning and losing control to one's emotions (Water). This time is dedicated to the dissolution of resistance and other impediments to *conscious union* of opposites within oneself.

The Conjunction — The King and Queen make love in the aqua Permanens. This refers to complete submersion in primal chaotic merging where the transcendent point of the dove is utterly lost in the union of opposites. The dove has disappeared into the ongoing unity—(Only to emerge later as the Divine Child).

The Fermentation — This "fermentatio" phase is a direct extension of the previous conjunction. Here King and Queen have sprouted wings as angels, signifying the conscious intention right from the start to unify opposition towards individuation. There is a great ripening and terrific energy is released. Fermentation has begun, thus finishing the Preparation, of Lesser Work, and giving way to The Greater Work initiated by the darkening black earth phase.

Death — The Vas Hermeticum has turned into a tomb, where King and Queen are joined as one. Here is the black earth "nigredo" phase resulting from the union of opposites. This new body lies in its dormant, potential state…rotting and germinating the seed of a new perspective, one which includes *both sides* of the self in its view. There is a cessation of movement and energy flow, often marking psychic stagnation and personal defeat. However, seeds germinate in the dark and the alchemists say, "The darker, The Better…" No life can arise without the dead of the old.

The Ascent Of The Soul — A child ascends from the corpse of King/Queen upwards into a cloud. The transcendent dove now returns to the realm of potential as a new seed concept which includes polar realities of self as an idea. Personally, this is a dark and disorienting time not unlike being out-of-the-body *or* in-a-dream, as the soul has temporarily vacated. As the soul approaches the fifth dimension, it is important during this time to exercise Patience and Faith in oneself, in spite of the subjective experience of Not Knowing Who or Where You Are. This emphasizes emptiness and alienation, so while this is happening…it is suggested practice to make use of it by *not* identifying with anything at all until your real self returns and heals you.

Purification — The cloud releases dew upon the old corpse in its tomb. This is the "albedo" or whitening phase resulting from the point of previous maximum condensation and blackness. Also referred to as the "mundificatio", this phase marks the moisture signaling the return of the soul. There is a strong spiritual intent to this phase emphasizing healing and de-emphasizing intellectual and rational preoccupation. It is a time to "throw the books asunder" and give into exaltation of Life Itself. For those that must know, it is essential you get out of your "head" during this time so the returning soul has somewhere to re-enter. Create space to live!

Multiplication — The soul is seen descending through the cloud down towards the corpse. This is a time for celebration and rejoicing as the soul re-integrates into the world. There is a renewed relationship to The Self in its Multidimensional nature. After the ego has been differentiated from its identification with Self, Life is re-affirmed in renewed relationship. Here is a mandalic awareness of the interconnectedness of reality in its multiple state...a mythic realization.

Rebirth — The Moon represents the previously unconscious elements of the personality, now integrated to serve as a support for the purpose of creation. 12 of the faces on the tree signify the polarization of the Human Body's bottom Six Energy Centers, with the additional face representative of the unified Crown or, Seventh Center. The chalice reflects the Vas Hermeticus and Human Body, wherein the living forces of Instinct, Feeling and Intellect (as serpents) are balanced, tamed and contained. The fourth, larger serpent held in the left hand (right-brain) speaks of the spirit or intuitive function of Intelligence. The bird is intellect grounded in the work of everyday living. The wings on the figure itself signify *conscious projection*...the ability to will one's consciousness outside of the physical body. The "final phase" is also called the "rubedo", or iosis, and implies a "reddening' The alchemists held it sacred, as it denotes the epitome of expansion on the plane of manifestation itself. It is not an end-all arrival but the beginning of life as a Human Being. In this stage, all previous phases are inherent, rendering a relativistic perspective of the greatest being contained in the smallest and both being of equal value.

20 | JUDGEMENT | △

ASTROLOGY
SCIENCE OF TENDENCIES

Astrology, is an ordering principle articulating the language of Mythic Intelligence as it applies to daily life. It is also a means of prediction through the synchronization of alchemical knowledge. Astrologically speaking, we are between epochs at this point in the Twentieth Century...signifying a major paradigm shift in our relationship to Just About Everything. This is referred to as leaving the Age of Pisces and entering the Age of Aquarius...the precise point of entry being somewhat difficult to pinpoint but suffice to say, signs abound around us heralding in the new age. The signs reflect a progressive Aquarian approach to living and relationship, leaving the diehard Piscean Fundamentalists with their last gasps for recognition. We will speak more about the various

Astrological styles later as we gradually unfold this path to understanding the Science of Tendencies.

Since about 90% of the available written material on Astrology is "Piscean-biased," the following presentation may take certain twists and turns unfamiliar to the traditional approach but perhaps more accessible to the newcomer. Some of these adjustments come as changing terms and others, a redefinition of the same, familiar terms. For example, the Astrological Signs are referred to hereafter as "styles" and the Planets, "forces". Each force conveys itself through a particular style. The Houses, as Traditional Astrology refers to areas of Life activity, are hereafter called, "states". Put it all together and you'll discover that each force conveys itself through a particular style within the boundaries of a certain state. Traditional Astrology also refers to the Sign preceding each House as the House Cusp Ruler, which will be referred to from now on as simply The Governor. An Astrological Chart is a map. It is a map conveying the United States of _____ complete with its separate Governors, Internal Forces and the Styles by which they are most effectively expressed. Each map also has a Ruler or President...which is determined by the particular force (planet) carrying the most clout and influence in the map (chart) as a whole.

OUR INTERNAL NETWORKING

Progressive Astrology is a model for the actualization of our *internal network*...realizing the contact points between the various aspects of the Multidimensional Self *and* their conscious synchronization with the events of the outer world. Astrology is a method of turning synchronicity into a *skill.* It is also challenging to our capacity for permitting uncertainty and bypassing dogmatic reaction. This is why Astrology is called here...The Science of Tendencies. It tests the flexibility of our conceptual framework. How open-minded can we be without our brain falling out, and how concentrated can we get without closing our minds?

Astrology is a kind of celestial psychology, giving the planets and constellations a series of characteristics. There are many different forms of Astrology practiced throughout the globe. Here, in the Western World, the most common being the *Geo-centric Natal* variety which is based upon your birth time and place from the perspective of the Planet Earth. In the Far East, there is a tendency to construct a chart from a *Helio-centric* basis or from the perspective of the Sun. Since this book is being written from the Western World, the Geocentric Natal Chart will be discussed as it applies to the Placidus House System.

We have now arrived at the stage of the process where you will require an Astrology Chart constructed for you, as we will not cover the technology of chart construction here. Call your local Metaphysical Bookstore to locate individuals offering this service; you will interpret the map yourself. If you can, request a computerized print-out. This way, you are assured of accuracy and you can re-draw the whole chart yourself as the print-out symbols tend to be exceedingly small. This is a good way to acquaint yourself with the map itself. If you are unable to obtain your own chart (due to loss of birth time, etc), the charts of three prominent individuals will be presented for demonstration purposes. These people were all selected on the basis of their outstanding contributions to the world from the realms of their own Mythic Intelligence.

There are four major layers to the map of your Astrology Chart: 1) The STYLES (the evolutionary phases of the Multidimensional Self) and the STATES they govern. 2) The FORCES (personal and transpersonal energies) and how each is expressed through a particular STYLE from a specific STATE, or area of the Self. 3) The ASPECTS, or Internal Network, relating the FORCES together and 4) The ALCHEMICAL & ENERGETIC DISTRIBUTION expressing the more general wholistic view of the chart. Astrology is a vast, complex Art & Science that cannot be comprehended immediately. Bits and pieces will be presented hereafter in the spirit of Picking Up What You Can. Your personal knowledge of Synchronicity and/or Alchemy will tend to deepen whatever you learn in Astrology...as all are codes for relaying the signals transmitted from Mythic Intelligence.

The following series of definitions have been distilled to convey overall style or qualitative approach. These styles act as Governors when seen at the outer periphery or a chart, as well as coloring the Forces placed within the various states of the map. *Every Astrology chart has every style and force within its boundaries.*

We are all these styles, simultaneously and may gain access to certain states by understanding their governing styles. Each style is assigned an element (Earth, Water, Fire or Air) and an energetic mode (Cardinal, Fixed or Mutable). Each style will be proceeded by a letter symbolizing its element (E is Earth, W is Water, etc.) and a symbol signifying its mode + Cardinal, - Fixed, = Mutable).

THE 12 ASTROLOGICAL STYLES

ጥ (+F) Aries: requiring the necessary control to be spontane-ous; decision making factor; bold, assertive, impul-sive; innocent

ஜ (-E) Taurus: requiring the necessary time to be thorough; stabilizing factor; physical, traditional, steady; dedicated.

Ⅱ (=A) Gemini: requiring the necessary variety to keep learning mobilizing factor; mental, ambiguous, curious; perceptive.

ꝏ (+W) Cancer: requiring the necessary tenacity to define its territory; protective factor; emotional, sensitive; depth.

♌ (-F) Leo: requiring the necessary pride to be generous; empowering factor; charismatic, drama, political; expressive

♍ (=E) Virgo: requiring the necessary intellect to be selec-tive; discerning factor; cultivated, refined, reserved; discreet.

♎ (+A) Libra: requiring the necessary diplomacy to remain social; balancing factor, loquacious, ceremonial, artistic; cultivated

♏ (-W) Scorpio: requiring the necessary strategy to penetrate the essence; activating factor; passionate, restrained & psychic Sagittarius: requiring the necessary direc-tion to keep moving; goal setting factor; outgoing, bright & hopeful

♐ (=F) Sagittarius: requiring the necessary direction to keep moving; goal setting factor; outgoing, bright & hopeful

♑ (+E) Capricorn: requiring the necessary executive power to attain its goals; organizing factor; dignified & reliable.

♒ (-A) Aquarius: requiring the necessary detachment to remain free; unpredictable factor; unorthodox, & progressive.

♓ (=W) Pisces: requiring the necessary flexibility to remain vulnerable; intuitive factor; pliable, receptive & sensitive.

THE UNITED STATES

The States are those areas on the map which appear as twelve wedges in the circle. Each one represents actual inner and outer territories of one's life. Every Astrology Chart has Governors placed at the point directly preceding or at the very start of their state. The states move counter clockwise from 1 to 12. The line from 1 to 7 signifies the horizon at the time of birth. The planets on the bottom half were unseen and the planets inhabiting the upper half, were above the horizon at birth. We will explore these meanings later. For now, here are the United States:

1) State of Self — overall approach to the world; personal and self image; your "act" or style of presentation; physical body and 5 senses.

2) State of Security — orientation to basic values; style of earning income; how security is defined; self-integration and establishment.

3) State of Mind — how one learns; communication and thinking styles; abilities to connect ideas together and relay them simply; concepts.

4) State of Home & Family — genetic heritage and extended family issues; rooting style and the home living environment, inner private self.

5) State of Fun — creative style and romantic requirements; adventure, vacations and simple pleasures; the child within and children.

6) State of Work — actual working conditions, with or without co-workers; Personal health & well being; orientation to service.

7) State of Partnership — relationship needs; mating style; business partners; inner "shadow" figures outwardly personified; marriage.

8) State of Transformations — what requires changing; death-rebirth process; sexual orientation; what comes to oneself without effort.

9) State of Perspective — spiritual orientation; philosophical outlooks and beliefs; physical and astral travel; principles lived for.

10) State of Career — professional ambitions and positions; public image; degree of recognition needed from society; status.

11) State of Social Activities — your circle of friends; degree of significance placed on finding a place in society; hopes and dreams.

12) State of the Unknown — relation to Factor X and mysticism, what is kept hidden from self and others; subconscious karma; blind spot.

SELF-ACCESS

Astrology is a tool for accessing the Self. The different States of oneself can be entered by understanding the Astrological Style which governs the particular State one desires to access. For example, the Governor of the 1st State of Self is the symbol to the extreme left of the chart, as the Governor of the 7th State of Partnership is to the extreme right. The symbol at the very bottom of the chart is the 4th State of Home and Family Governor…as the symbol crowning the top of the chart is the 10th State of Career Governor. The Governors communicate the particular style by which you can most effectively gain access to the actual territory.

On your own chart, locate the Governors mentioned in the previous paragraph. Then look these symbols up amongst the 12 Astrological Styles listed a couple pages back. See for yourself if there is any useful information from comparing these with what you know about yourself. Then, find out what other States you'd like to access knowledge about and look these symbols up in the same manner. For example, if Libra Governs your 7th State of Partnership…this is where you are required to be diplomatic in order to remain sociable. (This position dislikes making waves and/or fighting their partners and may require someone more cultivated than themselves to assure peace.)

In the following demonstration, we will present William's *Governors* and leave the study of his Forces to your own research later upon review. *1st State Governor* (Cancer): self-protective and emotionally expressive to distinguish his own personal world; a psychic in-depth approach and a highly sensitive persona, requiring a shell to protect him from external criticism. *10th State Governor* (Pisces): his public image was that of a mystic; he was extremely vulnerable to the public's response to his career; *4th State Governor* (Virgo): he was most selective of where he lived and how he lived, taking great pains to leave "the world" outside; much intellectual activity done at home; critical of family members at times; *7th State Governor* (Capricorn): marriage helped organize his otherwise chaotic lifestyle…wife was selected on the basis of meeting his life's goals.

WILLIAM BLAKE

THE 10 ASTROLOGICAL FORCES

The Forces run through us and they are us. Olde Astrology referred to them as Planets and indeed they are, except they are called Forces here in order for us to make their direct acquaintance. There are two varieties of Forces in Astrology: 1) *Personal Forces* and 2) *Transpersonal Forces.* The main difference between them is that we may *control* the former and we may acquiesce to the latter. However, when Transpersonal Forces emerge we can learn more about them through our conscious surrender to their influence by creating space for their expression. The Personal Forces are represented by: The Sun, Moon, Mercury, Venus, Mars, Jupiter, and Saturn. The Transpersonal Forces are referred to as Uranus, Neptune and Pluto. All the Forces, once again, are in every chart and at least latent in everybody.

Usually, human beings do not begin to access the Transpersonal Forces until after 29 years of age, when the Saturnian Force pays them a visit in the form of what Astrology calls The Saturn Return. This is a time where consolidating, crystallizing forces are deep at work shaping the personality to start manifesting its true shape. If this shape is unbearable to live with, this becomes an extremely stressful time. However, if you like the shape you're in during this period, it can be a highly successful phase in every respect. It is by understanding the Force of Saturn that we gain access to the Transpersonal Forces of Uranus, Neptune and Pluto and, not before. This is because the Saturnian Force is responsible for our capacity *to manifest* and the *work* it takes to start shaping our destinies. (There are, as usual, exceptions to the rule, an example being the synchronized outside shocks we receive from Uranus, Neptune and Pluto transits.)

THE PERSONAL FORCES

1) **THE SUN** ⊙ : *The Force of One's Identity*...basic sense of self, will and purpose, the Sun is rarely consciously realized. It's potential: Self-Actualization.

2) **THE MOON** ☽ : *The Responsive Force:* our daily *emotional* reactions and source of satisfaction, nourishment and well being. It's potential: Soul-consciousness.

3) **MERCURY** ☿ : *The Force of Thought:* how one *thinks,* talks and makes concepts of reality including self-image & learning. Its potential: The Illuminated Intellect.

4) **VENUS** ♀ : *The Magnetic Force:* how we attract *love,* beauty and art to ourselves, as well as our sociability & relating style. It's potential: Compassion.

5) **MARS** ♂ : *The Motivating Force:* how *action* is initiated through the basic drive, urge for power and sexual instinct. Its potential: The Will.

6) **JUPITER** ♃ : *The Exaggerating Force:* how we keep our minds open and expand consciousness through understanding and hope. Its potential: Optimistic Philosophy.

7) **SATURN** ♄ : *The Compressive Force:* the *pressures* of our fears, insecurities and commitments which are responsible for shaping our destiny & when embraced bestows us with the authority for shaping it ourselves. Its potential: The Teacher Within.

THE TRANSPERSONAL FORCES

8) **URANUS** ♅ : *The Freedom Urge* or *Liberating Force...unpredictable,* sudden changes shattering any forms not innate to the personal freedom of being one's unique self. Personification: The Liberator of Others...Genius.

9) **NEPTUNE** ♆ : *The Mystical Urge* or *Dissolving Force:* highest *inspirations* and greatest potential for *disillusionment,* thus, enlightenment to our oneness with all things. Personification: The Clairvoyant, Poet & Musician.

10) **PLUTO** ♀ : *The Transformative Urge* or *Restructuring Force:* transfigures whatever it touches by eliminating the useless, outdated patterns on the deepest structural levels of one's being, often with "ego-death" involved. Personification: The Healer and Initiator of Radical Change.

HIDDEN VARIABLES

There are three additional symbols not representing Forces of States per se, yet still significant in the information they yield. These are the "Hidden Variables" of Astrology: 1) *The North Node* 2) *The South Node* and 3) *The Part of Fortune.* Both nodes are related to the Moon *and* the North Node, to Uranus. The Part of Fortune can be obtained by subtracting the degree of the *Sun* from the summation of the *Moon* and *The Ascendent* (1st State Governor's degree). Most charts, once constructed, will have these included already. Some will not. If you don't know yours, look your birthday up in any *World Ephemeris* (available at your local Metaphysical Bookstore) and it'll tell you both North and South Nodes, which are always exactly opposite to each other.

1) **NORTH NODE** ☊ : *Future Memory:* this is one's Point of *Destiny* and how one progresses forward into the Future and the manner by which the present-life purpose can be made manifest; usually the most difficult and newest area accessible which is almost impossible without having first worked with The South Node.

2) **SOUTH NODE** ☋ : *Past Lives:* past orientation and upbringing in this life and previous ones; *karma* brought with us and what requires owning before true evolution can occur; our path of least resistance and what we may fall back on when regression is required.

3) **PART OF FORTUNE** ⊕ : *Being Rich and Happy:* the manner we bring both spiritual and material abundance to us *as one.*

The French surrealist poet and cinema artist Jean Cocteau, provides our next example as we focus on the *Forces* Mr. Cocteau activated in his life. *North Node & Sun* together in Cancer expresses his absolute need to realize his destiny through Self-Actualization in the State of Mind, communicating psychic truths (Cancer) for the common people. *Venus, Neptune* and *Pluto* all close together in the State of Self speaks of a mystical love for self-transformation…a theme permeating all his works. *Uranus* and *The Moon* in the State of Work tells of his requirement for total freedom in the work environment, where his Genius expresses itself, as well as where he derives the greatest emotional satisfaction. *Saturn* in between the House of Family and House of Fun, announces his total commitment to being part of a "family of artists" many of whom played in several of his films. *Jupiter* in the House of Transformation kept his mind open just so long as he kept transforming. How could he not?

JEAN COCTEAU

Our next level of understanding explores the internal connections between the Forces and how they conjunct, square, trine, sextile and oppose each other. These internal connections are called Aspects and they are important towards understanding the *dynamics* of a chart... where the action is. Looking at any chart, you'll notice a number wherever you see an Astrological Style...on the periphery as Governors and by the Forces themselves. These numbers signify degrees and there are 30° to each of the twelve Styles, making 360° total. The degrees let us know how the Forces are related and how they affect each other and consequently, us. These aspects will help communicate our inner tensions, free flows and power points so that we may better understand our own internal networking. There are many Aspects which Astrology articulates but we will only refer to five of them here. The others are extra-curricular research.

THE ASPECTS

THE CONJUNCTION ☌ : when 2 or more Forces are within 4° of each other, they combine forces to form a stronger synthesis; this is the most powerful aspect and more than 3 signify rare powers and potential abilities, as more than half of the Forces are fused together.

THE OPPOSITION ☍ : when 2 or more Forces are exactly opposite to each other, within 5°, it creates internal tension; oppositions signify polar aspects of ourselves waiting to be accessed and balanced; opposition is a preparation for balance and self-integration and is not necessarily destructive.

THE SQUARE □ : when 2 or more Forces are 90° from each other within a margin of 5°, there is a "creative tension" requiring extra effort and work to fulfill the direction of each Force in the Square; usually cultivates an appreciation for challenge.

THE TRINE △ : when 2 or more Forces are 120° from each other within a margin of 4°, there is a "free flow" of energy between them, making easy access to the trined Forces.

THE SEXTILE ✶ : when 2 or more Forces are 60° from each other, within a margin of 3°, there is an "allegiance" between the Forces in sextile; an easy-going aspect.

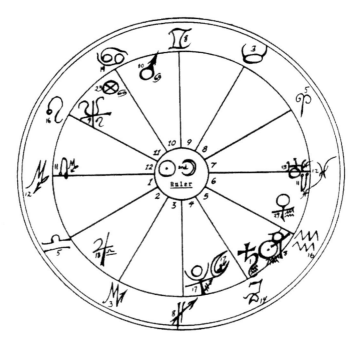

WOLFGANG AMADEUS MOZART

The musical genius of Mozart demonstrates every aspect except the Square. Pluto *conjunct* Moon tells us of his powerful personal magnetism and the emotional importance of home and family. Sun *conjunct* Mercury in the State of Fun in Aquarius speaks of artistic brilliance. This *opposing* Neptune in the Social State reminded him that his music was meant for Society to enjoy. Venus *trine* Mars gave him a free flow of Masculine & Feminine energies in Work and Career. Jupiter *sextile* Pluto/Moon gave a radical and personal bent to his philosophy, which he required to work.

OVERALL DISTRIBUTION

The Alchemical Distribution can be determined by counting the amount of Earth, Water, Fire and Air styles the *Forces* are expressed through. Mozart, for example, had no Earth and 50% Air. Just because a chart lacks an element does not imply it cannot access that particular quality. Mozart accessed his Earth through his Creativity, Spirituality and Self-expression—as the Earthy Styles of Capricorn, Taurus and Virgo governed those areas in his chart. His North Node was also in

Virgo, requiring a very deliberate, conscious and "picky" way of expressing himself in order to realize his destiny. So, check the State of Governors for further information on accessing a particular element in your chart. (See *ALCHEMY* for info re: The Four Elements)

The Energetic Distribution can be calculated by adding up the Cardinal, Mutable and Fixed Styles by which the Forces express themselves through. *Cardinal* is the degree of outgoing energy responsible for our capacity to take action and follow through with decisions and ideas. Fixed is the degree by which we are able to concentrate and focus energies over a duration of time; it is the "holding or fixing" power. Mutable expresses the degree of our overall flexibility and ability to adapt and take on different forms and roles. Both Alchemical and Energetic Distribution refer to the overall chart and provide us with another sense of the whole.

Our own Astrology Chart can provide a very precise instrument for understanding those tendencies which we are governed by and those which we may choose to govern. Through understanding its Forces, Styles, States, Governors and Aspects, it is possible to arrive at realistic conclusions as to where our real strengths and weaknesses are. If we attempt to access, for example, our CAREER in a very analytical way when our 10th State Governor is Pisces, then we may continue failing... unless, of course, the 10th State Governor happens to be Virgo. Then, our success would depend upon our communication skills and conceptual discernment. Each Governor relays the specific style by which an area can be entered from, even if Forces in that area are of a different Style. As we learn how to consciously synchronize ourselves, we gain access to the territory of our totality.

8

SPIRITUAL INTELLIGENCE

A PARADOX — B DREAMING — C FACTOR X

EIGHTH GRADE SPIRITUAL INTELLIGENCE

WHERE INTELLIGENCE ORIGINATES
ATOMIC NUCLEUS — THE VOID

Eighth Grade Spiritual Intelligence is meta-physiological by nature, in that it originates outside the boundaries of our physical body (above the head in the 8th Center) and is responsible for those experiences related to out-of-body states, or Dreaming, as well as energy in its pure, potential state...as in "void." Relationship to the void, or unknown, cultivates Spiritual awareness. Identification with void and the unknown develops Spiritual identity. Both relating and identifying with the unknown can be catalyzed for the purpose of deepening contact with Factor X, the irrevocable unknown. Subjectively, Spiritual Intelligence evolves with our capacity to *transcend ourselves.* It's the living sense of being everything and nothing (void).

ITS QUALITIES AND ATTRIBUTES
SINGULAR, PARADOXICAL AND PERVASIVE

Spiritual Intelligence is "non-local," or beyond time and space, and governs events within the time-space continuum. It's pure Conscious-ness, or Information, that travels at superluminal (faster than light) speeds. Bell's Theorem states that "whenever two particles have made contact once, they continue influencing each other regardless of time or distance in space." Its capacity for instantaneous recognition and know-ingness regarding the nature of a particular reality and the ability of information to *project itself out of energy* in order to enter "K-space" or void; the spiritual power of existing in *Potential* as a conscious entity.

FUNCTIONS OF SPIRITUAL INTELLIGENCE
THE PHYSICS OF ENERGY

Spiritual Intelligence is elusive to intellectual attempts at conceptual comprehension due to its infinite nature, which thrives on activity and *interaction,* rather than the illusion of separation. Whatever is Spiritual is truly related and alive.

PARADOX FOUND
FROM PARADISE CENTRAL TO PARADOX NON-LOCAL

A paradox is...two doctors fishing off a pair of docks with their pair of dogs when a pair o' ducks swim by and ask the pair o' dogs if they prey in the dark. Knowing paradox to be the rule of thumbs in those parts, the pair o' dogs told the pair o' ducks, "No, we bark in the day...do you pray in the dark?" The pair o' ducks quacked back at the pair o' dogs who simultaneously, barked and excited the pair of docs sitting on their pair of docks...while the pair o' ducks ate their worms, pulling the pair o' docs off their pair o' docks and into the waters where the pair o' ducks swam in spirals around the pair o' docks. This only excited the pair o' dogs more and in they jumped to join the pair o' ducks and pair o' docs in the wet, wild waters.

The word "paradox" is all to often used to describe anything currently larger than our categories...that is to say, paradox results from the expanding or contracting categorization of misunderstood information. This error in judgment mistakes the "paradox" as a thing in itself, rather than a symbolic tool for dismantling ineffective methods of categorization. For example, if being Human includes the sub-category of Law-Abiding Citizen, then if Law-Abiding Citizen turns into a Psychopathic Murderer, it seems there is some kind of "mysterious, fascinating paradox" because we forget that being Human precedes and includes the sub-categories of Law-Abiding Citizen *and* Psychopathic Murderer.

In Eighth Grade Spiritual Intelligence, our singular Human element (preceding all sub-categories) *awakens!* This kind of Intelligence originates "non-locally" or beyond the time-space continuum and governs all local activity in time and space. To the degree we are awakened and aligned to this type of Will is the degree Spiritual Intelligence is alive in our bodies. To permit the infinite nature of the Spiritual, a certain intimacy with The Void requires stabilizing. As we learn to relate with Nothingness, eventually it is possible to experience ourselves as The Void itself. We are nothing. And everything. This is an apparent "paradox" until we see that both nothing and everything are sub-categories of being Human.

Two Sufis met at a crossroads one day and one asked of the other: "What is more important than God?" The other pondered momentarily then replied, "Nothing." This aroused the curiosity of the first Sufi who then proclaimed, "Then, that is where we shall look!"

We shall refer to this Nothing as K-space to investigate further implications. K-space fills the heart of the atomic nucleus where the subatomic activities of quarks speculate amongst themselves whether or not they really exist. Or not. Here, in the Little Zen Heart of K-space, there is no energy…only the weird quality of manifestation in its potential state. K-space is beyond time and space and, energy requires time/space to manifest in. Looked at from another perspective, matter turns into energy when it travels at the speed of light (E equals MC^2). What happens to matter if it breaks the "light barrier"? According to Einstein's Theory of Relativity, nothing travels faster than the speed of light. That's right… NOTHING travels faster than the speed of light. K-space is "superluminal" (faster than light) because it's instantaneously everywhere at once. How can something be nowhere and everywhere at once? Some would say in drop-dead wonderment: "Wow…how paradoxical…" with jaws still gaping. Once again, these are still sub-categories of what it means to be Human.

What does it mean to be Human? As Fourth Grade Social Intelligence *Human* supports the Spiritual, it seems we can only find out by continual interaction amidst ourselves. The Spirit of Eighth Grade traverses between interacting Humans at superluminal speeds. Our awareness of its presence deepens as we de-emphasize the tendency to focus on individual personalities and instead, permit the Spiritual to emerge, circulate and come alive. Yet, without personalities, the Spiritual cannot express Itself through us…so, once again the apparent paradox. Being Human includes the sub-categories of Personality and Spirit, as well.

Strong egos (not big ones) can permit more uncertainty and so are able to become instrumental to the Spiritual. Walter Starcke's landmark book, *The Gospel of Relativity,* refers to this process as "double vision." It describes the simultaneous functioning of apparent contraries as a fundamental Human characteristic, i.e., "vertical" Spiritual love extends to "horizontal" Personal love and vice versa. The symbol of the crucifix demonstrates this further as our, perhaps, most Human symbol.

If part of being Human means that part of us is everywhere at once (K-space), then we have access to a Universal Source of Energy and Information. To the degree we realize ourselves as a "piece of Nothing," we are related to everything at once. The possibilities are endless. Sometime, in the Future, perhaps global and inter-galactic telepathy will replace A.T.&T. due to our innate Spiritual ability for instantaneous communication with each other.

DREAMING: THE DREAMER AND THE DREAMED

When you can personify your spiritual nature (without warping your mind too much in the interim), there emerges the opportunity to explore a process called Dreaming. By ordinary definition, Dreaming marks the transition between Sleep and Awakening. From another perspective, Dreaming is the predominant condition of being a Human Being on this planet. One way of demonstrating this observation is through understanding the following hypothesis: When we go to sleep at night, we dream. While sleeping, a "dream-ego" awakens and we have adventures and meet people in "dreamland." This much is obvious to everybody. Now imagine this: When you wake up in the morning, your "dream-ego" has gone to sleep in order to *dream you.* As you walk the planet's surface, you are being dreamed by your dreamself as it's sleeping in dreamland. Then, you get tired and go to sleep, awakening the dreamself *as you dream it.* Then, it tires and sleeps in order to awaken you to *its* dreaming. Back and forth, both sides of our totality dreaming themselves into existence through the mutual activity called DREAMING. Perhaps, there is only DREAMING. How many times has a dream seemed Totally Real? And our Daily Life…Utterly Dreamlike?

So, we are either dreaming or being dreamed. In Sixth Grade, we learned about the Human Aura. In Eighth Grade, your aura is The Dreamer. When you go to sleep, it leaves your body. As you wake up, it returns. The process of Becoming Awake (in all its possibilities) is your aura waking up in your body. Dreaming Rituals (activities exciting awareness of dreaming) exercise the auric body…who we are as beings of light; our angelic heritage. Dreaming is an angelic sport…one flexing the muscles needed for flight, illumination and awakening. As future angels, we are receiving spiritual instruction so that the rest of us may catch up to who we have always been—who we are—and will remain: BEINGS OF LIGHT. Dreaming Rituals are one method of catching up to the spiritual constancy of our totality as dreamers. This, of course, necessitates the intellectual permission to be in two places at once, as well as regarding our so-called "dream life" as real and awakening to the daydream we call "reality." This is the understanding required to execute Dreaming Rituals.

DREAMING RITUALS

DREAMING RITUALS are a kinetic method of non-interpretive dreamwork. They are dedicated to unveiling the "web of dreaming" connecting our so-called Waking and Dream states. The overall intent of a DREAMING RITUAL is two-fold: 1) To make creative contact with emotion through dream memory and 2) To realize a greater spiritual Constance through ritual. The process of DREAMING RITUALS entails the extraction of dream remnants for the purpose of their ritual enactment. To start the process, it is imperative we enter a "non-interpretive" attitude towards those dreams used for the purpose of creating DREAMING RITUALS.

THE PROCESS

1) Go to sleep with the intention of remembering your dreams when you wake up in the morning. From the dreams you remembered, select *1 movement*. Before going anywhere, replicate this movement to the best of your physical ability. (Select this initial movement from the basis of its emotional significance...or by the degree it just "stuck out" amidst the rest of possible movements.)
2) *The Dreaming Task:* Repeat your "dream motion" throughout that day between 3–6 times, stopping everything to give your total attention to its execution. Be receptive to any dream memory flooding your body &/or mind as emotions &/or images. Don't attempt to analyze their meanings, simply go through their motions and let whatever responses emerge on their own follow through.
3) Repeat phases #1 & #2 for three consecutive days, so that you have a total of 3 Dreaming Movements, which followed a sequential, day-by-day evolution. Remember and practice all three movements.
4) At the end of the third day or the beginning of the fourth, you will be ready to begin piecing the movements together towards a Dreaming Ritual. Before doing so, follow the instructions in Fifth Grade Ritual regarding *preparation,* so you will be flexible enough to make the best use of the new, incoming information.

CONSTRUCTING DREAMING RITUALS

1) After preparation for ritual is completed, enter No-Form and allow the first Dream Movement to emerge. Give your total attention to its execution. Resonate a sound which "matches the energy" evoked by the motion. Repeat this vocalized motion several times, letting the emotion &/or image surfacing become your psychic environment.

2) After phase #1, return to No-Form and repeat the mechanics of phase #1 with the *second* Dream Movement.

3) After phase #2, return to No-Form and repeat the mechanics of phase #1 with the *third* Dream Movement.

4) After completing the initial exploration of all three movements, begin again with the first one. Blend the first movement into the second by following movement #1 all the way *into* movement #2. Do the same for movement #2 as it follows through into #3.

5) Let whatever emotions & images emerge and animate the movement as a stimulus.

6) Repeat the 3-phase cycle that you created by piecing together all three Dream Movements. Find a way to blend movement #3 *into* #1 to stabilize the cycle as one continuous motion going through 3 phases.

7) Stay with this. The effectiveness of the DREAMING RITUAL depends upon the intensity *and* duration of your commitment to its follow-through. Let whatever energies are emerging *motivate* and compel your movement and sound. Keep following through until you enter trance. Trance dance. Implement InTensions wherever required. (See *RITUAL, InTensions.*) When you are resolved, return to No-Form outside your little circle.

8) Evaluate what happened. Talk about what occurred or write it down. Refrain from psychoanalyzing the contents. Create another ritual.

> *"What does it all mean, Mr. Natural?"*
> Flaky Floont

As with anything kinetic, the DREAMING RITUAL is not done for any other purpose than for the activity itself. What it happens to evoke can augment the actual movement by *motivating it.* This is an essential point to remember *it's an activity.* Suspend judgment and your translations altogether because if the DREAMING RITUAL is executed as a simple activity, an *inherent meaning* inevitably emerges. This means that you don't have to make one up or project one into the action. If there's enough patience and commitment to the activity itself, the ordinary magic of numinous evocation will provide a more eloquent interpretation than we could ever surmise.

Dreaming as a state of being also refers to any emotional and/or conceptual condition wherein we fail to recognize the difference between what is "real" and what is not. It is that interim of flux suspending our disbelief just enough to question our reality or authority. Certain forms of visionary, surrealist and poetic art create this effect intentionally.

In Quantum Mechanics, the word *information* has been redefined to accommodate high uncertainty definitions. Information, in New Physics, means "the unpredictability of a message." The more unpredictable a message is, the more information there is in it. Dreaming is a highly unpredictable state, flooded with information and unusual patterns of motion.

An element contributing much to the "structure" of Dreaming has been articulated and demonstrated by Dr. John S. Bell, who shows (if Quantum Mechanics is valid) that once any two particles have made contact, they continue to influence each other regardless of the time and space between them. This is the famous *Bell's Theorem* which did more to revolutionize Quantum Psychology than any other theory. Another term, *cosmic glue,* describes the quantum inter-cohesion which exists if Bell's Theorem is valid. Another more far-reaching notion, is the *Hidden Variable* theory which suggests that quantum events are governed by a sub-quantum system operating beyond time and space. Dr. E.H. Walker and Dr. Nick Herbert suggest the Hidden Variable to be Consciousness. Dr. Jack Sarfatti has gone so far as to call it...information.

WICKED, WICKED GRAVITY

To evoke more information on the process of Dreaming, we look towards two additional threads of the fabric: 1) *Gravity* and 2) *Spin.* Gravity is, perhaps, one of the more mysterious forces known to science. If we had figured it out by now, it wouldn't require so much thrust and fuel to get a rocket launched into outer space. Gravity permeates everything yet, like electricity, there is no real explanation for its presence. Physics describes Gravity as the faintest of the four primary forces, the other three being the Electromagnetic Force, the ultra-gravitational Strong Force holding an atomic nucleus together and the peculiar Weak Force of sub-atomic interactions. Gravity holds the status of being the weakest force in nature.

If we understand the basic qualities and principles of Gravity, it might yield the required knowledge for its self-regulation...introducing *levity,* as well. The overall texture of a dream seems to depend upon the degree of gravitational flux...how it oscillates between being "heavy" and "buoyant." If we can permit speculation, let us say that gravity is the innate intelligence of mass. "Mass" is the illusion cast when atomic particles form the molecular structures which bond into an apple, for instance. Gravity, then, is a name for that apple's innate intelligence on the level of its *mass*. As we learned earlier and with Einstein's E equals MC^2...mass turns to energy when its velocity, or pace, approaches the speed of light. Mass transforms its shape when it's challenged by acceleration. How does all this relate to our Human research into the nature of Dreaming?

High-velocity living challenges our definition...we tend to change shape as personalities when exposed to ultra-accelerated tempos and life changes. It is in this way that *Dreamers* are "shape-shifters." Dreamers are those people who have accepted Dreaming as a way of life and so, become more vulnerable to the constant influx of new information from the spiritual constancy pervading their lives. Upon surrendering to the momentum of the Whole...(the totality of one's being through dreaming and being dreamed)...one's center of gravity sinks into *one's own distinct being.*

SPIN

Spin Theory states that everything spins in at least two directions...as Bucky Fuller says, "It's either in or it's out." The two types of spin are called: 1) *Self-spin* and 2) *Orbitary spin.* In order to speak about spinning, we'll call that which spins a "point." A point is a center of gravity, from a speck of dust to a star. If a point exists *locally* in time and space, it is possessed of two poles, or directions, to spin. (Non-local points don't spin; they don't even exist and this is why thinking *about* K-Space is "pointless.") The more *motion* occurring between the two poles of a point, the more internal momentum is generated in the point as a whole. This increases the point's gravitational field and develops a self-spinning direction. Through the increased motion between the poles, the poles tend to shift and trade positions...generating more self-spin. If this self-spinning point comes into close enough proximity to another self-spinning point wit h a greater gravitational field (and more self-spin than itself), then our first point will shift into "orbitary spin" and spin around the stronger point.

This example of self and orbitary spin permeates every level of activity capable of existing, locally, in time and space...from our thoughts to black holes, from Human interactions to super novas. We'll spin *around* those ideas, feelings, groups, events and individuals who tend to have more self-spin than ourselves. This is where we learn orbitary spin.

Sometimes, we'll spin around another point long enough to build enough momentum to hop off and start self-spinning or choose to develop our orbitary spin around a more challenging point. Acceleration tends to challenge our gravitational sense...our shape shifts in higher velocities than we are habitually accustomed. To the degree we can flow freely between the polar aspects of our own nature, or point, is the degree we generate the essential internal momentum to cause a shift in our poles, thus, initiate the next level of self-spin. With every level of increased self-spin, our gravitational field magnetizes and pulls towards it...points of a lesser self-spin.

When two points of relatively equal self-spin and gravitational field meet, a kind of stellar dance ensues wherein each point circles around a third point expressed as the *area of their mutual gravitation.* Two-thirds of the galaxy's stars are believed to be orbiting around areas of mutual gravitation with their "star-mates." (Our own star, The Sun, is believed to have a partner the scientists call Nemesis.) Whether we are on self-spin, orbitary spin and/or mutual "G" spin, the way we realize our Spiritual Intelligence through Dreaming is through *harmonizing* with the universal force which brings us through each state and phase of our being. It is our very BEINGNESS which seeks the challenge of close proximity to more accelerated self-spinners. It does so because it innately knows that anything not intrinsic to itself will only burn off and be shaken out around greater gravitational fields than its own. It is none other than *FACTOR X* which offers the greatest challenge and promise of spiritual growth to the being within.

FACTOR X
THE IRREVOCABLE UNKNOWN

The phenomena of FACTOR X is impossible to write about without resorting to metaphors bent on exciting its influences. Astrologically speaking, you can look to your maps and locate the Governor of the 12th State Of The Unknown. This is one particular Style by which you may gain direct access to FACTOR X. Each of the 12 Astrological Styles have their own manner of approaching the unknown. A clue, here, is in reducing each Style to its fundamental animal instincts. For example, with CANCER as Governing Style, you enter the Unknown sideways and indirectly, like a crab. With ARIES, you would do best by charging straight ahead like a ram, without thinking twice or looking back once. CAPRICORN requires a certain degree of caution and dignity by which to enter the Unknown and LIBRA requires going with a partner. These are the Cardinal Styles of entering the Unknown. By studying the rest, you may come to your own conclusions and thus, proceed.

FACTOR X is always a test to your innermost being. Without FACTOR X, you would die spiritually. This is because FACTOR X expresses the bottom line of existence...*it's all unknown.* Any belief to the contrary runs in opposition and expresses itself always as *what is already known.* As those who "know"...the more we know, the more we realize how much we don't. As our knowledge increases, so does the potential for accessing FACTOR X...*if* the systems of our knowledge are open-ended enough to permit their expansion, growth and future evolution. If they are not, they will tend to excite entropy and internal collapse. FACTOR X has a tendency to excite "negative entropy" by introducing more and more *new* information. FACTOR X is absolute in its life-affirming influence. The question remains...*how much life can we stand?*

You may access FACTOR X by entering those situations wherein you are not necessarily in control (unless it is *unknown* for you to be), where you can relax your need to determine an outcome (unless it's *unknown* for you to determine outcomes) and to do something you've never done before. As a rule of thumb, FACTOR X comes to those who invite change into their lives and who welcome *the unexpected.* High Uncertainty Zones are especially fertile. The only way to effectively call FACTOR X into your aura is to move into the Unknown *with your totality*...and *remain responsible moment to moment.* This requires improvisatory skills, as you will be literally asked to make things up as you go along and draw upon the resources at hand. When entering a High Uncertainty Zone, it is suggested that you remain interactive, as you will have to immediately adjust yourself to the new information. (This is another example of how Social Intelligence is a ground support and stabilizer for Spiritual energies.)

If you bring your conceptual, manipulative mind into High Uncertainty Zones, you run the risk of getting your mind blown by the layers of new information and meaning constantly exploding before you. Suggested practice is to enter these Concept-Free Zones without preconceptions, ulterior motives and/or personal objectives save for the experience of being there as totally as you can. Give your thinking mind a break by coming to your conclusions *after* leaving the Concept-Free Zones. You will find that the "mirror of your soul" works much like a camera and will tend to take better "pictures" if you simply let the patterns of energy, light and information *impress* yourself first. Later, you can see how the photos turned out in the darkroom of your mind.

Your time in the Unknown is determined directly by how stable each of the previous centers, or functions, of Intelligence are. If a particular center short circuits or gets knocked off center, it is up to you to determine how much longer you can remain intimate with FACTOR X before your individual integrity deteriorates past the point of your approval. If you fail to recognize your own collapse, your body will obviously start signaling your mortal condition. If it is too late and you leave your body, go straight to *CHAPEL PERILOUS*...do not pass GO...do not collect 200 karmas...go to *CHAPEL PERILOUS*.

FACTOR X, like CHAPEL PERILOUS, is a challenge to everything you have learned and practiced throughout *ANGEL TECH*. The difference being that FACTOR X really is the Unknown, whereas CHAPEL PERILOUS emerges as a creation of our mind. FACTOR X is the only part of our mind which it did not have a hand in creating. FACTOR X exists independently of our thoughts about it and constitutes the delicious, black hole centers of our spiritual origins.

There is an old story about a Magician and his two apprentices. It starts out when both students of magic came to ask their teacher, what is the difference between white and black magic? The older Magician told his disciples that they both would have to go through exactly the same methods of training in order to discern the answer to that kind of question. Years passed and both apprentices learned precisely the same magical techniques and practices as the other, until one day the Magician called them both to his home. The apprentices were very curious because their teacher had never invited them both into his home at the same time before, so they knew it was an auspicious event. There, the three sat still in silence for a good amount of time until the Magician spoke. He said, "Today, you will discover what you came here for. You shall know the difference between white and black magic...as one of you will become a black magician and the other white."

This astounded both apprentices, as neither one had any idea which would become the white magician and which would turn black. Both trained in magical ways in the same way...both were approximately the same age and disposition. In fact, there were far more similarities than differences between them on the whole. Puzzled, they followed the Magician out to the Periphery of the World, whereupon they hiked to the Edge and waited for the Magician to speak. "This is the Edge of the

World. Beyond the Edge is the Great Abyss. For you to claim your last piece of magical knowledge from me, you must jump over the Edge and out into the Abyss." At this time, one of the apprentices leapt into the Great Abyss and the other turned around and ran the opposite direction, only to return a short time later. The apprentice asked the Magician who was the Black and White Magician. The Magician looked at him and spoke, "The White Magician leapt into the Abyss."

MYSTICISM

Mysticism is whatever you do to remain open to the Universe around you and its constant output of new information. FACTOR X is a mystical doorway permitting our entry to direct, open-ended contact and communion with the Universe. The locks on the door can be opened through the increasing *flexibility* of our physical, emotional, conceptual and social vehicles. This is due to the spiritual truth of our eternal nature, signified by FACTOR X. The mortal parts of ourselves would have to remain malleable to live *with* that kind of truth...the shock, of which, would perpetually remind these parts how transitory they actually are. FACTOR X, however, also possesses the influence of *diminishing* our mortal tendencies to crystallize and grow old. Our mysticism tends to keep us around longer than our conditioned habits would like.

There is a delicate balance between living forever and dying. Too much FACTOR X is not unlike "having too much of a good thing" and has rendered many a good mind frenetically crazed, because of the negligence of a certain finite body and its natural, genetically-programmed limitations. The sacred blessing of our physiological boundaries remind us how privileged we are to embody the human form. Our lives depend on it. (The mass of dis-embodied souls desiring human reincarnation makes our state welfare waiting rooms appear microscopically sparse by comparison.)

When working with FACTOR X, understand you are digesting the most powerful drug in the Known World: Infinity. Whenever you're in doubt about the correct dosage, consult your wisdom by asking, "Can I Bring My Body With Me?" As long as you're in the human form, you'll only be able to absorb as much energy and/or information as you can contain. On the other hand, not enough FACTOR X will have the effect of quickening the aging process. All you have to do to grow old is convince yourself that you know everything. It's as simple as signing on the dotted line and it's been working for thousands of years. Why, you can even obtain an Honorary Degree in Knowing from your local university and become an Expert.

FACTOR X also governs our access to the Collective Unconscious, the term Carl G. Jung used to refer to the subconscious mind of the race as a whole. (Fourth Grade Social Intelligence stabilizes the Spiritual by its emphasis on the Collective Consciousness) So, whether we are relating to our own personal contact with the unknown or the vast ancestral memories of our Human heritage, FACTOR X compels us to expand our definition of humanity and what we are capable of. It is our contact with the initial seed of being Human, before we became divided into sexes, races, nations, religions and so forth. FACTOR X recalls our originating singularity...inherently found in the nucleus of subatomic activities.

The major scientific breakthroughs of human history have not yet unfolded. When they do, humanity shall enter a phase so different from what has transpired that to call it anything but Post-History would be to underestimate its cosmic impact. These breakthroughs will occur in the field of Quantum Mechanics and New Physics, perhaps around the turn of the century (Terence McKenna says 2012), involving new understandings regarding the nature of time, space and gravity...enabling everything from time-travel to inter-dimensional materialization to a host of abilities undreamed of in our wildest science fiction stories.

When these scientific discoveries do occur, it will be a direct result of Spiritual Intelligence awakening in the depths of our modern scientists' innermost beings. It'll happen when Dreaming is understood as a vehicle for spiritual knowledge and Factor X confessed to being the basis of everything we know. Until these humbling revelations, it will be genetically necessary to continue smashing atoms, making bombs and shooting laser-satellites out of the sky. Why? Spiritual Intelligence is superbly well-timed and about as unpredictable as the information required to initiate the essential quantum leap in global consciousness. The key is *flexibility*...of the physical, emotional, conceptual, and social aspects of our lives. Perhaps, at this point in history, it rests with social flexibility...our ability to get along with each other as people. (It is Social Intelligence which provides the base support and stabilization for Spiritual Intelligence to enter and express itself.)

ANGEL TECH was designed for the purpose of flexing ourselves. By reclaiming each of the eight functions of Intelligence on our own terms, a certain flexibility is cultivated...the kind which permits the shock of new information. As we realize our futures daily, the pace of life cannot help but accelerate. There will come a time when people will be "flipping out" left and right because of their rigid inability to permit uncertainty and change...and the times will become highly uncertain and changeable before a new direction finds its cohesion and momentum. Science may cure cancer, AIDS, and other physical maladies but unless we learn to make ourselves whole again, we will be woven into the great dying beast of a schizophrenia of epidemic proportions. Confess your broken hearts, disappointments and failures, then get on with it...restructure your lives according to how your own Central Nervous System responds. In short, *define yourself or be defined.* When you feel strong and educated enough, follow the way of the White Magician and spiritualize everything you are. Jump!

The Underground Cinema of
ANTERO ALLI

from "Under a Shipwrecked Moon" (2003; 96 min.) by Antero Alli.
Sylvi Alli appears as "Sisu"

www.verticalpool.com/dvd.html

"Alli's films are not for the easily distracted. They are challenging and sometimes cryptic in their dissection of human emotions and societal interactions. Repeated viewings, however, reveal layers of wisdom and wit that may not have been obvious in the initial screening."
— Phil Hall, *Encyclopedia of Underground Movies*

I don't call myself an artist. The self-proclaimed "artist" is a modern-day delusion; that title is for others to decide. I see myself more as an accidental agitator. I do not agitate on purpose. My agitating is more like a gut response to being agitated. I am agitated by the soul-crushing bore-dom of any so-called "Art" produced by any individual, organization or Society of Spectacle depersonalized by imagination death. My aim is to agitate the insurrection of Poetic Imagination, the chief inlet for Soul in the Hypermedia Era.   — Antero Alli the

1988 afterword

to

Angel Tech

by

ANTERO ALLI

The response to **ANGEL TECH** has been simultaneously inspiring and disquieting. As I originally wrote this book for People in Trouble, it's no surprise that numerous letters have arrived describing your personal and psychic catastrophes. I am grateful **ANGEL TECH** has assisted so many people out of Hot Water yet I remain concerned that, like **any** body of knowledge, it encourages a kind of insular padding to direct knowledge of our actual life predicaments. ("The map is not the territory.") For example, this insular New Age Movement reeks, like its Fundamentalist Christian brotherhood, of **buffers.** Buffers to our inherent discontent, buffers to our human flaws and defects, buffers to our accumulating layers of buffers. Buffers are like training wheels on the Bicycle of Life. When you're ready for the Big Ride, you take them off.

Some of us have never taken our training wheels off. **We know who we are** and, if we are still alive, we feel a little shame. (Shame is not a "new age" emotion; it is a human one.) We are ashamed to admit it. Our training wheels have been locked on by the rust of habit and the reluctance to fly. Books are training wheels. The greatest satisfaction I can know as an author is that one of my books helped dismantle somebody's training wheels. Books, at best, can only hope to do as much. Otherwise, they're just Dead Paper Mothers nursing empty-minded vessels with the milk of someone else's big ideas. This is especially lethal in the area of Metaphysics...those principles we tend to live and die for hence, be controlled and governed by.

ATTENTION!

ANGEL TECHNICIANS are now required to register their dogmas
with the School of Metaphysics currently controlling their minds
for the bi-millennium reports to:

THE AKASHIC RECORD PLAYER.

Failure to do so will result in
the self-imposed penalty of Neo-Puritan Vanity.
If you do not know the dogma, grade or school you belong to,
the following Article of Identification has been provided
for your (re)edification.

NEW AGE CASUALTIES

FROM MEDITATION MONSTERS
TO KUNDALINI KRACK-UPS

There are basically two schools of metaphysics: **Disembodied** and
Embodied. The former originated amidst the more densely populated
regions of the world (India, China, Japan) partly as a method for attain-
ing temporary relief and occasional, personal transcendence from the
hideous crowding problems. The Disembodied School of Metaphysics
generally trains initiates in various degrees of out-of-body, or astral,
experience in addition to indoctrinating them into a hierarchical "psychic
caste" system to philosophically segregate "adepts" from the "masses."
This is especially true of the Hindu cosmology from which much of our
current Pop Mysticism and New Ageism originated, when it was introduced to America around 1890 by Madame Blavatsky, Alice Bailey and
Dr. Leadbeater. We have these people to thank for encouraging, under
the guise of somber authority, the ridiculously dangerous assumption that
there is a "higher" and a "lower" self, the latter postulated as "morally
inferior" to the former.

The Embodied School of Metaphysics originated in far lesser populated geographical locales (Native America and Northern Europe,
primarily), emphasizing spiritual union **in the body.** Examples include
all Native American "Indian" tribes and the nature-worshipping pagans
of Celtic, Irish and Slavic traditions. The Occidental exceptions to this
are the vast array of orthodox or fundamentalist Christian sects, which
are primarily **disembodied** due to their assumption of personal redemp-

tion in an afterlife (often requiring degrees of martyrdom or self-negation in the current one). These preach "evils of the flesh" and other ego-trashing dogmas for instilling a definition of virtue as "of the spirit alone," delegating the realm of the body to "hell" and other generally undesirable and fearful states to be in.

The danger of engaging any spiritual practice that did not originate in one's own spirit, or at least in the spirit of the land lived in, is that foreign metaphysical disciplines may be "genetically-wired" survival devices to adjust to the conditions of its culture. For example, Japan's Zen Buddhism strives toward the "samadhi of enlightenment" via the Gate of the Illuminated Void. Quite simply, zen cosmology revolves around The Void as **a goal**...an end-all, invitation to living forever in the present moment. This ingenious spiritual orientation suggests that the practitioner rely on his/her own being for spiritual authority and thus, an ideal solution to Japanese crowd control. With everyone becoming more inner-directed, a greater sense of space is honored and created...as can be witnessed in the myriad forms of Buddhist Art.

As those who've discovered Life After Zen know, the Void is a great place to visit but (like the Club Med...) you wouldn't want to live there unless, of course, you're Marlon Brando and just enjoy that kind of non-stop, exotic refuge from the World Game and, can afford it. The following sections address Americans practicing disembodied metaphysical disciplines who experience various stages of spiritual emergency and/or psychic crisis from long-term exposure to its effects. Our first in a series of New Age casualties:

MEDITATION MONSTERS

An especially perilous path is paved for those who make a career or religion out of disembodied metaphysics without knowing their motives and/or why they want to vacate their bodies in the first place. Transcendental Meditation, for one, is a highly effective tool when applied to daily relaxation, stress reduction and overall peace-of-mind maintenance. Some T.M. practitioners, who have been developing their techniques for seven or more years, have complained to me of a kind of "terminal buoyancy." A constant, overall disorientation seems to occur especially alongside the Advanced Levitation exercises. These meditation adepts report the disconcerting sensation that their heads are gone, or invisible, along with floating feelings...as if they're suspended above their bodies, looking down on themselves. They say they are preparing for a higher level of spiritual union. I would say they are Meditation Monsters suffering from a highly disguised and sophisticated death wish.

When identified with completely, any authentic spiritual practice turns to the absolute belief of dogma. **Dogma is a powerful drug.** See Chapter 4 of *Undoing Yourself with Energized Meditation* by Christopher S. Hyatt, Ph.D. (Falcon Press). We now know that millions of people have gone to war and killed millions like them all under the influence. When an advanced meditator is absolutely convinced they will reach their final spiritual goal by merging their identity with a disembodied metaphysical principle, they will tend towards realizing their destiny as a **disembodied entity.** (You don't have to be a psychic genius to know what this means.) The physical organism will react to this as a direct threat to its survival. **It knows it will die** someday and is in **no rush** to get there. It'll create lower back pains, sacrum discomfort, sciatic nerve spasms, and other blatant signs that alert the "soul" that the Survival Energy Centers are being abandoned. Sometimes, these distress signals are treated by the indoctrinated soul as just more "lower self obstacles" to overcome. Fortunately, the organism is linked *vitalistically* with other living organisms and so its S.O.S. does **not** go by ignored. Help, however, may not arrive in the most convenient and comfortable manner to the personality involved.

THE IDIOT WITHIN

Sometimes, the only antidote for stabilizing the volatile conditions brought on by this kind of spiritual emergency is **hard labor,** pitting the individual against the undeniable edge of pushing mass and feeling the pressure of the physical universe. The enigmatic philosopher Georges J. Gurdjieff often placed the "self-proclaimed spiritually evolved" directly to work in the garden, digging ditches and any other manual physical labor he saw fit for balancing their lopsided, lofty egos.

Gurdjieff's assumption about people in general was that we are all **sleep-walking.** This somnambulist state would maintain itself by our lack of complete operational functioning, i.e., some people would stay asleep by being conceptually adept but emotionally immobilized. Others…social geniuses but physical idiots. According to Gurdjieff, there are energetic centers within us all at various degrees of functioning and that our real work began the moment we confessed our area of true ignorance by proclaiming the **Idiot Within.** *He also was known to say* *that **vanity** was the most destructive vice he knew of insofar as its effectiveness at keeping us asleep at the wheel.*

Another remedy for reeling in wayward souls back to their grieving, angry bodies is **exposing** how they're preparing their own funerals. Sometimes the direct approach administers the **shock** necessary to stop us in our tracks and look at what we have set up for ourselves. Often times when this attack succeeds, it requires a follow-up of several hearty doses of hilarious humor. I'm not talking about puns and chuckles here but gut-busting, belly laughs that bring tears to your eyes. As the stomach spasms with explosive laughter, it seems to stimulate our ability to "digest" our more serious, denser foods. Take it from Henry Miller: "Laughter is the most direct route to God...filling our heads with Light as we go..." Besides, if something is **really true,** it's probably going to be really funny somewhere.

Another serious side-effect of disembodied spiritual practice can be seen in the current **Channeling Epidemic** where scores of otherwise normal people are learning how to throw their power away to the homogenized axioms of disembodied entities. One very common reason why some of us are drawn to communicating with the dead is that we don't have any real living friends to talk to. Establishing a link with our "guides" or "past lives" compensates for the lack of love, good sex and genuine human interaction in our lives. Spooks, like our childhood "imaginary" playmates, offer the strokes, status and the security of certainty missing from our social life. No doubt ghosts exist yet, are they any wiser than the living? Is death a Ph.D.?!

KUNDALINI KRACK-UPS

Whereas T.M. emphasized the activation of the upper energy centers, namely the sixth (third eye), seventh (crown) and eighth (above the head)...Kundalini Yoga focuses on the first center inside the base of the spinal column. Here, coiled in otherwise useless repose, is the "kundalini fire" that (when activated) burns its way up the spine and out the top of the head IF there are no blocks along the way.

If there is a block, the kundalini hits it and bounces down and out the center, or chakra, below it. For example, if you are not straight with where you are at with power and issues of the will, the activated kundalini moves up to the solar plexus (power center) and bounces down and out the sexual center (just below the navel). As the sexual center blasts open with the force of a small atomic bomb, the god of lust unleashes our erotic passions on the world around us. If our heart is closed, then the serpent bounces down and screams out from the power center arranging our world view into a non-stop political tour de force.

Kundalini Krack-Ups are not funny. Often times, they are painful as the physiological organs connected to each energy center are stressed beyond their threshold and occasionally break down entirely. Those of us suffering from some form of kundalini crack-up can seek occasional relief by finding, or inventing, outlets to express the activity pertaining to the over-emphasized chakra: security (parenting), sex (passion), power (leadership), love (relations), communication (art), vision (perspective)…until our condition eventually stabilizes. If we are creative enough, we get involved with situations to touch and inspire the lives of those around us with the resurrected intensities coursing through our individual bodies.

The activation of Kundalini does not always occur from practicing Kundalini Yoga, either. It has also been known to erupt spontaneously in those people on the verge of major spiritual breakthroughs, regardless of their ideas of how enlightened they are. In this case, "enlightenment" is unexpected and simply means you work like a dog or a God or Goddess…harder, longer and deeper than anyone else just to stabilize your hot, new metabolism so you don't completely lose it. When your brain is really and finally **on fire,** it's only natural to have to develop the command and discipline to keep it all together. There is literally no choice in the matter. Chaos surrenders to form and form gives in to chaos, and foo foo falls from the sky…

COSMIC FOO FOO

The obvious socio-politico-economic uncertainty of these times has elicited a real tendency to settle for easy answers, dogmas to cling onto and buffers against feeling our helplessness in the wake of relentless change. As New Agers continue over-emphasizing the spiritual and philosophical, they lose the perspective they sought to gain through metaphysics in the first place. When we're lost and disoriented, **feelings of inadequacy** are appropriate to our human predicament. When they're denied and repressed behind some New Age ideal of "divine perfection," we feed the delusion that "everything is wonderful and perfect no matter what" when, in fact, we're all too vain to accept our genuine shortcomings and flaws as **they are.** How can anything be wonderful and perfect all the time outside of Disneyland? The New Age is plagued with

Cosmic Foo Foo. Who will venture forth and take the cure before becoming cartoon parodies of themselves? What's it going to take to get real? Crystal suppositories?! This disembodied, New Age obsession with Wholeness and Perfection also reeks of death and stagnation. Its pathetic hankering over Clarity, Light and Harmony leaves us as transparent and cheerful as crystal skulls. Haven't you heard the news? **Pssst! The New Age is dead. Shhhh!** This act is over. A rebellious counter-movement stirs in the wings. They're real, live human dynamos who laugh, cry, inform and entertain…a motley, charismatic yet highly disciplined crew of players dedicated to navigating the turbulence of the times…in silence…effectively…without selling out. They've been working underground…hidden behind harmless smokescreens of flowery pseudonyms and New Age activities. Play a dirge for the changing of the guard. Enter now the Cyber-shamans, Warrior-Artists and Spiritual Anarchists…who nonchalantly sweep the stage with the limp, cheerful perfect corpses of the end of an era.

FROM ANTERO ALLI

A MODERN SHAMAN'S GUIDE TO A PREGNANT UNIVERSE

With Christopher S. Hyatt, Ph.D.

The Pregnant Universe is a Neural Cocktail party of a brain getting drunk on itself. It is the essence of slimy copulation between known and unknown forces. As the planet braces for a series of new contractions, bizarre and interesting forces are being born—brains with new centers, new chemicals, new visions—going far beyond the suited dinosaurs prattling their slogans.

REBELS & DEVILS
The Psychology of Liberation

Contributions by Antero Ali, Wm. S. Burroughs, Timothy Leary, Robert Anton Wilson, Aleister Crowley, A.O. Spare, Jack Parsons, Genesis P-Orridge, and many, many others.

"When he put the gun to my head at 16 I left home…" So begins this remarkable book which brings together some of the most talented, controversial and rebellious people *ever*. Not to be missed!

FROM ANTERO ALLI

PARATHEATRE
A Ritual Technology for Self-Initiation

Since 1977, Antero Alli has been developing a ritual technology for Self-Initiation—Paratheatre—combining techniques of theatre, dance and zazen to access and express the internal landscape. Paratheatre is highly transformative and has served as a critical source of inspiration for many of Antero's artistic endeavors, especially his films. (Two Audio CDs)

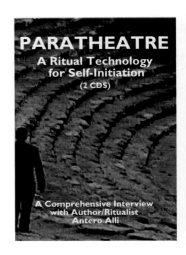

THE 8-CIRCUIT BRAIN

Antero Alli discusses his research results and a wide variety of perceptions on Timothy Leary's 8-Circuit Brain model for Intelligence Increase. Antero introduces the origin of this system and how his interpretations differ from Dr. Leary's and Robert Anton Wilson's, along with his insights on the vertical connectivities between upper and lower circuits, the function and nature of shock, the first and second attentions and much, much more. (DVD)

FROM ANTERO ALLI

TO DREAM OF FALLING UPWARDS

The elder Magus just passed away. Jack Mason, a promising young sex magickian cultivated to advance the lineage, loses it all when the elder Magus' biological son unexpectedly inherits everything with plans to commercialize and franchise the Temple. Jack plots deadly revenge and falls into a dizzying maze of encounters with underworld characters, desert brujas, and a twist of fate he never saw coming...or did he? (DVD)

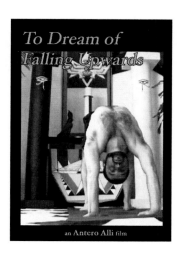

UNDER A SHIPWRECKED MOON

The power of a long-dead family secret is unleashed when the rituals of a self-made shamanic punk rocker catapult him into the spirit realm in search of his father, a ship's captain who drowned at sea. Meanwhile, back in the real world, he and his family gather around the bedside of his grandfather who has suddenly reappeared after a fifteen year absence. A surrealistic fable of love, giant hedgehogs, and the mystical depths of family bonds. (DVD)

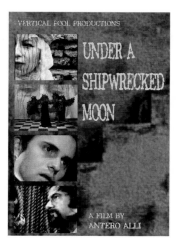

THE *Original* FALCON PRESS

Invites You to Visit Our Website:
http://originalfalcon.com

At our website you can:

- Browse the online catalog of all of our great titles
- Find out what's available and what's out of stock
- Get special discounts
- Order our titles through our secure online server
- Find products not available anywhere else including:
  - One of a kind and limited availability products
  - Special packages
  - Special pricing
- Get free gifts
- Join our email list for advance notice of New Releases and Special Offers
- Find out about book signings and author events
- Send email to our authors
- Read excerpts of many of our titles
- Find links to our authors' websites
- Discover links to other weird and wonderful sites
- And much, much more

Get online today at http://originalfalcon.com

Pure Consciousness
263

Dreaming
263

Void
264 (263)
Nothing = K-Space (265)